THE HEAD WAITER

THE HEAD WAITER

A biography of Harry Wragg

Michael Seth-Smith

Michael Joseph

LONDON

First published in Great Britain by Michael Joseph Ltd
44 Bedford Square, London WC1
1984

© Michael Seth-Smith 1984

British Library Cataloguing in Publication Data

Seth-Smith, Michael
  The head waiter.
  1. Wragg, Harry   2. Jockeys — Great Britain
  — Biography
  I. Title
  798.4'3'0924   SF336.W6/

  ISBN 0 7181 2443 X

Typeset by Alacrity Phototypesetters
Banwell Castle, Weston-super-Mare
Printed and bound in Great Britain by
Billing & Sons Limited, Worcester

Contents

List of Illustrations

Acknowledgement

I was approached by Geoffrey Wragg at Newmarket races in the spring of 1983 and invited to write the biography of his father. The principal 'ingredient' of the invitation was that Harry was anxious to help, for he had decided that the time had come for the story of his life to be set down in print. Such an 'ingredient' was very attractive and consequently I accepted the invitation without hesitation. During the autumn Harry recalled a host of memories for me, and showed me much hospitality at Abington Place. I would like to record that without his unstinting enthusiasm and assistance I could not have written this book. Geoffrey Wragg also gave me hospitality and provided much information about his father in addition to finding time to read and give valuable criticism upon the initial draft of the text.

Details concerning Harry's career were also given to me by Geoffrey's wife, Patricia, and her mother, Mrs Phil Lancaster; Arthur Wragg, son of Harry's elder brother; G. Hobson; Nat Frieze; Luke Seymour; Felicity Veasey, daughter of Chubb Leach; Renee Bell, widow of Captain Ossie Bell; Anne Irwin; J. Edward Vickers; and the Director of Sheffield Library. I wish to express my thanks and gratitude to all of them and also to the many others who gave me information, and to Clare Coney of Michael Joseph Ltd. Finally I wish to thank my step-daughter, Tina Matthews, who was born seven months before Psidium won The Derby and who without demur deciphered my handwriting and efficiently typed the original manuscript.

Michael Seth-Smith
Magnolia House
Hindhead

Foreword

Lester Piggott O.B.E.

I was born on Tuesday, 5 November 1935, a cold day when Harry Wragg was placed in two of the six races at Leicester. Before the season ended he had ridden six more winners including a treble at Derby, and finished in a blaze of glory by winning the Final Plate at his beloved Manchester. In those days I was too young to realise his artistry in the saddle, and in fact he had retired from the ranks of jockeys almost two years before I rode my first winner in August 1948, so I never had the opportunity and privilege of riding against him. However, in my years as a teenage jockey I often listened to trainers and jockeys who spoke of him with awe, especially when referring to his cool confidence on the occasion of an important race. I admired the manner in which he had so obviously planned how to ride each race, and had summed up the form of his rivals, and my admiration became even greater after I had ridden at Epsom and appreciated how his 'Head Waiter' tactics had made jockeys realise that it was not necessary to be in the first four at the foot of Tattenham Corner to win The Derby.

I first rode for him in 1950 and only wish that I had partnered Psidium in the 1961 Derby. However, I did manage to win the 1983 Derby on Teenoso trained by his son Geoffrey, and that victory gave me much pleasure. My own career has brought me nine Derby triumphs, but I still have to train an Epsom 'Blue Riband' hero before I can feel that I have surpassed Harry's record as a jockey and trainer! I have the good fortune to come from a racing family with Days, Cannons and Rickabys as my ancestors, but Harry had no such forefathers to inspire him.

Nevertheless he proved himself a genius in the saddle and on the training ground, and this biography by Michael Seth-Smith sets out the fascinating story of his life.

1

Childhood in Sheffield

In June 1902 the streets of Sheffield were bedecked with flags and bunting to celebrate the signing of the peace treaty of Vereeniging and the end of the Boer War. The forthcoming coronation was also causing excitement, with local tradesmen advertising trophies, flag poles and decorative emblems of every description suitable for the occasion. Sadly the coronation had to be postponed due to King Edward VII's illness and the necessity for him to undergo an operation for appendicitis, so that the anticipated festivities did not take place. Children found it difficult to understand why the parties that they had so eagerly awaited were cancelled, and parents had no easy task explaining to them why the decorations had to be taken down.

Two parents who had to face disappointment from their eldest children were Arthur Wragg and his wife Nellie, to whom a son was born on 10 June, and to whom the name Harry was given. He was their sixth child and followed Nellie, Alice, Ernest, Ivy and Florence. Two more boys, Samuel and Arthur, were to be born within the next six years to make up a large family who crowded into 26 Bolehill Lane, Nether Hallam. The drab semi-detached house was one of many identical red-brick dwellings whose front doors abutted the narrow, cobbled streets where children played hop-scotch and neighbours exchanged gossip throughout the day. The cost of living was a frequent topic, for poverty was known to the majority of the inhabitants of the street which sloped steeply down to the main road which ran through Crookes to the Bole Hills on the outskirts of Sheffield.

Yet at the commencement of the twentieth century Sheffield was a prosperous centre of manufacture, with the Sheffield knife and chisel renowned throughout the world as triumphs of quality and finish. Many of the 400,000 people who lived and worked in the city were skilled in choral singing, with chapel services a main focus point of their life. They formed brass bands, went to political meetings and cherished a genuine devotion for the beauty of the hills and the moors that girded their borough upon which the title of City had been bestowed by the Crown in 1893. However, their intellectual contact with the outside world was spasmodic and insufficient, and they made little attempt to learn from others. A visiting architect claimed that there was not a building of outstanding merit in the entire city, which comprised a jumble of narrow streets, courts and alleys, and that even if an architect designed a fine building it would be ruined by being given an inappropriate site. The claim was strengthened by the comment of a local journalist: 'Sheffield may be likened to an untidy house. It has been enlarged several times but the entrance is still through the kitchen. You knock on the door and say, "Will you be good enough to show me over your house, sir?" and the answer comes, "Ay, and welcome lad. Come thee out into the garden."' There was no garden, however, at 26, Bolehill Lane, nor was there much space in the overcrowded house for the cups that Arthur Wragg had won for athletics and boxing as a young man.

At the time of Harry's birth, Arthur Wragg was working for Laycocks, one of the largest firms of cutlers in Sheffield, being employed as a brass buffer. His task was to polish brassware on a machine which had a felt buffer on a constantly spinning wheel. He was a tall, heavily-built man, who was well-known for his fine baritone voice and for his love of dancing. On Sunday afternoons in the winter he would insist that his family joined him singing hymns and songs in the front parlour where a coloured print of Mary Queen of Scots adorned the wall above the fireplace. His favourite song was 'Bonnie Mary of Argyll' which his children learned by heart. He followed all local sport especially athletics in summer, and enjoyed telling his children of his achievements as a boxer. He also looked forward to his annual pilgrimage with his friends to Lincoln for the first handicap of the Flat Season, never missed the St Leger at Doncaster, and in the autumn would usually make a trip to Newmarket for either the Cambridgeshire or the Cesarewitch. However, he had no especial interest in racing and seldom had a bet.

He always claimed that his ancestors had arrived in Sheffield in the mid-eighteenth century from Scotland when General Murray, a member of a renowned Scottish family from Tullibardine Castle, decided to build Banner Cross Hall at Eccleshall. The General brought many servants with him, amongst them a man named Wragg and his wife. Their daughter, Molly, went into domestic service as a maid, and eventually settled as a nurse and midwife in a cottage at the top end of Brincliffe Edge. Molly was much loved, and was believed to be the curer of all ills. Whenever anyone was sick the cry went up 'Fetch Molly Wragg' and locally Brincliffe became known as 'Molly Wragg Lane'.

Harry Wragg's mother, Nellie, was a resourceful, hard-working woman who outwardly was strict with her children, but inwardly was soft-hearted. Anyone going to her with a hard-luck story would be given her last penny. When she went to the wholesale market for food supplies her children were popped into the empty barrels and baskets on the flat cart for the trip into Sheffield to ensure that no one went astray on the journey. She insisted that her children were taught the value of money and had to work to earn it, with household duties and chores to be completed before they were allowed to play. The nearby recreation ground was a popular meeting-place for the children because amateur football teams played there, and invariably drew a crowd of spectators. Harry's eldest brother, Ernest, found a method of making a few extra pennies due to these football matches. He enlisted the help of his sisters and Harry, scavenged for empty tins, and when they were found would knock in a few holes with a nail, collect some twigs and coke from the local tip and thus make a miniature brazier. These warmers were sold to spectators for twopence each.

Weekends during the summer usually found the Wragg children down in the valley, paddling in the stream or fishing for tiddlers. They also walked for miles onto the moors, collecting blackberries and bilberries. Their mother loved flowers, and marguerites were her favourite. To the children these flowers were known as 'moon pennies' and they would frequently pick a bunch for her. On occasions they played truant from school, but the gift of freshly picked 'moon pennies' on their return home at the end of the day brought so much pleasure that the deserved beating was often overlooked.

Harry grew up as a sturdy, determined but reticent boy who knew little of his mother's worries. She realised that the cost of supporting an ever-growing family was too great a drain upon her husband's wages whilst they lived in Bolehill Lane, and knew that they must move to a home which would be cheaper to maintain. She heard of a house in Pitt Street which had a small fruit shop attached to it, became convinced that she could make extra money by running the shop, and persuaded her husband to move. The children enjoyed their new home, where Harry astutely discovered the trick of taking a bite out of an apple or a pear and then replacing it so that customers could only see the presentable portion of the fruit. If he was caught he was spanked, but on many occasions it was impossible to prove that he was the culprit.

Harry showed an athletic streak early in life. Even when a child he joined in the games organised by his father on the Bole Hills, and although too young to participate in the running competitions which were held there, he often watched them. At home his father insisted that he was taught to box. The kitchen table would be pushed out of the way, and Arthur Wragg would demonstrate the art of self-defence to his sons and daughters. These sessions often ended in uproar with someone either losing his temper or getting a bloody nose. Only once, however, was there any risk of serious injury. This occurred when Harry, frustrated that he was the smallest, picked up a flat iron and hurled it across the room. Luckily the iron did not hit anyone.

In 1912, when Harry was ten, tragedy descended on the family soon after the birth of Arthur. Nellie became ill and died. She had been the lynch-pin which had united the family and her unexpected death left Arthur Wragg helpless and distraught. He had never been a man with great will-power and strength of character and seemed to go down hill once he became a widower. The fruit shop and home in Pitt Street were sold and a move made to Solly Street where the lessons in self-defence that the children had been given stood them in good stead. Solly Street was one of the toughest and roughest areas in Sheffield, and was part of a rabbit-warren of narrow streets and back-to-back houses, some of which had only one room upstairs and one down. The front doors of the houses were so close together that a favourite game played by the children was to tie the handles together, knock on the doors and run away. The community were either rugged, outspoken Yorkshiremen or Irish Catholics who bickered constantly, and who were amongst the poorest of Sheffield's citizens.

Harry, who was a healthy child and seldom misbehaved, was sent to the local school where his marks in each subject were 'average' and where the masters accepted him as a placid, thoughtful, quiet boy who caused little trouble. During the school holidays he would take his father's lunch to the cutlery works and collect bluebells on the way home. Money was always in short supply, and only occasionally was there the treat of going to the theatre, taking with him a banjo — a bun with chips in the middle. If Harry had earned a few extra coppers he would take a penny bus ride before paying threepence to watch Sheffield Wednesday on their home ground. Often he saved money by waiting until half-time when he would find the gates open and gain free admission. He would then enquire how the match had progressed in the first half. He enjoyed watching soccer matches, and although he had little idea as to his future, he contemplated the possibility of becoming either a professional footballer or boxer. He felt that he could succeed in either sport, for he knew instinctively that he was quick of foot and brain, even though he was content that others did not realise that he possessed these attributes.

Harry left school at the end of the summer of 1916. The war did not seem to be progressing in the Allies' favour, for Gallipoli had been evacuated; there had been a Sinn Fein rising in Ireland; Lord Kitchener had been drowned in the North Sea when the *Hampshire* struck a mine; and the Battle of the Somme appeared to be a stalemate in which casualties were on a colossal scale. Only victory at the Battle of Jutland brought cheerful news to the people of Sheffield, who were working night and day on armaments production. Crankshafts, armoured plate, torpedo parts, steel-turbine forgings and shells, especially for the Royal Navy, were keeping the local factories at full stretch.

Fourteen-year-old Harry had no regrets at leaving school and relished his new-found freedom, whilst having the good sense to appreciate that it was essential that he found a job. His father advised him, 'You have got to graft, and stand on your own feet. There is no union to help you, so help yourself and do better than your mates.'

Some of his schoolboy friends thought him 'happy-go-lucky' but, although outwardly he may have given them that impression, in reality he had far more determination to succeed than the majority of his contemporaries. Understandably his horizons were narrow and he lacked both money and any form of sophistication, but some almost indefinable sixth sense gave him the benefit of a feeling of security and confidence in his future.

It was this almost sublime confidence which brought him his first job, even though he had little conception of the fact that there was full employment in Sheffield due to the vast number of government orders for vital war supplies. He had no real idea as to where he intended to apply for employment when he left his home after breakfast one September morning, but as he walked past the entrance to Willey's he decided to find out if any work was available. To his pleasure but not his surprise he was given a job — not that it was anything special, or required any skill. One of the processes in the Sheffield Forge and

Rolling Mill was to stretch big thick iron bars until they extended to almost forty feet in length. It was Harry's job to help drag these bars away so that another batch could be stretched. He worked quietly and competently, got in no one's way, and found that he had the necessary strength even though at the end of the day his arms ached and his back felt bent.

On the first Saturday morning it was announced that anyone willing to work on Saturday afternoon would be paid 'time and a half'. Harry expressed willingness but discovered that different work would be allotted to him — work known as a 'pulling-out job'. He had to stand in front of a furnace, pulling red-hot bars of iron from it, before passing them on to another worker who put them through the mill. It was a horrific task, reminiscent of Dante's Inferno, for a young boy who stood no more than five feet in height and who was offered no protective clothing for the task which could have terrified many a man of greater height and strength. The tongs which he was given for the job of pulling the red-hot bars from the furnace were almost too heavy for him to lift, and he found that he could not cope. Somehow he managed to pull eight bars from the furnace, but received burns on his arm whilst doing so. Enough was enough, so that he gave his notice and began to look for another job.

His second job proved more to his liking, for he was offered a job in the Samuel Smith Flour Mill in Carlisle Street at twelve shillings a week tying up bags of flour. The work was far less arduous than slaving amidst the heat and hustle of a steel-rolling mill and he was content. All he had to do was to ensure that the bags of flour, once tied, were hauled up to the top floor. Harry only had to contend with twelve bags an hour, so there were plenty of rest periods. He made friends with other employees and often went round the flour mill with one of the mechanics who had two floors of machinery to look after. Harry thought that the mechanic was impressed by his alertness and industry when extra tasks were given to him, but the truth was that the man was willing to allow the innocent Harry to carry out his work whilst he relaxed. Nevertheless Harry was happy and hoped to earn promotion, for he realised that due to the war many of the young skilled employees were being called up for the armed forces, and their jobs in the flour mill needed to be replaced.

After he had been at the mill for eight months a job became vacant and was offered to him when the mechanic made it clear that Harry had the ability to carry it out. Harry was in his seventh heaven for his wages now rose from twelve shillings a week to more than two pounds, and he believed that he was on the road to fortune, particularly since Europe was now at peace.

However, by the autumn of 1918 Sheffield, although the steel capital of the empire, and the first city in Yorkshire, seemed likely to become a depressed area. Foreign competition was growing stronger; the order books of Firth's, Cammells, Vickers and Steel Peech and Tozer, which had been bursting at the seams during the war years, were becoming empty; price cutting was prevalent; mechanisation was depriving many first-class grinders of their livelihood; and the world demand for Sheffield steel was slackening, with the cutlery trade the hardest hit. Admittedly the streets of the city were now lit by electric light, national newspapers were delivered every day and slum clearance was steadily progressing, but nevertheless depression was biting deep into the lives of all Sheffield's citizens. For the young, who were unqualified, the retention of jobs was no easy matter, and unemployment with all the ensuing hardships stared them in the face.

Fate now decided to play a part in Harry's future. Arthur Wragg was drinking in The Bell in Fitzalan Square one night when he struck up a conversation with a man from Newmarket who had come to Sheffield to collect an apprentice. He told Arthur Wragg that the lad had got 'cold feet' when it actually came to the point of leaving home, and that his master, Mr Robert Colling, would be furious when he returned without the expected apprentice. To Arthur Wragg these words seemed like manna from heaven, for the home in Solly Street was bursting at the seams with his children, and his eldest daughter, Nellie, was finding it no easy task running the home in her mother's place.

Arthur Wragg proposed, therefore, that the man followed him to Solly Street where he could assess Harry's size and physical condition. If he approved, all that would remain was for Harry to be persuaded to go to Newmarket. His father wheedled, cajoled, and pleaded to such good effect that eventually, but with the greatest reluctance, Harry agreed to leave Sheffield, his home and his family.

His father bought him a small suitcase, and even though he had never seen a racehorse and knew nothing about stable work Harry departed for Newmarket where he arrived after dark. He was lonely, homesick and desperately hoped that someone would be at the railway station to meet him. His hope was unfulfilled and eventually, feeling lost and despondent, he found his way into the High Street where he asked a stranger to direct him to Waterwich House where Mr Colling trained. Following the instructions given to him he trudged into Wellington Street and up the Water Course. Still feeling dispirited but equally determined he finally arrived at the huge wooden gates guarding Bob Colling's stables.

The gates were locked but he found a small open doorway in the middle of the massive gates through which he scrambled with his suitcase. His eyes were by now accustomed to the darkness but he had no idea about the layout of the stables which were as silent as the dead. Choosing a door in what seemed to him to be a series of similar doors he opened it before quickly shutting it in fright when he realised that inside was a snorting beast! After opening and shutting several more of these doors behind each of which was a horse, he gave up the unequal struggle and began to retrace his steps. As he did so, three young stable lads appeared on the scene and immediately asked him what he was doing and who he was. Harry explained that he was a new apprentice and that he was lost. They offered to help, showed him to a dormitory and gave him a bed. Tired and exhausted after his journey from Sheffield, he was soon asleep, comforted by the knowledge that the three stable lads had promised to tell him what to do, but somewhat alarmed that his day was to start at 6.00 am.

The following morning he was introduced to the head lad who gave him two horses to look after and groom. He soon learnt how to muck out the boxes, being taught the rudiments by the other lads, but felt miserable when he was left in the yard as the string of horses and their riders went onto the gallops each morning. After a fortnight he plucked up his courage and asked the head lad if he could ride out. The head lad, who knew little or nothing concerning Harry's background, was a kindly man and suggested that when Mr Colling called for his hack, Harry should take it to him, explain who he was, and request that he be allowed to ride out. Harry seemed to have no awe for his employer and was merely nonplussed that no one was taking a blind bit of notice of him. Consequently when delivering the hack to Mr Colling and telling him that his name was Harry Wragg, he had no compunction in claiming that he knew how to ride when asked if he did so.

It was a foolhardy but understandable claim which caused him to be given a mount the next morning. In reality, Harry, although observant of the manner and style of those whom he had watched ride out every morning, had not the slightest idea of how to hold the reins or what to do with his feet when he was slung into the saddle by another lad, who wrongly assumed that riding horses was second nature to him. The next stage was that he was expected to take his place in the string as they walked out of Waterwich House onto the Severals. Harry found that his mount was dancing all over the place and as they began to trot around in a circle he felt exceedingly unhappy. In his ignorance he thought that these preliminaries were the sum total of the morning's exercise, and once the trotting ended turned to his neighbouring rider and exclaimed, 'Thank God that's over.' When the reply was, 'We were only doing a little trot. You'll find it much more exciting when we gallop,' Harry confessed that he had not the remotest idea how to ride a thoroughbred. Once across the Severals and the Bury Road, Bob Colling's horses began to gallop up Long Hill, keeping Sefton Lodge, the church and Abington Place on their left. Harry was scared but had the sense to tell the head lad that he had no conception of what he had to do. Preoccupied with other matters, the head lad took little note other than to order Harry to hang on grimly and follow the other horses up Long Hill. Somehow Harry managed to do so, but as his mount pulled up he fell to the ground.

Bob Colling witnessed his fall and came to investigate. Angrily he ordered Harry and his horse to be taken back to Waterwich House in company with another disgraced colt and his rider. It was winter and beginning to snow, and Harry's misery was at its zenith. Shamefacedly he admitted to his companion that he had no control over his mount, and when told to get him in front, asked how he should do so. When it was suggested that he should merely hit his mount with the reins, Harry obeyed, and was promptly thrown to the ground as the horse bucked him off. He was knocked unconscious and taken to hospital. He remained unconscious for days with a fractured skull and was not discharged until nine weeks had elapsed.

The incident was as inauspicious a start to a jockey's career as had ever occurred, and there were those at Waterwich House who believed that Harry would never return. They totally misjudged his character for although his skull had been fractured and his head was still swathed in bandages when he was released from hospital, it had hardly entered his mind not to continue. Whilst in hospital he had considered the alternatives as to his future, and other than to return to Sheffield there seemed no choice but to remain at Newmarket. His power of observation had aided his decision to return, for it had not escaped his notice that there were those in the world of racing at Newmarket who seemed affluent beyond belief.

Several of the lads at Waterwich House admired his decision to come back and did all in their power to help him learn to ride, but it amused him that others were under the impression that he had mastered the art of horsemanship whilst in hospital. However he was determined, and by the spring of 1919 he was beginning to show some competence in the saddle. He was riding out regularly and although he suffered the ignominy of more falls, none of them were serious and be became an apt pupil, taking in every piece of advice offered to him.

*   *   *

Robert Weston Colling, to whom Harry was apprenticed, was born in Marske, North Yorkshire in 1872, and was the son of a hunting farmer. Brought up in an atmosphere of hunting, horse-breeding and horse-loving, where sport was paramount and where horsemanship was counted as a cardinal virtue and almost a passport to heaven, Bob was riding a pony to hounds at a very early age. Determined to be a jockey, he was apprenticed to R. W. Armstrong at Penrith and rode his first winner at Newcastle when a boy of seventeen. He never rode a Classic winner but won the Stewards Cup at Goodwood on Marvel in 1892. When increasing weight compelled him to relinquish his jockey's licence, he began training near Sinnington and established his own pack of hounds. He lost little of his popularity one Sunday morning when exercising his hounds and they got on the line of a fox that hurtled into the local churchyard closely followed by the pack in full cry at the exact moment that worshippers were leaving the church.

In 1899, Colling commenced training at Spigot Lodge, Middleham. He was an unorthodox trainer who never had any time for the touts, and on many occasions galloped his most fancied handicappers at night. He would finish his evening meal, washed down with a liberal intake of claret, and would then drink more than his fair share of vintage port, before saddling his 'good thing' with the help of his head lad. The horse would be taken onto the moors and trained by the light of the moon! Towards the end of World War I, he moved to Waterwich House at Newmarket, and was still in the process of settling down in his new stables and in need of apprentices and stable lads when young Harry Wragg — long-lipped, hazel-eyed and wide-mouthed — appeared on the scene.

Harry's character was now developing and he was spending more time than ever thinking deeply about his future. He was anxious to keep fit and to improve his skill as a boxer so that he could defend himself if the necessity arose. He was perfectly prepared to accept the occasional clip over the ear for a minor misdemeanour, but had heard that in the town there were several bullies who tried to terrorise young apprentices. Sensibly he thought that if their paths ever crossed it would be to his advantage to be proficient as a boxer. Every Sunday he and Bob Colling's two sons, Jack and George, and their three great friends, Felix, Jack and Chubb Leach, would have boxing matches. They all enjoyed these bouts, especially as Bob Colling would give them a few shillings as a form of extra pocket money. Harry was probably the best boxer of the six and would skip and dance about the ring, go on the ropes and shadow box. He acquired a punch ball and improved his prowess by constant use of it.

One afternoon a few days before the Two Thousand Guineas meeting a man entered the stable yard and explained that if anyone wished to enter for a local boxing competition he could provide the entry forms. Harry, inclined to weigh matters up from a mercenary angle, asked him if there were any prizes, and was informed that if he won his first bout he would receive five shillings, ten shillings if he won the next round, and more money the nearer he got to the final. Harry promptly entered for both the 6-stone and the 7-stone competitions, calculating that by so doing he might double his winnings. The first night he had two fights in each competition and won them all. The next night he fought in two semi-finals, and was victorious in both. The second of them had been fiercely contested and Harry did not feel that he could fight both finals. He decided to give his opponent a walk-over in the 7-stone competition, but was persuaded that he mught fight as his supporters had backed him heavily to win and insisted that he stood his ground. His opponent was almost as skilled as 'the Waterwich Kid', as Harry was known, and only in the last round did Harry assert his superiority to gain the verdict. His fans now refused to allow him to withdraw from the other final, which he duly won to become the hero of the hour. He received his two trophies, but to his disgust the promised prize-money was not forthcoming. However, he received enough to celebrate by treating himself and some of his pals to his favourite meal of egg and chips and a bar of chocolate before going to the cinema. For the most part the stable lads existed on starvation rations, with their final

meal of the day consisting of bread and butter at 4.00 pm.
Newmarket landladies were only given about one pound a week
by trainers for the stable lads' board and lodging, so they were
not to blame for the lack of liberality.

Harry's supporters from Waterwich House told him not to
ride out the following morning for he deserved a rest, but he
refused. The reason was that he thought that there was a
possibility that he might be given his first ride in public the next
day. One of Bob Colling's fillies had been earmarked for an
apprentice race at Newmarket and Harry expected to be chosen
to ride her. He imagined that if he did not ride out on the
morning after his triumph in the boxing ring then the mount
might be given to someone else. He could have enjoyed a
'morning off', for as he rode out he was told that the filly was a
non-runner. He was obviously disappointed, but the incident
convinced him that boxing should never take priority over his
future as a jockey. He was finding that he was riding out at
exercise on many occasions alongside George Colling, who
taught him much for he was a generous-hearted young man.
However, there were very few opportunities for Harry to ride in
public, partly because of the scarcity of apprentice races in
the Calendar and, more to the point, the fact that George
Colling was so talented an apprentice that his father gave him as
many mounts as possible. Nevertheless, Harry rode for the first
time in the Bury Handicap at Newmarket in July 1919, a month
after his seventeenth birthday, which gave him an inkling of the
glamour attached to a career as a jockey. He weighed less than
six and a half stone. In September he rode a three-year-old
filly in the Burton Apprentice Plate at Derby:

> The filly, who was owned by Major J.B. Paget, was named
> Flying Duck and had already run five times without
> success at distances from six to twelve furlongs. Nobody
> wanted to make the running, and so I went to the front,
> setting a slow pace whilst the other four jockeys seemed
> content to follow me. Things carried on exactly as I had
> hoped until we were about to enter the straight which
> had a short three-furlong run-in. One of the other jockeys

tried to come up on my inside so I cut him off and as we entered the straight I went for my life. They never caught me and I won by six lengths, but they flew by me the moment we'd passed the winning post.

Now that did me a lot of good, even though the season was more than half over. I finished second on Flying Duck in another apprentice race at Stockton in October and on the final day of the season finished third in a Nursery handicap at Manchester. Steve Donoghue and Brownie Carslake were riding that day, and as I cantered to the start I wondered if I would ever be as famous as they.

2

'What a business this is . . .'

By the spring of 1920, Britain was attempting to shake off the horrors of war. King George V had ratified the Peace Treaty; homage to the Glorious Dead had been paid by a two minutes' silence for prayer and remembrance; Dame Nellie Melba and Mr Charles Chaplin were the stars of the entertainment world and the soaring cost of living was bringing storms of indignation. Tetratema was thought to be the best colt in England and in the Free Handicap published the previous autumn had been given 12 lbs more than the second horse, Orpheus, owned by Mr Hugo Cunliffe-Owen. In the Honours List a baronetcy was conferred upon Mr Cunliffe-Owen, with a similar honour being awarded to three other well-known racehorse owners, Mr James Buchanan, Mr Abe Bailey and Mr Edward Hulton. Racing appeared to be booming, for crowds were flocking to the racecourses, betting turnover was on the increase, and there seemed to be plenty of opportunities for young jockeys. Harry Wragg was given a mount at Lincoln on the first day of the season and forty-eight hours later rode in the Lincoln, having the mount on Cylgar. Although not given the opportunity to ride at Epsom or Royal Ascot he had several mounts at Newmarket and showed such promise that he was offered a ride in the Cumberland Plate at Carlisle. He realised that:

> It was a wonderful thing to be able to get onto the racecourse. That way you'd got a chance of meeting people, probably you might get a spare ride. This happened to me one day at Nottingham. Before the Nottingham meeting we had been racing at the Craven

Meeting, Newmarket and that was my first break. We were running a little filly, a tiny little thing, called Winsome Ciss, owned by Mr P. F. Heybourn. Brownie Carslake was supposed to be riding her and he came down to exercise her the morning before the race. When he saw the animal he was going to ride he said 'Gracious me, you don't want me riding that, you want to put that kid on,' which Mr Colling duly did and I was allowed the ride on Winsome Ciss. The most extraordinary thing happened. There were fourteen runners and as we were going into the starting gate — she ducked her head. It looked like being a start, I thought it was anyhow, and away I went. Some of the field on the high number side of the course didn't jump off, but we had gone on our side. At least I had, and the chap with a flag in the middle of the course who was there to send you back if there's a false start did not do so. So I went on. Two or three other jockeys followed me, not many because a lot of them pulled up and went back. The Stewards had me in after the race and asked me — did a feller with a red flag move, was he off the course when I got there? I said yes, he'd gone for his life. He had to. Anyhow I kept the race.

In the Calendar it was stated that the Starter reported to the Stewards that some of the jockeys pulled up their horses because the tape broke as the gate was released. But as this had not interfered with any of the horses, he did not consider that it was a case in which he should have made use of the recall flag. The Stewards heard the evidence of the winning jockey and other jockeys who rode in the race, and considered that the jockeys were very much to blame for pulling up their horses without the recall signal having been given.

Then came my success at Nottingham in July. I'd taken a horse to run the next day and I was just scouting around and touching my hat to people, trying to talk to people, trying to get a ride when I was on the stands watching a race. There were two owners and a trainer talking to a young jockey and I overheard him saying that his Uncle Dick wouldn't let him ride this thing. I thought by Jesus, he's refusing the ride, so I made signs to him and I kept implying that he should put me in for the ride.

To my annoyance he didn't look like taking any notice
at all. I was wanting him to tell the owners that he didn't
want to ride it but that there was a boy who would, but he
never even mentioned it. So eventually I thought I should
take the bull by the horns. I went in, 'Excuse me, sirs,' I
said, 'if you're looking for a jockey for tomorrow, I could
ride.' They said, 'Who are you?' I said, 'I'm Harry Wragg,
I'm the boy that rode that winner in April at Newmarket
when there was a lot of talk about a false start, I won that
race.' The point was that their horse, Voxol (who had run
eight times unplaced in 1919), had got a very light weight.
'What weight can you do?' I was asked. I replied 'I can do
any weight.' 'Well, this has got 6-12', I was told. I said, 'I'll
do that on a 10lb saddle.' So they said, 'OK, you'll ride
him.' Anyhow, when I got on the horse they told me he
pulled and that's why this other boy didn't want to ride
him. I said, 'All right, I'll just take him down very quietly,'
which I did. I gave him a lot of rein and he lobbed to the
post.

He was an old rogue and in the race I'm making the
running and I'm leading at a nice sort of pace. Voxol
always seemed to me to have got a very good chance and
when we got over the road and there were about two
furlongs to go, I started to increase the pace a little bit.
Started pushing him, and as I did so his head went back
and I thought, oh dear. So I stopped immediately and got
hold of him and started to ride him as if I didn't bother any
more and sat so still that the horse started to go better and
better and better. So eventually I hung on like that but I
daren't pick my stick up or push him, and I was just sitting
still. Anyway, we passed the post — winning by three-
quarters of a length at 33-1.

It was a biggish race and before I left the races that day
the trainer, Captain J. R. Renwick, came up to me and
wanted to know if I was going to Pontefract at the end of
the week. I said, 'Yes, I can go anywhere, but I shall have
to let my guv'nor know about this sort of thing.' Actually I
didn't know how I was going to get there. I'd got no
money, no clothes nor anything. So I talked to the valet. I
told him what it was all about — this feller wants me to
ride tomorrow, I don't know how to get there. So the valet
said, 'I'm going that way — I'll give you a lift.' So I spoke
to my head man and I told him what had happened. I'd

got a ride tomorrow and the next day at Pontefract, so he said, 'OK, I'll tell the boss when I get home.' So that was another start to help me on the way.

I had a couple of rides at Pontefract, but I didn't do any good — I think I got a third but Captain Renwick asked if I could ride again at Catterick at the end of the week. So I said, 'Yes, that'll be alright.' So I told the valet again and he looked after me and agreed to get me to Catterick. On the Friday and Saturday I went to Catterick where I rode two winners — Easy Accession and Ring O'Roses — for Captain Renwick.

Captain Renwick thought that Harry had ridden with coolness and sense, and approached Bob Colling with the proposal that his apprentice should be loaned to him. Colling discussed the matter with 'Cannie' Watts, one of his closest friends, and a man famed for his skill at picking winners, working commissions and backing horses in running. Watts was convinced that Wragg had a great future but that he would have no chance at Waterwich House due to the fact that Bob Colling's son George was showing such prowess in the saddle and following in the footsteps of his elder brother, Jack. Watts advised Bob Colling to allow Harry to ride for Captain Renwick and his advice was heeded.

Forty-three-year-old John Renwick trained at the historic Whitewall outside Malton in Yorkshire. Eldest son of Sir George Renwick, the renowned Tyneside ship-builder, he had closed down his famous stables from where John Scott had sent out so many Classic winners in the nineteenth century, and served with an ammunition column in the Northumberland R.F.A. Brigade during the 1914-18 war. The Armistice signed, he re-opened his stables, once again took over the Goatland Hounds, which hunted over rough boggy moorland and of which he had been Master before the war, and set about training thoroughbreds. He was regarded as a peerless judge of a yearling, but he openly admitted that he infinitely preferred hunting to the Turf, which he considered smattered of commercialism. From his point of view the Turf also provided a

precarious existence, and the bailiffs were often interested in his
whereabouts. If he knew they were coming to Whitewall he
would walk to those stables which had been converted into a
garage and sit down on the back seat of a large comfortable
motor car. His butler would bring him his newspapers and a
bottle of port, and then cover the car with a massive tarpaulin.
Renwick would remain in hiding until after the departure of the
bailiffs.

Harry spent much time riding for Renwick during the next
six months. He noticed during his months in Yorkshire that the
people who were held in the highest esteem were the rough-
riders, for they were real horsemen with the skill and the
strength to school even the wildest of colts. Harry attempted to
copy them, even though it meant that the head lad frequently
gave him a box over the ears for seemingly 'fooling about' when
in reality he was trying to follow their example.

Before the end of the 1920 season, Harry had finished third on
Eastern Valley in the Ayr Gold Cup, had ridden in the
Cesarewitch, and at the Liverpool Autumn Meeting had won
the Grosvenor Cup on Internationale, beating George Colling
on Lord Derby's March Along by a neck. Colling was one of the
best apprentices of the era and in 1919 had ridden seventy-two
winners which put him fifth in the Jockeys' Table, but there
were those who thought that Harry was becoming his equal.
Proof that he was in demand came in the final three days of the
season when after four mounts at Manchester he was sent to
Lingfield where he had three rides on the last afternoon.

Harry was now on the threshold of his career as a jockey and
his name was mentioned whenever the question of leading
apprentices arose:

In the early parts of my apprenticeship days, all we
apprentice boys would go about in groups especially when
we were going to the Park meetings near London. When
we got to Liverpool Street we had to get on the Under-
ground and it's amazing how well and how quickly we
could get on when we were going in groups. We got into a
way of doing things, we were really always on the trot, we

weren't really just walking and looking at signs, we knew where we were going — and to go across London we could go as quick as any of the best taxi-men. We knew where we'd got to change on the Inner Circle and we could do it in very quick time. We always caught trains, we never missed them.

All we kids were very good dancers. We needed to keep fit, and if we were racing at Leicester, Derby or Nottingham and staying overnight we would spend the evening at the local Palais de Danse. We always tried to stay in the same digs, and we would never be late back in case we upset our landlady. Usually our 'gang' consisted of Bobby Jones, Dick Perryman, Charlie Smirke and Tommy Weston. When we arrived at the Palais I would buy about ten tickets, each one of which entitled you to a dance with a girl. I would spot a girl dancing who I thought was adept and go and ask her for a dance. If we got on well I gave her the other nine tickets and booked my dances with her until it was time to leave the Palais. I was very keen on music and really loved dancing.

Gradually, although we were in groups, we found that we had especial pals. I had one called Bobby Jones.

It was due to Bobby Jones that Harry was accepted as a lodger by the Robinson family on his return to Newmarket from Whitewall. Robinson, who was head lad to Alfred Sadler, lived at Beaumont Villa in Rous Road with his wife and two teenage daughters. Bobby was already 'in residence' and suggested that Harry should join him. The two young men became the best of friends, with Bobby far more of an extrovert than the thoughtful, cautious Harry. Bobby was the son of a gardener, had been born in Beverley, and was the youngest of three brothers, all of whom were jockeys. His eldest brother, Peter, was to die in October 1923 from injuries received when his mount, Maid of Middleham, fell at Bogside. Bobby was apprenticed to Alfred Sadler who was training at Abington Place after leaving Freemasons Lodge.

The two Robinson girls thought the world of both Bobby and Harry, although Harry appeared far less dashing than the debonair Jones, but they were grateful that he often took the trouble and thought to bring chocolate and flowers for their mother on his return from a race meeting. Occasionally he gave them a tip — which was immediately passed on to their father. A shrewd, kindly man, who was a superb horseman and an equally fine servant to Alfred Sadler, Robinson won considerably more money than he lost by following the tips that Harry gave.

Much of Bobby and Harry's spare time was spent playing billiards and snooker at the Craven Club in Newmarket, and also on the local golf course. Bobby was a talented player, whilst Harry improved steadily by dint of concentration. They had no proper lessons from the local professional, Charlie Kennett, but were adept at picking up hints as to grip and swing by watching him in action.

1921 By the spring of 1921 there was no doubt that Harry's career as a jockey was 'set fair'. He won the opening race of the season when he scored on Glenaster to become Champion Jockey for half an hour! And to show that this victory was no flash in the pan, he rode another winner for Mr G. Renwick the next afternoon. During the spring racing lost thirty-four days due to a coal strike, but Harry rode at Epsom for the first time on the eve of The Derby, and on Oaks Day, having been second in the first race, took the mount on Mr J. S. Courtauld's Donna Branca in The Oaks. At Royal Ascot he won the first race of the meeting on Lord Astor's Plymstock and later in the week scored again when he forced Santaquest home by a short head in the Wokingham Stakes, beating Tommy Weston on Lemonade by a short head. As Lemonade was owned by King George V, it was not considered the most popular of results! However Harry was quickly forgiven in Royal circles, and rode Lemonade in the Stewards Cup at Goodwood. He had mounts in both the Cesarewitch and the Cambridgeshire at Newmarket in the autumn and ended the season on a high note by winning three races at the Manchester November meeting. He won on Knee Cap, his final mount on the Saturday afternoon, to give him a remarkable double of having won on his first and his final

mount of the season. He also finished second to Brownie
Carslake in both the first race and the Manchester November
Handicap, to bring his name to the attention of the racing press.
He had ridden fourteen winners during the year, and as an
apprentice his reputation was as high as that of Gordon
Richards, who was apprenticed to Mr Martin Hartigan,
Tommy Weston whose master was Mr E. McCormack, and
Edward Charles Elliott whose master was Mr J. L. Jarvis.

Harry had more sense than many of his contemporaries and
was always willing to learn. One man who helped him was Jim
Bell, who had once trained at Hambleton:

> Jim Bell was an interesting character who came into my
> life early on. When I was an apprentice he often came
> down to Bob Colling's and he used to pick me out and I
> remember him saying to me, 'You've got to realise when
> you're riding a horse that you're the master, like at school
> when you're the master, so you've got to teach him the
> rights and wrongs. If you carry out the job well you may
> make him into a horse — you'll never ruin him — anyhow
> you'll be able to do some good.' Jim was a real character
> and he used to get horses that nobody else would train and
> nobody wanted to train and he would do all kinds of
> things, including tying them to a tree and leaving them
> there. But he did have some crackerjack jumpers — horses
> that had got ability and weren't showing it on the Flat.
> The moment he got them and started training them he
> made them into good horses. Anyhow, I thought he helped
> me quite a bit, taking me on one side and instructing me
> how to make a horse do what he should be doing.
> Constantly he would remind me — he's at school, you're a
> school master and he's got to be taught, even to learn how
> to walk.

Harry's final year as an apprentice began less auspiciously than **1922**
1921 and he did not ride a winner until almost a month of the
season had been completed. However, the winner brought a
significant milestone in his career for it was Will Somers, owned
by King George V, on whom he won the Leicestershire
Handicap Plate — his first success in Royal colours. Later in the
year Harry was to win on Will Somers at Nottingham in July

and again at Leicester in August. He was unplaced in both the Two Thousand Guineas and The Derby on Mr F. Bibby's North End, a horse who always seemed to contest races in which he was hopelessly outclassed. At Ascot Harry rode Selene, the future dam of Hyperion, in the Gold Vase won by Charlie Elliott on Golden Myth who was brought out again to win the Gold Cup two days later, but in many ways Harry's final season as an apprentice brought him no important success, even though he again ended the season on a high note by winning two races at the Manchester November meeting.

However, during the summer an incident occurred which almost ended his career as a jockey and one which, understandably, embittered him. Luckily Frank Haslam, one of the rough riders who worked for Bob Colling and a man for whom Harry had the greatest respect and whose style and tactics he tried to copy, came to his rescue.

One morning Harry went to see Bob Colling in his office to be paid the money that had accrued to his credit during his apprenticeship. He had calculated that there would be a considerable amount out of which he intended to buy his father a small house in Newmarket and also give presents to his sisters. He knew that he had earned much for Bob Colling, particularly during his final season as an apprentice, for Colling had always demanded the odds to at least twenty-five pounds from those owners outside the stable for whom Harry rode a winner, and Harry assumed that he would leave the office a comparatively wealthy young man. As the interview progressed it slowly dawned upon an astounded Harry that he was to receive nothing. Bob Colling told him how excellent an apprentice he had been, began a long dialogue about Harry's future prospects, and proposed that Harry was given a retainer to ride some of the stable's horses the next year, but of money owed to him there was no mention. Eventually, heartbroken and crying, Harry departed with his world shattered and his confidence in human nature destroyed.

One of the first people that he met was Frank Haslam, to whom he blurted out his misery. Haslam pointed out that he was not in the least surprised, for Bob Colling was renowned for his parsimony, but somewhat helped Harry's ego by adding that in the opinion of many Harry was one of the best apprentices in Newmarket. Nevertheless, Harry made it clear that he had decided to give up all idea of making his future as a jockey and that he would return to Sheffield. Haslam exploded with indignation, told Harry that he was an idiot even to contemplate such a notion, and reminded him that he had two rides at Alexandra Park the next afternoon. Harry muttered that he would not go to the races, but such was the strength of Haslam's personality that he insisted that Harry change his mind, and personally escorted him to the station, bought his ticket and waited with him until the train departed.

Harry duly reached 'Ally Pally', where he won the London Cup on Captain Bewick's Vindictive. Such a success put new heart into him:

> Then my father came down and brought the indentures and the contract for me to read. There it was in black and white, the only money that was mentioned was that I was to receive a shilling a week and it increased to two shillings the subsequent year and three shillings the following — that's the only money that was mentioned — not a thing in the contract in the case of any money I earned. Nothing concerning any riding fees, which was a very unnatural thing. There was nothing I could do about it, it wasn't there so I didn't squeal, I just thought what a business this is, from now onwards I've got to really work, as Frank Haslam says, and get everything I can earn and put it into the bank.

Harry might have been wiser to bring the entire matter to the attention of the Jockey Club for the sake of other apprentices. However, such a course of action would have been easier said than done.

3

A budding career

1922 was the first year since 1913 that racing in England suffered no interruption, although there were indications that the post-war boom was almost over. Racecourse attendances were down, except at Epsom on Derby Day and at Newmarket for the Cambridgeshire and the Cesarewitch, and the fact that over a million men were on the dole meant that to attend a race meeting, especially in the North of England, was a luxury beyond the financial resources of many lovers of the sport. Their interest remained stimulated by the racing information in the newspapers, and by sixpenny bets made on street corners.

1923 However, it was hoped that the 1923 season would see an improvement. Harry was in his first season as a fully-fledged jockey, and earning the respect of Stanley Wootton, a man renowned for 'not suffering fools gladly'. Ironically, Harry's first winner of the season was on a filly owned and trained by his former master, Bob Colling. At Epsom, on Derby Day, he won the race which immediately preceded 'The Blue Riband', which he watched from the grandstand as Papyrus won from Pharos. Three weeks later at Ascot he was second in the Bessborough Stakes on His Majesty's Bowood and third on Lady Feo in the Coronation Stakes, also in the Royal colours. At Goodwood he won the Chichester Plate on Joss House for the King, and in doing so upset a gamble on 'Archie' Falcon's Orderly. He also won for King George V on Carmel, a two-year-old filly by Friar Marcus, at the Newmarket July meeting and again scored on the filly at the second October meeting.

Harry had been recommended to succeed Herbert Jones as the King's jockey by Joe Childs. Childs had been approached by Richard Marsh, the royal trainer, and the King's racing manager, Major Featherstonhaugh, and told them that he thought that Harry had all the makings of a first-class jockey. Many of the King's horses had been badly handicapped in the post-war years due to the fact that even if they had no chance of winning or being placed they were ridden out to the bitter end since they were carrying the Royal colours. On one of the first occasions that Harry rode for the King he dropped his hands once he realised that all chance of victory had gone. As he returned towards the area where unplaced horses were unsaddled he espied Richard Marsh approaching him in obvious fury. Quickly he dismounted, told the stable lad to walk the horse up and down and when Marsh arrived, promptly said, 'He looks sound now, sir, but I had to pull him up as I thought he had rapped a joint.' The resourceful explanation was accepted without demur.

In the spring of 1924 Harry rode Knight of the Garter for the **1924** King in the Two Thousand Guineas but was unplaced, and Carmel in the One Thousand Guineas when the filly was no match for Plack and Mumtaz Mahal. At Newcastle on Easter Monday Harry had shown his potential ability by riding the first four winners of the afternoon, and for good measure scored two more victories at the meeting the next day. It was a fine achievement and one which equalled similar feats in previous years by Steve Donoghue and Frank Bullock, although W. Higgs had won five races at Newbury in one afternoon, and Fred Archer all six races at Lewes. Less than three weeks after his Newcastle feat Harry rode three winners in an afternoon at Ayr — a fine performance for a twenty-two-year-old jockey, who by mid-August was second in the Jockeys' Table, only five winners behind Charlie Elliott. Those who knew Harry were beginning to appreciate his strength of character and temperament, although his fellow jockeys, who admired his sense of balance, considerable powers of concentration and his alertness to exactly how each and every race was being run, thought that he did not seem to achieve his success through flair and instinct but by dint of perseverance.

However, much to his disgust, in the Cesarewitch he was not allowed to ride the race he wished, for entrepreneur and financier Jimmy White insisted that he handled Norseman — who had been second in the Ebor Handicap at York to Flint Jack and second in the Bessborough Stakes at Ascot — as he, the owner, demanded.

'You must come on the outside all the way,' stated White, 'for two jockeys are going to try to get at you.' 'If I do so,' replied Harry, 'I shall have no chance at all.' 'Never mind,' said the determined owner, who had backed his horse to win a fortune. 'If you ride the horse your way and win there is no present for you. But if you do as you are told and ride him my way, I shall not mind if you lose.' Such an astonishing comment left Harry totally in a quandary — but he decided to ride Norseman how he thought fit until within sight of the grandstands. Only then did he pull Norseman onto the outside. As he did so the horse started fighting for his head, lost ground and eventually finished fifth to H. H. Aga Khan's Charley's Mount. Harry was convinced that ridden correctly Norseman would have won.

1925 During the early spring of 1925 Harry signed an agreement with Solly Joel, for whom he rode Applause in the One Thousand Guineas. Solly and his brother Jack had been born in the East End of London where their father kept a public house — the King of Prussia. As boys they had shown their ingenuity by selling homing pigeons to unsuspecting bystanders in Piccadilly Circus and Leicester Square. Within hours the birds had flown home to their loft at the King of Prussia and were sold over and over again! By the age of thirty both Solly and Jack Joel were millionaires due to their acumen and their understanding of the fortune to be made in the diamond industry of South Africa. In 1896 Solly bought a house in Great Stanhope Street, Mayfair, which became his London home and three years later registered his 'pink and green stripes'. In 1903 he acquired Maiden

Erleigh near Reading which became his country home and his principal stud. It was here that his famous parties on the Sunday before Royal Ascot were held.

By the mid-1920s he had won the 1915 Triple Crown with Pommern: the 1905 Doncaster Gold Cup and the 1906 Ascot Gold Cup with Bachelor's Button; and the 1906 Champion Stakes and Cambridgeshire with Polymelus. He had won the Lincolnshire Handicap twice, with Long Set (1912) and Soranus (1921), and the 1913 Royal Hunt Cup with Long Set again, who also credited him with the 1911 Cambridgeshire. In 1922 Solly, who had headed the list of Winning Owners the previous year, bought the Moulton Paddocks at Newmarket from Jimmy White who had acquired the estate from Sir Ernest Cassels at the end of World War I. Two seasons later he installed Walter Earl at Moulton Paddocks as his private trainer. Solly was immensely generous, stubbornly loyal to his friends and a wonderful host. He loved gambling, would bet on every race, and enjoyed nothing more than to sit up all night at Monte Carlo or Deauville playing chemin-de-fer, but his knowledge of the breeding industry and the finer points of bloodstock were far less than that possessed by his brother.

At Epsom Harry Wragg rode Solly's 100-1 outsider St Napoleon in The Derby and finished virtually last. He fared little better in The Oaks on Applause who finished ninth of twelve behind Lord Astor's brilliant filly, Saucy Sue. However he had better luck at Royal Ascot and after finishing second on the big and handsome Polyphontes in the Royal Hunt Cup, he won the Ribblesdale Stakes on Solly's colt Glommen. Polyphontes, sired by Polymelus, was a very useful horse who had won the 1924 Eclipse Stakes at Sandown ridden by W. McLachlan. He had been fifth in The Derby to Sansovino, and third in the St Leger to Salmon Trout.

A month later as Harry Wragg rode Polyphontes down to the start of the 1925 Eclipse he noticed that there was as big a crowd at Sandown as anyone could remember and that the King and Queen were present. Lord Astor had two runners, although his filly Saucy Sue was an absentee due to heel trouble, and

H. H. Aga Khan also had two runners. Harry was content to let
Polyphontes remain in the middle division until half way up the
straight when he drove him up to the leader, Zambo. It was
expected that Polyphontes would surge ahead, but so gallantly
did Zambo struggle that Harry only managed to force Polyphontes into the lead in the last few strides to win by a neck, to
thus become the third horse to win the Eclipse in successive
years — the others being the Duke of Westminster's Orme (1892
and 1893) and Lord Astor's Buchan (1919 and 1920). For Harry
it was his first success in a major race, and one which gave his
morale and confidence a boost.

'Glorious Goodwood' proved equally successful with Harry
winning the Seller on the opening day for Solly and later in the
afternoon the Richmond Stakes on Pantera and the Gratwicke
Stakes on Glommen in his colours. The starting price of the
treble — let alone the doubles and single bets — came to almost
100-1, so that the bookmakers were hammered, and Solly left
the races a very happy man. The money that he had won was of
little consequence to him, but his pleasure at defeating the
bookmakers was boundless. The great run continued the next
afternoon when Harry won on The Monk for Solly, but the rest
of the afternoon was not so successful and three fancied runners
were beaten — much to the bookmakers' relief. However, their
relief was comparatively short-lived, for Solly and Harry won
with the full brother and sister, Fodder and Dodder, at the
Doncaster St Leger meeting to bring off a 76-1 double. As Solly
thought nothing of having thousands on his horses, Doncaster
also provided temporary misery for the bookmakers.

However, Harry was almost responsible for saving them from
a colossal pay-out over the Cesarewitch-Cambridgeshire
double. Mr A. K. Macomber had doubled up his Cesarewitch
contender, Forseti, with his Masked Marvel for the Cambridgeshire. Forseti won by one and a half lengths and if Masked
Marvel won the second leg, the bookies were liable for a pay-out
exceeding £100,000. On the eve of the Cambridgeshire, Solly
bought the three-year-old Pons Asinorum, who had run
creditably in the St Leger, from Mr Albert Lowry, and backed

him heavily. Masked Marvel took up the running at halfway and was never headed although inside the final furlong Harry forced Pons Asinorum nearer and nearer to him and would have won in another hundred yards. Nevertheless, Solly Joel ended up second in the Winning Owners List for the year — only £146 behind Lord Astor.

In an effort to overhaul him, Solly entered six horses at the Manchester November meeting, but to no avail as the meeting was abandoned. On the first and third days the track was frozen hard, and on the second day when racing would have been possible, it was cancelled due to the funeral of Queen Alexandra being held in the afternoon.

Harry was justifiably pleased at his success throughout the season, for he had ridden 78 winners from 594 mounts and had finished fourth to Gordon Richards in the list of Winning Jockeys. A fortnight after the season ended he was best man to Bobby Jones at All Saints Church, Newmarket, when he married Helen Cartwright, whose father was head lad to Reg Day. After Christmas Harry went to India to enjoy a 'busman's holiday' on the courses there before returning in time for the Flat Season. It was his first experience of riding abroad and made a great impression on him.

1926 brought little success to Harry, who rode Pantera in both **1926** the Two Thousand Guineas and The Derby behind Coronach. There was no racing from 2-29 April due to the General Strike and both the Two Thousand Guineas and the One Thousand Guineas were held on the same day. Harry had no notable victories until Goodwood, where he won the Goodwood Cup on Solly Joel's Glommen, who was now a very good four-year-old, but one with a will of his own. Harry had already won on him three times that year: at the Manchester Whitsuntide meeting, at the Newmarket second July meeting, and at the Liverpool summer meeting. He was well fancied for the Goodwood Cup but there was a distinct possibility that the mount would be given to Brownie Carslake.

He was a one-eyed horse — they were going to get Brownie

Carslake to ride him in the Goodwood Cup. So he came down to ride Glommen work. As we went across the Limekilns to Waterhall, he reared up and went down on his knees and began to eat the grass. It frightened the life out of Brownie and he didn't want any part of it, and so he said to the head man, 'Look, get me off this thing and get this kid Wragg on it.' So we changed rides. I rode him in a gallop and when we got back the head man told the trainer, Walter Earl, what had happened. He said Carslake didn't want any part of him. So I rode him in the Goodwood Cup and he won. And I didn't mind, as a matter of fact, if anybody wasn't satisfied with my riding, I didn't give a damn really because I didn't think anybody could improve on me — so naturally I was very pleased to keep on him because he was a very good horse.

Others beside Harry were also confident of his future, and the Hon. George Lambton commented, 'I very much like young Harry Wragg's quiet way of winning races. There is never anything theatrical about his finishes, and I think that he has sometimes been blamed unjustly for being a trifle slow, but when the same horses have been ridden by another jockey there has been no improvement in form. He has a great future.'

The next day Harry dead-heated on Pantera with Henri Jelliss on Thistledown for the Gordon Stakes. When the deciding heat was run Harry was beaten six lengths. He objected on the grounds of crossing, but his objection was over-ruled and his deposit forfeited. This objection emphasised the opinion that some critics were forming that Harry was beginning to get somewhat 'swollen-headed'.

Such swollen-headedness was to some extent excusable in jockeys who were constantly in the news, and who were fêted as celebrities. Certainly Brownie Carslake was vain and self-opinionated and thought by many to be sardonic, but he could be the staunchest and most generous of friends. Aquiline of features, with a long nose, jutting chin and high forehead from which his black hair was brushed back, he was invariably dressed immaculately, and gave acquaintances the feeling that he should have been an actor. A useful cricketer and a competent boxer, he loathed cold weather and rode his best in mid summer. He had made his name as a jockey in Australia where his father was a trainer at Caulfield, but came to England in 1905. For much of the next ten years he rode on the Continent and once wrote, 'All was pomp and elegance, aristocracy and wealth. Marvellous uniforms on the grandstands, beautiful women in the paddocks. Princes and Grand Dukes, Counts and Barons. Generals, Captains, dashing Cavalrymen and gallant Hussars. What a pageant a German or Austrian racecourse was — just like a show in Daly's Theatre.' He spent the war years on the Continent, and arrived in England virtually penniless in 1918. However, he soon made a name for himself riding for the Hon. George Lambton and 'Atty' Persse and at the end of the season it was prophesied that 'the chances are that Carslake will succeed to the vacancy created when Danny Maher and Frank Wootton retire.' By the end of 1924 he had won five Classics, but the drama of the St Leger which he won on Salmon Trout after strong rumours that the Aga Khan's colt would be beaten and that he was heavily committed with bookmaker Moe Tash, gave the incident a 'Nat Gould' flavour and left a stigma on Carslake which he never completely shook off.

In August York proved a successful meeting for Harry, winning the Ebor Handicap on Pons Asinorum, who started favourite. His success was fully expected, for Harry had ridden him to finish third to Solario in the Gold Cup at Ascot, having previously won the Newbury Summer Cup. The next afternoon Harry won the Gimcrack Stakes on Mr H. Shaw's Bold Archer, a half-brother to Derby winner Papyrus. Mr Shaw lived at Beenham Court near Newbury and Bold Archer had been leased to him by Sir John Robinson, who had not thought the colt to be in good enough condition to be submitted with other lots from his Worksop Manor Stud at the Doncaster St Leger Sales.

At Doncaster Harry won the Doncaster Cup on Glommen but much to his indignation was disqualified. Freddie Fox, who rode the runner-up, Lord Rosebery's three-year-old filly Bongrace, objected on the grounds of bumping and boring. The objection was sustained even though there was considerable criticism that the objection should not have been made. Harry was content to keep Glommen at the rear of the field until the straight was reached, but half a mile from home he took close order on the leaders. It was evident that there would be a struggle for supremacy between Glommen and Bongrace, who had disputed the lead with Wykeham, but two hundred yards from home Glommen swerved and bumped the filly almost onto the rails. But for this misdemeanour, Glommen would have won easily — and in fact he passed the winning post four lengths ahead of the filly.

The two horses met again in the Jockey Club Cup six weeks later — but at a weight difference of 16 lbs as compared with the 35 lbs difference at Doncaster. Small wonder, therefore, that Glommen was considered certain to defeat Bongrace. However, in a slow-run race she beat him by a neck — with the excuse being offered by the supporters of Solly Joel's horse that he had suffered a gruelling preparation for the Cesarewitch between the two races with Bongrace from which he had not recovered. Brownie Carslake had ridden him in the Cesarewitch and failed to reach the leaders, but Harry was re-united with him when Glommen failed to take his revenge on Bongrace. She was a filly full of courage who needed a tremendous amount of work, and was laziness personified. Every time that she ran she required a smack with the whip to remind her of the task in hand. At stud she became the dam of Ribbon when she was seventeen years old.

One of the best two-year-olds of the 1926 season was Hot Night, a colt bred by the Sledmere Stud and bought by Sir Victor Sassoon for 3,800 guineas. Described as a tall, light-fleshed colt, he raced only twice during 1926, making a winning debut at Newmarket before running a frustrating race in the Champagne Stakes at Doncaster where he took up the running at halfway, his rivals apparently at his mercy. Suddenly he seemed to become disenchanted, dropped his bit and to the disgust of his jockey, P. Brown, refused to race. In consequence he was deemed a colt of exceptional promise, but one whose temperament might be his greatest enemy. His owner had only recently come into racing, with his entry being due to his friendship with J. H. Crawford, a veterinary surgeon and amateur rider in Bombay who had returned to England in 1922 to train for Mr Mathrados Goculdas.

When Goculdas, a cotton magnate, found himself unable to meet his liabilities — largely due to unsuccessful betting — Sir Victor Sassoon, who had recently inherited the baronetcy from his father, took over his racing interests, bought the Fitzroy House stables at Newmarket where he installed Crawford as his private trainer, and also acquired the Bungalow Stud at Wood Ditton. He began purchasing yearlings on a lavish scale and at the 1925 Doncaster sales bought ten yearlings for 28,350 guineas. One of them he named Hot Night. Within minutes of buying Hot Night, a colt sired by Derby winner Gay Crusader, he met Martin Benson, better known as bookmaker Douglas Stuart. He asked Benson to lay him £1,000-£1 that Hot Night won the 1927 Derby. Benson agreed to accept the bet — each way — but only to the stake of a penny. Benson's much published slogan was 'Duggie never owes' — a much more subtle wording than 'Duggie always pays', which he had intended to use until a friend in the world of advertising suggested the alternative wording.

In January 1927, Harry married Marjorie Hobson whose father kept the Queen's Hotel in Roundhay Road, Leeds. He had first met Marjorie the previous year when motoring through Leeds with Charlie Smirke. The car in which they were travelling broke down and they were compelled to stay the night at the Queen's Hotel. Deciding to go for a meal to the nearby Majestic Restaurant they met Marjorie's brother, George, who was dining with George Hulme, the Aga Khan's jockey. After dinner they went to George Hobson's home for coffee where Harry was introduced to Marjorie. Less than a year later they were married. They went to Egypt for their honeymoon, staying at Shepheard's Hotel in Cairo. Marjorie was keen to see the pyramids and to make trips up the Nile, whilst Harry was

happy to ride on the local donkeys. He was astounded at the
treasures of the tombs of the Pharaohs, and wistfully longed for
even a small portion of their wealth, for he realised that capital
could unlock many doors in life.

Nevertheless, Harry was beginning to accumulate a little
capital, which he invested wisely but with great caution after
the most careful consideration. Virtually a non-drinker of
alcohol, he had made a study of the drinking habits of others
and came to the conclusion that there were large profits to be
made by those who provided liquor, particularly whisky.
Consequently he invested £500 in the Distillers Company. It
was an investment which was to pay him handsome dividends.

Shortly after returning from his honeymoon, Harry heard
that two lodges at the entrance to Duchess Drive in Newmarket
were for sale and bought one of them, North Lodge. The lodge
had several acres of land attached, and Harry gave a piece to
'Darkie' Thompson who kept the Jubilee Café in the town.

One of Harry's first capital acquisitions had been his motor-
bike, which was his pride and joy, but secretly he longed for a
motorcar. One day he was staying with friends who kept a hotel
in Harrogate for York races. They owned a 12 h.p. Wolseley
which they offered to let Harry drive and, if he wished, borrow
to take back to Newmarket. He did not accept the offer, but
nevertheless became determined to own a car, especially after
he had seen a brand-new Wolseley in a Harrogate car show
room. He bought the car for £300 and decided to drive it to
Sheffield to see his father and his sisters and hopefully to
persuade them to return to Newmarket with him. His persuasion
was successful, but when the journey was almost completed they
ran out of petrol on the Cambridge road near Egerton Lodge.
None of them had the slightest idea how to refill the petrol tanks,
so they had no option but to leave the car and walk into the
town!

1927   Prior to the beginning of the 1927 Flat Season, Harry signed a
contract to ride for Sir Victor Sassoon, which meant that he
would have the mount on Hot Night throughout the season. It

was an exciting prospect and he was delighted when he rode Hot Night to a six-length victory at Lingfield in mid-April, for he knew that the colt would be his mount in the Two Thousand Guineas.

Understandably, Hot Night was tremendously fancied for the first Classic, but failed to gain a place behind Adam's Apple, Call Boy and Sickle. It was a frustrating performance, for at halfway he was travelling so well that he seemed the probable winner. However he did not quicken when Harry asked him to do so, and was passed by several of his rivals. Suddenly he began to eat up the ground and at the winning post was fourth and catching the leaders with every stride. Consequently not all hope of victory in The Derby was lost, particularly when he won at the York May meeting. Crawford deliberately chose to run him at York rather than at Newmarket to give the temperamental colt more experience of travelling. Everyone at Newmarket knew that Hot Night was a horse of immense ability, but one whose character and courage were highly suspect. At Doncaster the previous autumn he had become far too excited before the race, and then disinterested during it. In the Two Thousand Guineas he had hardly behaved better. However, at York he behaved in exemplary fashion, and beat Mr Washington Singer's Chantrey by a head, conceding 18 lbs. Chantrey*, trained at Manton, was thought to be a very useful colt, and the fact that Hot Night had defeated him — and in so doing broken the course record by more than four seconds — made those at Manton believe that Hot Night was a certainty for the Derby. At the Derby Press Club Luncheon, Sir Victor Sassoon, who had arrived from India days earlier, told his listeners in the course of his speech, 'Yesterday Hot Night was walking round his paddock in a manner showing either that he is no longer temperamental or else that, like a well-known film-star, he is saving up his temperament for next Wednesday. At

---

*Subsequently Chantrey was to win the Prince of Wales Stakes at Ascot by fifteen lengths, run second in the Irish Derby and win the Welsh Derby. In August, when he was a much-fancied contender for the St Leger, he tragically died of a twisted gut.

any rate I have a hope — it is only a hope — that on Wednesday he will have the right to carry his head as high as some of you maintain that he does in his races.'

The weather on Derby Day was overcast, but at least there was no rain to ruin the occasion. In the previous three years spectators had been drenched to the skin as they watched Sansovino, Manna and Coronach win, but at Epsom on 1 June 1927, although the sun did not break through the clouds, the afternoon was dry. The new grandstands had been completed in time for the meeting, thanks to frantic last-minute efforts on the part of the builders, and for the first time a radio commentary on The Derby was being given. For Harry Wragg it was the most important day in his career as a jockey, for he had no doubt that he was riding the best horse in the race. Only Call Boy, owned by Mr Frank Curzon who everyone knew was a dying man, was at shorter odds in the betting, and in his heart Harry was convinced that Hot Night could beat him. He had little fancy for Adam's Apple, Sickle or Lone Knight, and believed that only misfortune could rob him of victory.

Perhaps he would have had less confidence if he had realised the significance of a conversation between Sir Victor Sassoon and Frank Curzon forty-eight hours before the race. Sassoon called upon Curzon who was too ill to go to Epsom and who sadly told him, 'I just hope that I live long enough to hear on the wireless that he has won.' On hearing these words Sassoon replied, 'I hope so too, and to make sure, I will not back your horse as I always lose. But I'll break the habit of a lifetime and have a hundred on mine. That should settle it!'

It did settle it, for Call Boy ridden by Charlie Elliott beat Harry on Hot Night by two lengths, with Shian Mor eight lengths away third. Yet the result was wrong in that Hot Night was far superior to Call Boy, but once again proved his own worst enemy. Call Boy set a tremendous gallop from the moment that the tapes went up, but Harry was content to keep Hot Night covered up, especially as his experience told him that he had at least a stone in hand. He did not want to hit the front too soon and waited until the final furlong before he delivered his challenge. When he did so, Hot Night swept into the lead with his race apparently won. Harry was riding a copy-book race and victory seemed assured — but the wretched Hot Night had other ideas. He put his head up in the air and when the courageous Call Boy, answering every demand of his jockey, tried to get back on terms he capitulated without a struggle.

Bitterly disappointed, Harry was sufficiently diplomatic to tell the press, 'I was full of hope as Hot Night drew level with Call Boy, and then got his head in front, but the slight rise near the finish, which should never be lost sight of, was too much for him. Higher went his head, and I soon realised that it was not to be. Call Boy kept on pulling it out. He is a bad 'un to beat.' But in the privacy of his bedroom that night Harry wept. He had never had such a good ride in The Derby, knew that Hot Night was easily the best horse but that he had refused to try.

Mr Frank Curzon had changed his mind about not attending Epsom, and supported by his trainer and his secretary met his champion at the entrance to the Winner's Enclosure. Almost on the verge of collapse he received the congratulations of his friends, and by dint of will-power and strength of character managed to find the energy to obey his Sovereign's command to go to the Royal Box for further congratulations. A month later he was dead.

A sidelight on The Derby was the almost ludicrous prize money awarded to the owners of the runner-up and of the third horse. Mr Frank Curzon received £12,615, a record sum in the history of The Derby, whilst Sir Victor Sassoon was awarded a mere £400 for being the owner of the second horse, and Major Courtauld exactly half that sum as the owner of Shian Mor.

Hot Night's next race was the Trial Stakes at Royal Ascot for which he started a very short-priced favourite. Punters made him one of the bankers of the meeting but, despite all Harry's persuasion, he let them down by failing to finish in the first three, giving a feeble display totally lacking zest. Crawford was still convinced that Hot Night's 'natural backwardness has been the greatest obstacle for him to overcome'; that he would not reach his peak until he was a four-year-old; and that he could not stand a great deal of training. Consequently he was only given a light preparation before the St Leger, a method of training which brought Crawford severe criticism from Newmarket gallop touts. In the St Leger Hot Night ran a replica of his Derby performance. Harry persuaded him to join issue with Book Law three furlongs from home, and match strides with the filly, but once again he showed his lack of resolution by refusing to carry through his effort. Undoubtedly the best colt of his generation he could have been hailed as a 'Triple Crown' winner if he had been more courageous. However, Book Law's success enabled veteran Manton trainer Alec Taylor, who retired at the end of the season, to conclude his great career by saddling his twenty-second Classic winner.

A high note during the season for Harry was riding five winners in two afternoons at Hamilton Park in mid-July. His younger brother, Sam, rode a winner at the same meeting. Sam, born in 1909, had also been apprenticed to Bob Colling, despite the infamous treatment given to Harry, whilst Arthur, youngest of the three brothers, was apprenticed to Stanley Wootton at Epsom and had ridden his first winner, Burning Thoughts, at Warwick in the spring of 1927. Harry often discussed jockeyship and riding tactics with Sam and Arthur. He believed that:

> To become a successful rider, a top jockey, you've got to really study lots of things. For instance, you've got to study the jockeys, their strong points, their weak points, you've got to know in a long race who to follow. You pick on people that you know are having good runs. You don't want to get behind somebody that's riding as if he's in a traffic jam — stop and go business. All things like that you've got to work out — especially your danger in a race. Try and track him if you possibly can.
>
> Amongst other things that you've got to study are the starters. The starters make a terrific lot of difference and it's all anticipation. When you get to know how a starter likes to be starting, you adopt the same sort of tactics.
>
> Captain Allison was one of the main ones I could always guarantee. If I was half a length behind, he would know that I was ready and he would pull the gate when he thought it was right for all the others. Major Kenneth

Robertson was another one — he would let you go sometimes. You'd got to be aware that he would let you go six lengths off the gate, ten lengths perhaps. So long as you were straight he would pull that gate, so you'd got to be alert, you'd got to be thinking of those type of starters. But it is all anticipation and all jockeys try to pinch a little bit at the start, always try to get a march on the others. I remember one day at Warwick I flew the gate and I thought I had got a flyer, but as I looked across to my right I saw Gordon Richards — he was the quickest feller ever at the gate. He was fiddling for his irons for he had left the gate without one foot in the iron but he was still level with me.

There was some similarity between the background of Gordon Richards and Harry, who was almost two years older than his great rival. Both were from a family of eight — although Gordon's mother also gave birth to four more children who died in infancy — and both came from homes where little interest was shown in horseracing. Gordon's father was a coalminer, but a man determined to succeed in life, whilst his mother was the daughter of a miner who was a devout Methodist and a lay preacher. Gordon enjoyed a happier childhood than Harry, whose early years were clouded by the sudden death of his mother, and by his father's failure to gain promotion in his work. Perhaps the most significant difference between Gordon and Harry in their formative years was that Gordon had ridden pit ponies as a boy, dreamed of becoming a jockey and had been encouraged to write to Mr Reid Walker applying for a job in a racing stables. His mother was adamant that he should not become a miner and was happy at the thought that he was to make racing his career. Harry, on the other hand, had never sat on a horse until he arrived at Newmarket, and the thought of becoming a jockey had not occurred to him.

4

Felstead and Blenheim

1928 The frustration and disappointment suffered by Harry in 1927, due to the unwillingness of Hot Night to exert himself, was amply compensated for in 1928. Before the season commenced he signed a retainer to ride for Captain 'Ossie' Bell, son of Sir J. P. Bell, of Dalby, Queensland. Ossie had been born in Australia and as a young man had taken walers — Australian horses — to China where they proved too speedy for the Chinese ponies who opposed them in races. He then spent three years as Secretary to the Hong Kong Turf Club before setting up as a trainer in India where he enjoyed considerable success. He came to England in 1911, ostensibly to study training methods, and took over a small stable at Epsom which he closed down during the war in which he served in the Worcestershire Regiment. He was very reserved, content to say little, and admired any thoroughbred which could trace its line back to Carbine. Many of his friends thought that he should have been a diplomat, for his suave manner could charm and mollify his owners at their most indignant. A very tall man, he never rode up to the gallops on a hack, preferring to drive a motorcar. He had a delicate stomach and throughout his life had to be very careful as to the food that he ate. At the end of the war he acquired College House and the Delamere stables at Lambourn, before eventually moving to Stork House where Sir Charles Nugent had trained.

His principal owner was the newly-knighted Sir Hugo Cunliffe-Owen, the chairman of British American Tobacco. Born in August 1870, Sir Hugo had commenced racing in 1918.

He was a keen yachtsman and a fine shot, lived at Bray in Berkshire and established the Weir Bank Stud close to his home shortly after the Armistice. At the end of the year he married Helen Elizabeth Oliver of New York. She registered her colours as 'Scarlet, white hooped sleeves, quartered cap'*, and enjoyed her first major success when Mount Royal won the 1920 Goodwood Cup. Sir Hugo had beginner's luck when Orpheus carried his colours into third place behind Spion Kop and Archaic in the 1920 Derby, before twice winning the Champion Stakes. Like many rich men he could be cussed but was seldom mean, although outspoken and blunt to the point of rudeness. At times a heavy gambler he landed a large bet when his colt King Sol won the 1919 Stewards Cup at Goodwood. His advice to punters included, 'Use your eyes and not your ears', 'If you lose, find out why', 'Never back a horse that sweats' and 'Don't plunge on the last race of the day'.

In 1926 he won a great deal of money on the French colt Highborn II who had been sent over by his owner, Mr Edward Esmond, to run at Royal Ascot. Highborn II won the Fernhill Stakes on the Wednesday and was promptly bought for £10,000 by Sir Hugo Cunliffe-Owen in whose 'green, white hooped sleeves, quartered cap' he won the King's Stand Stakes forty-eight hours later. At Goodwood Highborn II was beaten half a length by Solly Joel's Oojah in the King George Stakes before winning the Nunthorpe Stakes at York. In November Solly Joel matched Oojah, ridden by Brownie Carslake, against Highborn II, ridden by Joe Childs, for £2,000 a side at Newbury. Highborn II won by ten lengths, much to his owner's delight.

In 1924 Sir Hugo Cunliffe-Owen had acquired the six-year-old mare Felkington, who had been covered by Spion Kop, and the name Felstead was given to the colt foal born in April 1925. The facts surrounding the purchase of Felkington by Sir Hugo Cunliffe-Owen are tinged with sadness. She had originally belonged to Mr John Watts of Newcastle, and won six races in

---

* When Harry Wragg first registered his colours in 1946 he chose identical colours.

his colours when trained by Dobson Peacock at Middleham. Due to ill-health he decided to sell up his bloodstock, including his broodmares which were kept at the Meddler Stud near Newmarket. His son, who thought the world of Felkington, bought her at the 1924 Tattersalls July sales without telling his father. The price was 2,100 guineas and Sir Hugo Cunliffe-Owen was the under-bidder. When the news of the purchase was given to Mr John Watts, who was dying, he implied that he was very disconcerted and that the transaction was contrary to his wishes. In consequence his son reluctantly agreed that it would be unwise to retain Felkington if his father was worried, and sold her to Sir Hugo Cunliffe-Owen who had also kept his mares at the Meddler Stud before establishing his own stud at Bray.

Felstead, a lengthy colt with white stockings on his hind legs, and a white blaze on his forehead and nose, possessed hocks and knees which were unusually low to the ground and he was regarded as rather ewe-necked and slackly put together. He made his debut in the Fulbourne Stakes at Newmarket on 1 July 1927. He was ridden by Michael Beary and was unplaced behind Flamingo. Nine days later he ran at Chepstow where he finished second of four, ridden by L. Brown. Unplaced in the Molecomb Stakes at Goodwood, again ridden by L. Brown, Felstead had his final race of the season when unplaced in the Rous Plate at the Doncaster St Leger meeting, ridden by Steve Donoghue.

He wintered well, and when Harry rode him for the first time in public, he started a hot favourite for the Spring Maiden Plate at Newbury. There were nineteen runners, but Felstead won easily by three lengths. Captain Bell decided that his next race should be over the final seven furlongs of the Derby course, and consequently ran him in the Prince of Wales Plate at the Epsom spring meeting. He started favourite and was beaten into third place behind Caballero and Golden King — neither of whom had any pretentions to class. The race was marred by the fall of Harry's brother, Arthur, on Silver Sue, but luckily neither he nor his mount were injured. Understandably, the avoiding

action that Harry was compelled to take in order not to gallop
over his stricken brother put paid to any chance of victory.
Felstead next ran in the Two Thousand Guineas where he made
no show behind Flamingo. His next public trial was the Davis
Stakes at Hurst Park's Whitsuntide meeting which he won
easily, thus highlighting that he was in good heart. However, it
needed a man of great confidence to envisage that he would win
The Derby. Nevertheless Harry Wragg was delighted by the
performance and a few days later told 'Ajax' of the *Evening
Standard* that Felstead was improving all the time, that he had
more than an outside chance of being placed at Epsom and that
by September would be a fancied contender for the St Leger.
Despite Harry's assurance it seemed reasonable to assume that
The Derby lay between the brilliant Fairway, Flamingo, and
Sunny Trace who were the three most heavily backed colts,
although Ranjit Singh, Royal Minstrel and Gang Warily had
their supporters.

Derby Day proved a 'sizzler' with the sun shining from an
almost cloudless sky. A vast crowd thronged the Downs, and one
reporter noted, 'Motors have now almost taken the place of
horses in the tremendous flow of traffic from London to Epsom'.
In the daily newspapers cigarette advertisements blazoned the
headlines that 'Players Please' were ten for sixpence, that the
latest model 21 h.p. Renault car cost £455, and that the Cornish
murderer, John Maynard, had been sentenced to death. For the
first time the result of the race was to be transmitted to the
Empire by means of beam wireless, with the majority of
spectators believing that Fairway would be the name on
everyone's lips once the result was known.

One man who did not believe that Fairway would win was
the Hon. George Lambton who saw the Derby horses having
their early morning canters on the course. As he was driven back
to London for breakfast he told his chauffeur that he was
convinced that Fairway did not appear 'right', but such
comment may have been coloured by the fact that Frank
Butters had replaced him as Lord Derby's trainer. In the
paddock and the parade Felstead was noted as 'A nice horse and

how well he looks' whilst critics of Fairway complained, 'He's light in his quarters and his body'. Flamingo and Sunny Trace were both thought too small to win The Derby, and Royal Minstrel was considered to lack the stamp of a true stayer.

There were three false starts, but once the magic cry 'They're off' reverberated across the Downs, Flamingo and Charlie Elliott and Sunny Trace, the mount of Gordon Richards, set a cracking pace. As Harry Wragg stated in retrospect:

> I worked myself through onto the inside and I was getting a beautiful run. I was a good way behind the leaders but gradually I was picking up horses as I moved through on the inside, and coming up towards the seven-furlong marker I was still on the inside. I looked and saw a bunch of horses on my right but the only feller in front of me that I could guess was stopping my passage was Joe Childs on Royal Minstrel. I worked up to him just coming to the six-furlong pole. There were ten or twelve horses on my outside and I screamed murder. All I wanted was two or three inches, which Joe gave me and I was through there like a shot and I'd landed myself on the inside of about ten horses.
>
> I was running into third or fourth place coming down to Tattenham Corner and then I started to get a view as there were two jockeys in front of me, Gordon on Sunny Trace and Charlie Elliott on Flamingo, and they were really having a real battle. I thought, well I'd better let them carry on with that and if things go on like this I'm going to win The Derby. So I gradually crept a bit nearer coming round Tattenham Corner. I ran say three or four lengths off them, running very smoothly. They still had this battle going on and I kept talking to myself — don't be in too much of a hurry to take on those two, let them fight it out, first let them finish their battle before you really go. I sat happily like that, smoothly, just getting a little bit nearer, and a bit nearer. Then we come to about a furlong from home. Charlie had just gone past Gordon and was going on to win his race when I gave my horse a couple of slaps and whoops, here I go. I went straight by him and won a length and a half.

Sir Hugo Cunliffe-Owen was reputed to have won £25,000 in bets over Felstead's victory at 33-1 and to have rewarded Harry generously for the calm, thoughtful and unflustered manner in which he had ridden his Derby hero. Sir Hugo was one of the speakers at the subsequent celebration dinner given by Harry, and at which Gordon Richards and Johnny Dines proved themselves as comedians, having their audience convulsed with laughter. Ossie Bell, usually imperturbable, and a trainer who never made excuses for his horses when they were beaten or blamed his jockey, was also at the party and surprised many fellow guests by letting his hair down. Jack Jarvis, Flamingo's trainer, always thought that his horse would have won The Derby but for Elliott's senseless duel with Gordon Richards.

Felstead did not run again after his Derby triumph, for he was plagued by training mishaps and was withdrawn from the St Leger, much to the disappointment of his owner, trainer and jockey. The colt, whose sire, grandsire and dam's sire were also Derby winners, was almost sold to the U.S.A. for £100,000 before the end of the season, but Sir Hugo decided to keep him, much to the amazement of Ossie Bell who did not believe that any thoroughbred was worth such a sum. Felstead stood at the Lambourn Stud which had been established in 1924 jointly by Sir Hugo Cunliffe-Owen, Ossie Bell and Captain G. H. Drummond, and remained there until he died in 1946. Captain Drummond was a member of the famous banking family, one of whose members had lost £20,000 to Beau Brummel playing faro. He had bred Ox and Ass, a colt which received his unusual name because the Drummond family were claimants to the Oxford peerage, a title taken by Mr Asquith.

Towards the end of the 1928 season Harry won the Beckhampton Handicap at Newbury. Ever observant, he noticed a colt who finished in the ruck whom he thought could have won by the proverbial street. Consequently he beseeched Sir Hugo Cunliffe-Owen to buy the colt, Moontoy. His advice was taken and Moontoy proved a money-spinner in 1929, scoring first time out at 10-1 ridden by Sam Wragg, winning at the Newmarket second July meeting ridden by Harry at 5-1, obliging again at Stockton at 4-1 and ending the season by winning the Newcastle Autumn Handicap at 5-2. On each occasion the stable gambled heavily on him.

1929 Harry's prospects in the first months of the 1929 season appeared poor, and although he won the Woodcote Stakes at the Epsom Derby meeting on Lady Cunliffe-Owen's Lady Abbess, trained by Felix Leach Snr, nothing seemed to be in his favour until Royal Ascot where he won the Royal Hunt Cup on Lord Michelham's Songe — a French-bred five-year-old, trained by Ossie Bell, the Bessborough Stakes for Lord Howard de Walden on Siegfried and the King's Stand Stakes for Mr Jack Joel on Tag End, beating Doch-an-Doris.

In the Ascot Gold Cup he rode the American four-year-old Reigh Count into second place behind Invershin. Reigh Count had enjoyed a remarkable history, and the enterprise of sending him across the Atlantic was a very sporting one. Described as a 'homely chestnut, high on the leg, and standing over a lot of ground', he was a marvellous galloper and despite the fact that Sundridge, the very fast sprinter, was his paternal grandsire, Reigh Count possessed an abundance of stamina. In August 1927 as a two-year-old, having won six races, he went to Saratoga where he won again, and in doing so made such an impression upon Mr John Hertz, the wealthy owner of the Chicago Yellow Cab Company, that he bought him for $12,500 and gave him to his wife as a present. The purchase proved a bargain for Reigh Count won the 1928 Kentucky Derby, ridden by 'Chick' Lang. Later in the season he won the Jockey Club Gold Cup at Belmont Park and was hailed as the American Champion three-year-old. Although he was only saved in the nick of time from being burned to death when a barn in which he and fifteen other horses were housed caught fire in October, it was decided to send him to England to be prepared for the 1929 Ascot Gold Cup. In December he was shipped to England and quartered at Jack Leader's stables at Newmarket, where his American trainer joined him.

In the spring of 1929 Reigh Count made his English debut in the one-mile Lingfield Handicap. He was set to concede more than a stone to each of his twenty-four opponents, yet was installed favourite. The attention of all eyes in the paddock as a representative of International Racing, he was ridden by Chick Lang, who had never previously seen an English race-course. Reigh Count ran fast for five furlongs and then gradually faded. A fortnight later in the one-mile Newbury Spring Cup he performed moderately behind Athford in the colours of Mr W. Barnett, and spectators were inclined to believe that he was grossly over-rated. Their belief was consolidated when he failed again in the Kempton 'Jubilee' won by Athford.

Then came Epsom, and on the day after Athford's full brother Trigo won The Derby, Reigh Count contested the Coronation Cup. There were nine runners including Athford, whom Reigh Count was meeting on level terms instead of conceding him 12 lbs as he had done at Kempton. In a desperate finish Reigh Count, ridden by Joe Childs, defeated Athford ridden by Michael Beary who wished to lodge an objection for bumping. Mr Barnett refused to allow him to do so, and Reigh Count became the hero of the hour and did much to foster Anglo-American sporting relations.

The next race for Reigh Count was the Ascot Gold Cup in which he was ridden by Harry. There were thirteen runners including Invershin, winner of the 1928 Gold Cup; Cacao, winner of the Prix du Cadran in the colours of Baron Edouard de Rothschild; Ox and Ass; and Palais Royal II and Cyclonic, two more French challengers who had finished second and third to Fairway in the 1928 St Leger. Palais Royal II had returned to England to win the Cambridgeshire. In the event Invershin won from Reigh Count by two lengths with three lengths separating Reigh Count and Palais Royal II.

Reigh Count — he was a brilliant horse, a pulling sort of horse — but he could have been a great horse if he had been brought up over here in England. We could have taught him how to control himself and settle in races and produce him, because he had brilliant speed. But all these horses when you train them although they've got brilliant speed it doesn't last for long, so you've got to time it right.

You mustn't hit the front more than half a furlong from home because the speed doesn't last in distance races and this horse had been used to running distance races in America. All horses have got a certain amount of speed and if you can reserve that for the very last moment you're going to beat anything providing you've got good control and the horse is working with you. Reigh Count, he was alright in his own country — you can afford to lay up and make the running there because they run on sharper courses, where it's an advantage to be in front as it's an advantage to be going round the turns on the inside. But with the distances we have on our courses it's a little bit different when you start thinking of running two and a half miles at Ascot — up hill and down hill and right the way out there in the country — it's a different object.

Reigh Count had first of all his American jockey riding him and they decided on a straight mile at Lingfield. The opposition wasn't very great and he was odds-on and naturally wasn't going to tell us a terrific lot because he was going to beat these a long way. He was making the running and something was tracking him and then he faded quickly, which was a terrible start really for him. Anyhow, he got a very bad press and his Ascot Gold Cup rating went right through the window. They didn't even rate him.

The press got hold of the trainer and told him a few things and I said, 'Look, if that horse is going to get anywhere in this country you've got to have him settled, you've got to have somebody like Joe Childs or myself schooling him, teaching him his business, how to settle and what to do.' From then on this feller — he was a good trainer — realised that he's got to make amends for the poor showing he put up at Lingfield. He got a good deal of help from the Newmarket trainers with lead horses and things like that, and got Joe Childs and I occasionally to go down and ride him. I remember one day I was riding Reigh Count on the Limekilns, a mile and a half straight, and we had lots of lead horses. I got him covered up and had him settled part of the way and eventually I came down like that with two handfuls all through the gallop and about a furlong from home I pulled him out from behind and he sprinted by his rivals. He really did impress me and he beat them by about something like ten lengths.

I reckon he must have been running the last furlong in twelve seconds.

In the Coronation Cup they picked Joe Childs to ride him — Joe had him at the rear of the field for the first part of the race and had him covered up a goodish way back. When he got to the six-furlong marker coming down into Tattenham Corner Joe thought, I've got a bit to do here, and pulled him to the outside of his field and he took off. He really sprinted down there and he hit the front — he joined the leaders within a furlong as they went round Tattenham Corner and really got the race well in his pocket. In the final furlong he started to wander and Athford came up and challenged him — it was a very near thing and he just wandered onto the horse a little bit, nothing much really.

The next race in Reigh Count's sights was the Ascot Gold Cup and Joe and I both decided that he was a real good horse providing you could control him so we kept having a lot of rides on him. On work day, either he or I would go out and ride him. And so this thing went on until it was time for the Ascot Gold Cup. I'd ridden him most by then, and they decided they were going to let me ride him. So I've got a lot on my plate because at Ascot in a race like this they don't go much of a pace. This horse was used to running each furlong of his races in twelve seconds or better, and here they were going to run the first furlong in about fourteen seconds, and I've got my hands full to keep him covered up. The other jockeys all know what a problem I've got and so naturally everything they can do to upset my plans they will definitely do.

During the race they went very slowly and he was giving me a difficult ride until I'm going into Swinley Bottom — I've got him covered alright but not really settled. I was right on the inside with about three horses upsides in front of me and the lead horse that was in front just on the rails. As the leader wandered off a bit my feller saw the opening and we looked like going through there — I had to really stand up on him to hold him back. The next thing is we're going along coming towards the home turn — the jockeys starting to get more interested when one French jockey came alongside me flapping his whip and shouting. That disturbed me again and Reigh Count looked like going through another opening. Coming into the straight two and a half furlongs from home I've got so much in hand it's unbelievable, but my horse won't last if I hit the front — so I'm back again just in behind the leaders and so I stay until about a furlong from home. One of the leaders started to wander off the fence again and with that Reigh Count took charge and I got about half a length behind the other leader and I thought, well there's nothing else I can do — I can't possibly take him back now, but he just could not reach Invershin.

The Gold Cup was Reigh Count's final race in England for in July he was shipped back to America where he received a hero's welcome when he gave a lap of honour at Arlington Park.

Writing from Miami Beach a few months later, Mr John Hertz commented, 'The day that Reigh Count won the Coronation Cup showed us that the English racegoing public are sportsmen of the highest type. The fact that Reigh Count was an outlander meant nothing to the stands. That day they only knew that we have travelled 4000-5000 miles to throw our hat into the ring for the love of sport.' He continued: 'His defeat in the Ascot Gold Cup did not bother us one bit. The horse did well and made a game and gallant effort. The only mental reservation we had with this race is that Childs, who was familiar with his ways, was not permitted to ride him. We will always feel that if he had, the result might have been different.' Such a comment seemed grossly unfair to Harry and should have been refuted at the time. In fact Joe Childs was compelled to ride Lord Lascelles' St Jerome in the Gold Cup as W. R. Jarvis had a retainer on his services.

After Ascot Harry seemed in the doldrums until he won the Cheveley Park Stakes for Lord Carnavon on Merry Wife, although he had won again on Lady Abbess at the Doncaster St Leger meeting. In her next race, the Hopeful Stakes at the Newmarket first October meeting she was beaten one and a half lengths by a colt belonging to H. H. Aga Khan and to whom the name Blenheim had been given. He was to finish second in the Middle Park Stakes a fortnight later.

Blenheim was ridden by thirty-five-year-old Michael Beary,

the irrepressible, irresponsible Irishman with a soft persuasive
brogue who was a stormy petrel of the Turf. He had charm and
magic in his personality, but was utterly improvident, and
thought nothing of staying at the most expensive and exclusive
hotels irrespective of the state of his bank balance. In 1913 he
became apprenticed to Atty Persse at Stockbridge, but returned
to Ireland for the duration of the war. He rode for Senator
Parkinson who told him 'put everything you make in this game
into Guinness' but Michael never took the sound advice.
Following the Armistice he returned to England but in May
1923 his licence was suspended after he had been found guilty of
foul riding at Kempton. Eighteen months later he was made
bankrupt. Discharged in May 1925, he restored his reputation
by brilliant victories on Solario, Lex and Verdict — but his
licence was withdrawn twice more within the next five years —
and although he won the 1929 St Leger on Trigo he was
annoyed that he had not ridden the colt in The Derby when he
was given the choice of rides by Dick Dawson.

Michael Beary was to be even more annoyed when he chose to **1930**
ride Rustom Pasha in preference to Blenheim — who was a half-
brother to Trigo — the following year in The Derby. He had
ridden Blenheim in both the Greenham Stakes at Newbury and
the Two Thousand Guineas, and on both occasions H. H. Aga
Khan's colt had been unplaced although in the first Classic he
had finished fourth. Rustom Pasha seemed the better horse, for
he had won over a mile at the Epsom spring meeting, and
appeared to have inherited stamina from his sire, Son-in-Law.
It was believed that he would have won the Two Thousand
Guineas if he had contested that Classic, and no one had any
doubts that Beary had chosen the better of the two Whatcombe
colts as his Derby mount, allowing Harry to ride Blenheim.

> Dawson asked me down to Whatcombe to have a ride on
> Blenheim. It was a very interesting gallop — about eight
> horses altogether — and we went a very quick pace.
> During the gallop I gave Blenheim a good sort of chance.
> He was a beautiful horse to ride — you could put him

anywhere you liked, he was a real gentleman — and when eventually towards the finish, Michael Beary on Rustom Pasha went up to the lead horse very easily and had the trial won a furlong from home, I was finishing very well to run second to him about three lengths off. But it's a very funny thing that a Derby trial at home, such as at Whatcombe, can be very different to the Epsom Derby itself and all the time I was thinking to myself that I've got a very good chance really in the Derby. Epsom's a very tricky track and if Rustom Pasha happened to go and hit the front too soon — I knew he had got a terrific lot of speed but he had started to tire towards the end of this gallop — I had a good chance, and this fact kept going through my mind.

I went from riding that gallop to ride at Doncaster, and when I got to the races I met Lord Carnarvon — who was the breeder of Blenheim. He owned Malva, a very good broodmare I was riding for Sir Hugo Cunliffe-Owen at Doncaster and they asked me how the gallop went — what did I think about it — so I told them that I thought Blenheim had a great chance.

Derby Day was hazy, with the sun trying unsuccessfully to break through the clouds. The previous day had been King George V's sixty-fifth birthday and he was given an especially great cheer when he arrived on the course. Harry fancied Blenheim even though he was easy to back at 20–1 and thought that if Michael Beary took Rustom Pasha to the front too soon, Blenheim would beat him. That is exactly what happened for Beary elected to keep Rustom Pasha in the front rank from the start. At the foot of Tattenham Corner he shared the lead with Diolite, winner of the Two Thousand Guineas, but 'cracked' more than a quarter of a mile from home, and Beary's subsequent excuse that he was 'waiting in front' from the outset was scorned. Harry always thought that Michael Beary made an appalling error riding Rustom Pasha the way he did and believed that if held up for a final sprint, then Rustom Pasha would have won. On Blenheim he was content to bide his time and delayed his challenge until the final furlong was reached. Keeping Blenheim perfectly balanced he brought him with one long uninterrupted run on the outside, cut down his rivals, swept past Iliad and Diolite and won by a length — with his jubilant owner misguidedly shouting the name 'Rustom Pasha' since he imagined that it was his more fancied runner who was the Derby hero. Harry described the race:

> I was drawn on the extreme outside but one, and when the starter pulled the lever I would be standing about a length behind. That would not have mattered much, but my horse jumped off to the right instead of straight forward, with the result that I was last of all to leave the gate and a few lengths behind the others. I at once took a firm grip of his head, for I did not want him to jump into his bit. Once I had him balanced I let him go along on the outside of the field, and I got him running very smoothly but well within himself.
>
> By the time we had got to the mile and a quarter starting-post I found I had moved up a few places, and I continued to go on the outside, for I wanted to steer clear of trouble. At the mile post, still going on the bit, I was about seventh. There were three horses racing almost abreast, and then another three in somewhat similar formation. Just behind those two groups was Steve Donoghue, so I pulled in a bit with only Steve between the rails and myself. Having got there without trouble, I was quite satisfied. It was just the pitch I wanted, and I sat quite still.
>
> Noble Star was now racing on my outside, but there was no danger of my getting shut in. Thus we raced to Tattenham Corner. There were then in front of me Rustom Pasha, Diolite, Ballyferis, Trews and Iliad. Once we had got into the straight Ballyferis and Trews seemed to collide and they dropped out. I once more pulled to the outside, and for a moment I was inclined to make my effort. But I saw Bobby Jones on Iliad get out his whip and dash after the two leaders, and I realised that if I did the same my horse might not last it to the end. So I promptly changed my mind and went in behind Iliad again. When I saw Jones go and make his effort I was not alarmed, for I felt I could go and beat him when I wanted. He soon overcame Diolite, and that was the signal for me to get really busy. It was not more than a furlong and a half from the winning post when I pulled out and went after Iliad.
>
> There was nothing spectacular about the way Blenheim

did his job. It was only by a very gradual process that I
made up the leeway. Stride by stride I crept nearer, but all
the time I knew I was going to win. I had to bring out my
whip and help the game colt as much as I could, but he had
a bit better speed than Iliad, and when I got on terms a
hundred yards from home the race was mine. I had taken a
look over my shoulder before making my final burst, and
that satisfied me I had only Iliad to beat. I was going right
away from him in the last fifty yards to win by a clear
margin. I have to give Blenheim his share of the credit. He
was a lovely little horse to ride. I found I could put him just
where I wanted, and he did everything I asked him in the
most gentlemanly manner. I thought he would get the
trip. He did.

At an altitude of 3,000 ft the seventeen passengers in an Imperial
Airways plane flying from Croydon to Paris heard a commentary
by R. C. Lyle of *The Times* on the race through a portable
wireless set, and so too did passengers on the Flying Scot en
route for Edinburgh.

It was at a celebration dinner held at the Savoy Hotel in
London, when the health of Harry, of the Aga Khan, who had
given Harry £5,000, of Dick Dawson and Blenheim had been
drunk over and over again, that Steve Donoghue introduced
Marcus Marsh to the Maharajah of Rajpipla who asked him to
train his horses with the happiest of future results. At the dinner
Harry admitted that he loved riding at Epsom, especially on
Derby Day.

Of all the racing days I think that the one I used to enjoy
most of all was Derby Day. When I grew up and I started
getting good rides I used to think it was my day. I had such
confidence and I thought I knew my way round there
much better than anyone else, it was rather fun to study
people, which I used to do a lot, and I knew that every
other jockey was on edge. One thing you've got to have at
Epsom is confidence — you've got to have a lot of
confidence — you've got to know you must not allow
things to worry you, and when you walk into the weighing
room you can see that most of the jockeys are worried stiff.
They're cracking jokes, saying all kinds of things trying to
amuse themselves. But they're all fidgety, and that's why I

used to like it so much. I used to keep as calm as anything. I remember going to the post thinking of things to occupy my mind and I'd look up at the stands where I knew my wife would be and let my eyes wander across the place to where I thought she was. Eventually I would come across a green hat — that's it — and give a wave. She'd wave back — she'd seen me.

Things like that calm you down. I knew where I was, I knew where I was going and what I was doing. Now you don't find that in the race and I found in the race so many things happen that you wouldn't believe.

Harry's conviction concerning the true ability of Rustom Pasha was vindicated in the Eclipse. Understandably, but unwisely as it proved, Michael Beary chose to ride Blenheim:

So the next race to come along for the Derby horses was the Eclipse Stakes, and this was the next one in line that they'd got Blenheim going for — at least, Mr Dawson had. He was going to run both horses again, so Michael Beary, who was the stable jockey, naturally got the choice and this time he decided to ride Blenheim. Mr Dawson told me this and I said, 'Well, I don't mind that, matter of fact I think ... Sandown ... yes, I think at a mile and a quarter, I might probably beat Blenheim. I think I will beat him, as a matter of fact, because Rustom Pasha's got such brilliant speed, and I think if he's given that chance he would. Yes, I am very happy to be riding Rustom Pasha.' Anyhow, when it came to the day of the race, they're making Blenheim favourite — I was going to the racecourse and the first thing I was told was that Blenheim wasn't going to run — he wasn't too sound, something to that effect, so he wouldn't be running. I thought, oh dear, never mind, because I thought that I was going to lose my ride and Michael Beary would jump back onto this horse, which was only natural. So I went into the weighing room and the travelling man came up and gave me the colours. I said, 'No, he doesn't run.' He said, 'I know he doesn't run but you still ride Rustom Pasha.' I said, 'I don't believe it.' 'Oh yes, the guv'nor said that you've still got to ride it.' I said, 'Thank you very much, he'll win and I think he'd have beaten Blenheim as it was.'

Anyhow, he ran a super race, he was just as brilliant as I thought he was and I was riding third, fourth, something like that, through the race and with about a furlong to go there were two horses, Walter Gay and Lovelace, in front of me and I'm just tracking the two of them. Then they split a little and I went straight between the two of them and really won on the bridle — won without even going for my stick — a wonderful race — he was a brilliant horse, and I'm sure he would have beaten Blenheim if the Derby winner had run. If a horse has got class and he's got brilliant speed, you can do anything with him, but you've got to wait for that very last bit and if you can finalise that and just do that nicely you can make horses run much better.

Michael Beary was really furious after the Eclipse because Rustom Pasha had won so easily — well, I'm pretty certain he'd have done the same in The Derby if he had been ridden that way, I am certain of that. Anyhow, I made Michael very angry which meant later that he really wanted to have a dig at me.

There was no doubt that Harry rode a brilliant race on Rustom Pasha to win by a neck from the French challenger Lovelace II, who had been second in the French Derby and sixth in the Grand Prix de Paris. After the race the Aga Khan made it perfectly clear that it was not a personal matter — or, rather, only 'personal' to Rustom Pasha. 'Beary rides for me again next year, and for many years, I hope.' Diplomatically he added, 'The idea of giving a temperamental horse, who may easily remember one punishing race with his regular rider on the back, a change of jockeyship, is nothing new. Did not the unknown Herbert Jones, and not Morny Cannon, ride King Edward's Derby winner, Diamond Jubilee? Anyway, the experiment with Rustom Pasha has come off, and that is the main thing. Beary remains, too, in my opinion, as great an artist as Wragg on both horses.'

Harry rode Rustom Pasha in the St Leger to finish third to Singapore and Parenthesis — with Michael Beary unplaced on Ut Majeur, also owned by H. H. Aga Khan, and who started at a shorter price than Rustom Pasha, having beaten him in a trial gallop at Whatcombe. Rustom Pasha and Harry went on to end the season on a high note by taking the Champion Stakes from

Grace Dalrymple and Fair Isle. Blenheim never raced again after his Derby victory, but Michael Beary had some compensation when he rode Ut Majeur to win the Cesarewitch.

At this stage of his career Harry had seldom received substantial presents from owners for whom he had ridden winners — although he received several thousands of pounds from Sir Hugo Cunliffe-Owen and H. H. Aga Khan after the Derby victories of Felstead and Blenheim. However, he was cautious where the spending of his earnings was concerned, and invested his savings wisely. His first venture into the Stock Exchange had proved shrewd and over the years showed a substantial profit. However, another venture into New York Central Railroads was less profitable. The Aga Khan had recommended these shares and explained that the value of the railway land in New York was totally undervalued, but the shares proved worthless. Even worse was the failure of his Newmarket accountant to make ample provision for the demands of the Inland Revenue where 'presents' were concerned, and eventually he received a horrifically exorbitant demand from them. His accountant advised him to explain that he could not possibly pay so huge an amount, but that he would settle immediately for an agreed sum. Agreement was quickly reached.

Frequently when riding in a seller he was told by trainers, '£25 if you are second, nothing if you win,' for there was an unwritten law that trainers did not bid for winners saddled by their friends. As a result, selling races became the medium of gambles, with the winner bought in at the subsequent auction. One Lambourn trainer who loved a gamble on his selling platers was Ted Gwilt, who trained at Saxon House for Mr J. C. Gaulstan, an Armenian with business interests in India. Eventually Gaulstan, who betted in thousands of pounds, went bankrupt, but he will long be remembered for coining the phrase, 'Come on Steve,' as Donoghue urged the horses that he had backed to victory.

During 1930 and 1931 Harry was associated with an extraordinary handicapper named Auction Pool who was trained by Bertie Holland at West Horsley in Surrey:

At Alexandra Park I was going with Brownie Carslake into the paddock and I looked at the horses as they paraded. 'By jingo,' I remarked, 'there are some funny-looking objects here.' We were picking them out and criticising them. Brownie said, 'Look at that one, number 29, he ought to be at Watney Combe and Reid — he's a beer horse.' I realised that number 29 was my mount so I walked across to Bertie Holland and said: 'What have you done to me, Bertie? This ugly clumsy brute won't even get round the track.' He replied that Auction Pool would give me a good ride.

Anyway, the race started and as we reached the first turn my mount got onto the fence position. He was almost taking the paint off the rails and was scooting round the bends. I was doing nothing, he was doing it all himself and we won. I was amazed. I talked to Brownie after the race, and we agreed that Auction Pool was a rum customer whom we did not wish to know, but Bertie Holland was delighted by his performance.

However, when Auction Pool next ran the racetrack was Gatwick, a wide galloping course. Brownie Carslake rode him and finished last, for the old rogue of a horse did not try. Brownie's disgust was heightened when Harry rode Auction Pool again at Alexandra Park and won, and this disgust was increased still further in the future, for after Dick Perryman had been tailed off on the horse at Nottingham Harry proceeded to win for the third time at 'Ally Pally':

> I started to think — I'm always thinking about horses and what they do — and there was no doubt about it, that wretched horse was more scared than his jockey when he was running at Alexandra Park. He was scared out of his life and that made him run. He was squeezing all the time on the inside and ran as though the devil was on his tail.

Auction Pool won so many races at Alexandra Park that they named a race after him. Many of these races were on a Saturday and racegoers called him 'the dinner stakes', for the money they won on him paid for their Sunday lunch. Eventually he was sent jumping but proved useless.

*   *   *

In the autumn of 1930, Harry began to ride for Jack Jarvis and **1931** the following summer almost won his third Derby on Sandwich, owned by Lord Rosebery. Sandwich had only had one run as a two-year-old when he contested the Imperial Produce Stakes at Kempton in October. He had finished unplaced and a disconsolate Jack Jarvis said to Harry, 'That's that, I'll take him out of the Classics.' Harry told him not to be so hasty as he had given him a 'certain feel', and added that the winner, Doctor Dolittle, and the runner-up, Jacopo — who had won the Molecomb Stakes at Goodwood and the Windsor Castle Stakes at Ascot — were very useful two-year-olds.

> It so happened I was riding Sandwich when he was a two-year-old at Kempton. Now this time of the year there are always a lot of forfeits for the next year's races, and trainers have got to make up their minds whether they are going to leave the horses in the following year's Classics, for it's very expensive. It saves a lot of money if you take horses out that have no chance. After the Kempton race Jack Jarvis came up to me and said, 'Well I'll be damned, but I suppose that's that.' I said, 'Look, I wouldn't say that. As a matter of fact there is something I like about the horse. If you ask for my advice I would leave him in next year's races.' He said, 'What?' I said, 'Leave him in.' 'I wouldn't dream of it,' he said. 'Do you realise that he will be tailed off last?' I said, 'No. There is something there, I can't explain it, but he has certainly given me some kind of feel. Something that may come out later. Perhaps next season.' That night Lord Rosebery rang me from Edinburgh and asked 'What is the row between you and Jack Jarvis, what's it all about?' I explained that I hadn't had a row with Jack Jarvis, but he told me that Jack had telephoned him and said he was furious with me. I admitted that I had noticed that when he left me after asking how Sandwich had run that he was hitting the ground with his stick as if what I'd said had not pleased him, but he'd asked me for my opinion and I'd given it to him.

Somewhat mystified Lord Rosebery left Edinburgh on a night sleeper, met Harry at the races and successfully poured oil on the troubled waters which seemed to exist between his jockey and trainer. The matter appeared to blow over and Sandwich

stood his ground for the Classics. In the 1931 Two Thousand
Guineas, when ridden by W. Nevett, he was unplaced to
Cameronian. Harry rode Concerto for Sir Hugo Cunliffe-Owen
and was also unplaced. Sandwich, again ridden by W. Nevett,
then won the Chester Vase and came into the Derby reckoning.
Bred by Mr J. J. Marr at his Confey stud near Dublin, Sandwich
was a half-brother to Manna, and had been bought by Jarvis for
3,600 guineas on behalf of Lord Rosebery. It was obvious that
the colt had more than an outside chance of winning The
Derby, and at the annual Press Club lunch Lord Rosebery had
no problem in stating that he had thoroughly enjoyed the
Club's hospitality, but that he hoped he would enjoy a
Sandwich at Epsom on Derby Day even more! His enjoyment
was dashed, however, for Harry, who was given the mount, for
once rode an injudicious race. His patience was proverbial, but
the supporters of Sandwich were aghast to see how far behind
the leaders he was as Tattenham Corner was approached. His
chance seemed hopeless for he had failed to come down the hill
or to keep his balance and action, and no one gave any thought
to him as Cameronian tracked Gallini and Armagnac into the
straight. As the final quarter-mile was reached, Cameronian
struck the front with Orpen the only apparent danger. Suddenly
Sandwich could be seen gaining with every stride, and his belated
challenge only failed by one and a half lengths. After the race
Harry told the press:

> I was an unlucky loser. When they went off at such a bat up
> the hill I was delighted, for I knew they would not last out
> at such a pace. I did not mean to get so far behind, but
> could not help it, because they were crowding round me
> all the time. When I did make to improve my position,
> every time I went to the outside something went across me,
> and back again I would go on to the rails. I must have been
> seventy-five yards behind at one time, and I was nowhere
> near the leaders when we entered the straight. I pulled to
> the outside once more and gave my horse a crack with the
> whip. The response was of such a nature that I thought I
> was in a train instead of being on a horse! When finally I
> did get a clear run, I switched across to the inside, behind

the two leaders, so as to escape further trouble. My horse was travelling at such a rate that I thought even then I might get up, but the gap was too wide to be bridged in such a short space of time.

Jack Jarvis was not at all amused, and thought that Harry's words 'I was an unlucky loser' were the understatement of the year. Equally, Harry was displeased that Jack Jarvis never made any reference to the fact that if he had not advised against the action, Jarvis would have scratched Sandwich from all his Classic engagements after his Kempton debut as a two-year-old. Sandwich went on to win the King Edward VII Stakes at Ascot before running third to Lord Derby's Caerleon in the Eclipse Stakes at Sandown.

The surprise result of this race and the enquiry held by the Stewards headed by Lord Lonsdale had far-reaching repercussions. Lord Derby had always mistrusted Lord Lonsdale and his dislike of a man whom he described in a letter to the Hon. George Lambton as 'his mind is failing. I have been told that before and what little intellect he had, has entirely gone' was now heightened. So too was his belief that when his trainer, George Lambton, was ill, Cicely Lambton masterminded the training of his horses at Stanley House. This he could tolerate to a limited extent. What he could not tolerate was the possibility that Cicely Lambton brought off betting coups on horses running in his 'black, white cap' colours. Certainly the success of Caerleon at 25-1 upset him, for any stigma attached to the running of his horses was anathema.

The Eclipse was run at a crawl for the first six furlongs, which did not suit Sandwich whose stamina was his forte — and he showed that he was one of the best of his generation two months later when he won the St Leger by four lengths in effortless style to prove that he possessed limitless speed and stamina. Orpen had been coughing, but for some inexplicable reason the Newmarket touts succeeded in putting most people off Sandwich, despite Jack Jarvis's confidence and openly-expressed belief that he represented marvellous value at 9-1. Cameronian had stormed down to the start looking more like a highly-strung sprinter than a colt who was about to contest a long-distance race, and ran abysmally. He had developed a high temperature by the evening, and many critics believed that foul play could not be totally ruled out.

At Goodwood Harry won the opening race of the meeting on Lord Abergavenny's Knight of the Vale and an hour later watched from the grandstand as his brother Sam took the Stewards' Cup on Sir Hugo Cunliffe-Owen's Poor Lad. Before the meeting was over Harry had also scored on Blandearna for Sir Abe Bailey, Rivalry for Mr R. C. Clifford and Lord Bill for Sir Alfred Butt.

On more than one occasion during the season the Wragg brothers carried all before them, and at Warwick in September Harry rode the first two winners of the afternoon and Sam the last three. It should be added that the only other race of the afternoon was for amateur riders!

The Ebor meeting at York proved significant for Harry as he triumphed in the historic Gimcrack Stakes on Miracle, who at the outset of his career was a big overgrown baby with lop ears. The lottery of bloodstock breeding, ownership, and turf ventures as a whole was never more emphasised than on this occasion when the Senior Steward of the Jockey Club, Lord Rosebery, won with Miracle, and thus qualified to be the chief speech-maker at the December banquet of Ye Ancient Fraternitie of York Gimcrackers. Respected as an owner-breeder, he had bought Miracle at public auction for a paltry 170 guineas. The colt had already rewarded him by winning £1,650 and obviously had Classic aspirations for 1932, for the well-bred son of Manna-Brodick Bay, according to Harry, had made all the running in the Gimcrack and beat the deadheating Inverman and Totaig very easily, even though the judge gave the distance as only three-quarters of a length.

The £.s.d. of Lord Rosebery's purchase of Miracle demonstrated the unpredictability of racing. The fee alone of his sire was 400 guineas, and Brodick Bay had fetched 3,800 guineas when she had been sold in December 1930. Lord Beaverbrook had bought her from Lord Derby when he was founding his

Newmarket stud. She bred Miracle, who was one of Lord Beaverbrook's yearlings sent over to Ireland as an experiment for a change of air. Obviously the experiment did not agree with the big ungainly colt, for when he arrived in the sale ring few noticed him. Lord Rosebery, a wise student of breeding, took a chance and bought him.

Eldest son of the 5th Earl, who had married Hannah de Rothschild and become Prime Minister in 1894, Lord Rosebery had inherited the Mentmore Stud on the death of his father in 1929, the same year in which he became a Steward of the Jockey Club. Three years later he was elected President of the Thoroughbred Breeders' Association in succession to Lord D'Abernon. Never the easiest of men to face up to, partly because his intellect and quickness of mind did not allow him to suffer fools gladly, he could be the staunchest of allies and the most formidable of foes. Sadly he was unable to speak at the Gimcrack Dinner after Miracle's victory due to the death of his son a few weeks earlier.

Miracle wintered well, but was unplaced in his first race of the **1932** 1932 season — the Two Thousand Guineas, behind Orwell. Nevertheless Harry was not despondent, for he knew that the horse was not fully wound-up, and his confidence in Miracle's Derby chance was heightened when he rode Lord Rosebery's colt to win the Newmarket Stakes by four lengths. Jack Jarvis however was surprised at the ease of Miracle's victory, for he had been upset that Lord Rosebery's colt had only managed to finish eighth of eleven in the first Classic, and wrongly assumed that the horse was not as good as he had thought. The fact that Miracle had beaten Bulandshar, winner of the Chester Vase, so easily, was tremendously encouraging — but the truth was that Harry had decided to ride the long-striding Miracle in a totally different way to that he had adopted in the Two Thousand Guineas. On that occasion he had allowed Miracle to go with the leaders, whereas in the ten-furlong Newmarket Stakes he had restrained him until the final quarter-mile was entered. As a result of this victory Miracle was heavily backed for The

Derby, for which Orwell ridden by Bobby Jones was installed a
red-hot favourite. Bobby Jones had already won the 1922 St
Leger on Lord Lonsdale's Royal Lancer and the 1926 Oaks on
Lord Astor's Short Story — but he was not destined to win The
Derby on Orwell, for the colt ran deplorably, and finished ninth
behind Mr Tom Walls' April the Fifth, H.H. Aga Khan's
Dastur, and Lord Rosebery's Miracle. Dastur, ridden by
Michael Beary, took up the running soon after Tattenham
Corner, but was challenged by Miracle at the furlong pole. The
race seemed to be a duel between them when suddenly April
the Fifth came flying on the outside and stormed past both of
them to win by three-quarters of a length, with the judge
awarding second place to Dastur by a short head. In retrospect
Harry stated:

> I told you I would have won had the race been run at
> Newmarket. Now, make no mistake about it, my horse was
> not beaten for stamina, but for finishing speed. I was
> staying on all right, but could not match the winner's
> speed in the last few strides. I suppose the judge is right,
> but I was confident in my own mind that I beat Dastur. I
> should say the winner obscured me from the judge's view,
> but that does not matter. I did not win. Yet I had a good
> ride. I saw to it that I had a good place all the way. I had
> just the position I wanted at the top of the hill, and as we
> made the descent I was racing almost in line with Dastur
> and Royal Dancer, with Spenser, Firdaussi and Portofino
> in front of me. In the straight Dastur shot past me, and I
> knew I would have to get to work. My big fellow took some
> time to find the full length of his stride, but when I really
> got him going I could see I would catch Dastur. I had the
> leader 'set' half a furlong out, but when Fred Lane came
> along my horse could not produce the same turn of
> finishing speed. I still think Miracle may be the best of
> them all on a galloping course; he must have that to show
> him off to the most advantage.

Fourth in The Derby was Jack Jarvis's other runner, Royal
Dancer ridden by Sam Wragg. Jarvis always claimed that his
two colts collided early in the straight and that they would have
finished first and second but for this unfortunate incident.

Harry's version was that he had told his brother before the race
to follow him. Perhaps it was not surprising, therefore, that as
Miracle was taken to the outside so that he had a clear run up
the straight, Sam Wragg decided to do so at the same time.

> I pulled out to win my race and just as I did so Sam began
> his run, but it meant that he had to switch to my outside. It
> just meant that he had that bit further to go. I did not
> interfere with him. He should have anticipated that I was
> not going to wait all day riding a big, long-striding colt. If
> he had waited a moment more before delivering his
> challenge the result might have been different.

At Ascot Miracle started odds-on for the Prince of Wales's
Stakes — but was beaten by Sigiri, owned by the popular
Frenchman M. E. St. Alary, and to whom he was conceding
12 lbs. However, Harry had a very successful meeting, winning
the Queen Anne Stakes on Unlikely, the Ascot Stakes on Son of
Mint, the Churchill Stakes on Orpen and the Wokingham
Stakes on Sir Hugo Cunliffe-Owen's Concerto.

Miracle enhanced his reputation with a fluent victory in the
Eclipse Stakes at Sandown. It was a fine performance for the
thirteen runners included Goyescas, winner of the Hardwicke
Stakes at Ascot, Firdaussi and Sandwich, even though
Cameronian was withdrawn after being jarred up at Ascot.
Miracle slammed his opponents, and would have won in any
event, but the tactics employed by Harry gave him an added
advantage:

> This was an important meeting, and as I rode down for the
> first race — it was a long-distance race, a mile and five
> furlongs — I noticed that the inside of the track had been
> watered well, whilst the outside was all dried up. During
> the race I was running last down the back straight and I
> decided to pull my horse Timber onto the outside.
> Immediately I started to run right into the heels of the
> other runners. So I took him back again and dropped into
> the inside until we got round into the straight where I was
> probably twenty lengths behind the leader. I pulled out to
> the left to go up the firm ground and once again started to
> race far faster than my rivals. I thought rather than give

the show away now and let everybody see what I'm up to, I would go back and join the field. I didn't allow Timber any chance to go and finish on the fast ground because I thought I might be showing up my tactics for the Eclipse, and finished fifth. Eventually the big race came along and I went in the paddock to meet Lord Rosebery and Jack Jarvis. I said, 'I'm going to tell you something — what I did in the first race today — and I believe if you let me do what I want to do it'll make a difference — Miracle will run ten lengths better than what he's ever run before. What I'm going to do when I come in the straight is I'm going to pull wide and come up right on the outside away from the field. I'll guarantee you he'll run ten lengths better.' They said, 'OK, you do that.' Well, it so happened the same sort of thing occurred again. I waited just behind the field when I got in the straight, I pulled wide and I was sitting still and Miracle was running straight through them, eventually finished up by winning very easily. He started at 10-1 and the press made a hell of a shout about it. They said it was a bit of a fluke and it was all to do with watering the track. They were asking me about it and I said, 'Now look, I think this horse will run much faster on dry ground than he will on soft ground.' So it was the Sandown racecourse executive that came into a real belting from the press through watering the track. The papers were full of it.

The next day they had a race — the Anniversary Cup — and I was riding Abbots Worthy for Frank Hartigan. I told him the story about what happened the day before when I won on Miracle and I said I would do the same sort of thing. I came last into the straight and pulled on the wide and I went through the field again. There was only one jockey following me and I didn't spot him until I just got up to the post and he was on my tail following me. It was Michael Beary on Apperley. But we'd beaten the field by two lengths.

Some years previously Harry had observantly noticed a similar state of affairs on the five-furlong course at Sandown:

I noticed when I walked the track that they'd been doing some watering and it was all green in the middle of the track and on the outside of the track it was yellow, burnt up, really firm. So naturally I thought a horse must race

ABOVE
A courtyard
house in Solly
Street,
Sheffield,
where Arthur
Wragg and his
children lived
after the death
of his wife in
1912

BELOW
Seventeen-
year-old Harry
on the
three-year-old
Jolly Flying
Buck, his first
success as a
jockey when
he won the
Burton
Apprentice
Plate at Derby,
September 4th
1919

LEFT Tennis at Bedford Lodge with, *left to right*, Dr Basham, who had been on duty at Newcastle races when Harry had his horrific fall, Harry, Freddy Fox, Fred Lane

BELOW Harry hits a perfect drive, watched by his wife, Marjorie

Harry's first Rolls-Royce, 1934 Sports Saloon Vanden Plas, 20/25, with Marjorie at the wheel and daughter Susan

ubilant Sir Hugo Cunliffe-Owen leading in his Derby hero, Felstead, the first Classic ridden by Harry, 1928

Harry with his two brothers, Arthur (*left*) and Sam (*centre*) at Newcastle races, June larry finished first on Cornwood, Arthur second on Bodyline and Sam third on Myton.

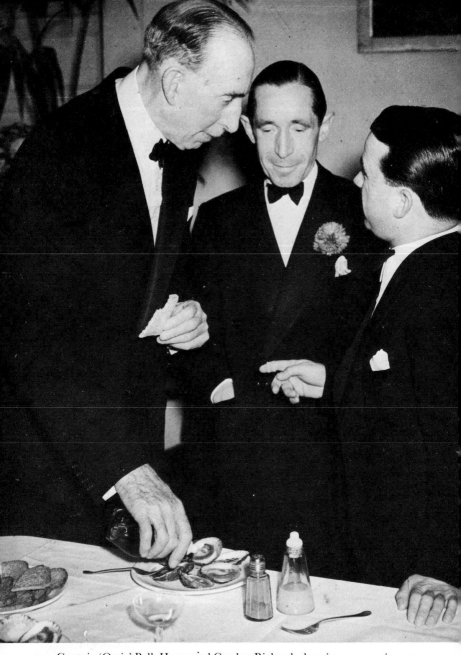

Captain 'Ossie' Bell, Harry and Gordon Richards deep in conversation at an end-of-season Champion Jockey's dinner

much faster on that particular ground. This was the first race I was going to ride in — five furlongs — and I was drawn a high number but I'd like to be drawn low so that I could come up this good part of the track that's been burnt up. When I got down to the start they're lining up and as they're lining up I said to the starter, 'Look, sir, this horse might kick if I start a high number. If I start by the rails — ' The jockeys immediately said, 'Good gracious no, if this horse kicks let him start on the outside.' That's where I want to be. Anyhow, I said, 'I don't mind where I go.' So anyhow they let me start number one and I went up the left side where I saw all the burnt-up part. They didn't see which way I went. I won by six lengths. So I thought, that's it — I've discovered something there and so a bit later on I'm sitting in the weighing room thinking over that thing because all the time the horses always race on the right-hand side at Sandown. This was something new to see a horse come up on the left side. Brownie Carslake came up and sat down by the side of me and said, 'Listen brains, what was all that about?' I said, 'What was all what about?' 'What made you go up there?' I said, 'Oh, that horse, he's a funny sort of feller. I've got to keep him away, if he gets near other horses he turns it up he does something screwy.' 'Now look, there's more than that,' Brownie said and he walked away from me. I thought, by jingo he's really caught on to me already but I'm not going to say anything at all about this.

Anyhow, a bit later on in the day Brownie came to me again, sat down beside me and said, 'Look, I've got a two-year-old in the final race and it means a terrific lot to me — I just wondered if I ought to do what you did?' 'Well,' I said, 'I told you the truth about it.' 'I can't make any mistakes, I don't want you lying to me.' I said, 'Look, if it means so much to you, come up where I did. You'll go by.' So anyhow the race came along and he came up where I'd been and of course he won by six lengths.

The Eclipse proved to be Miracle's final race, for he broke down a few weeks later, was scratched from the St Leger, and was sent to his owner's Mentmore Stud where he stood at a fee of 250 guineas — but proved a total failure as a stallion. Harry rode Udaipur, heroine of The Oaks, in the St Leger and finished fourth in a remarkable Classic which brought first, second, fourth and fifth places to horses racing in H. H. Aga Khan's 'green and chocolate' colours, and which caused King George V to comment in a letter to his new racing manager, 'I hear they called it the Indian Circus.'

Until autumn 1932 Harry had never suffered a serious accident as a jockey. However his younger brothers had not been so lucky. Sam had been hurt when his mount Imp, owned by Sir Hugo Cunliffe-Owen, rolled on him at Alexandra Park in August 1928. He was hurt again the following year when riding Typhoon at Leicester. There was a collision and three horses fell. Arthur Wragg was also unlucky when Silver Sue fell in the Queen's Birthday Handicap at Windsor in May 1928 and he fractured two ribs and ruptured a kidney.

The fates decreed that Harry was to be badly injured when riding a two-year-old filly Donatia to the start of the Astley Nursery Handicap at Newcastle on 19 October. He had won the previous race for Lord Londonderry and was hopeful of completing a double, thus taking his total number of winners for the season to 102. Suddenly Donatia pecked and he was thrown to the ground, his right leg exceedingly badly smashed. News that he had suffered serious injury with compound fractures to his leg was made known to dismayed racegoers but the general public did not realise the full extent of his plight, for detailed information was never divulged. He was taken by ambulance to the Newcastle Nursing Home in Windsor Terrace, with one of the racecourse doctors remaining with him throughout the journey. This wise doctor appreciated that it would be fool-hardy to allow anyone to attempt to remove Harry's boot or breeches until he was examined by Mr Gordon Irwin, Senior Orthopaedic Surgeon to the Royal Victoria Infirmary.

Mr Irwin was celebrated for being very much aware of the enormous anxiety of sportsmen and athletes when their future was at risk, and would spend endless time and energy helping them return to their pre-injury expertise. He was not especially interested in horseracing — his personal preferences were for golf, shooting and fishing — but he knew that a celebrated jockey was now in desperate need of all his medical skill. It took some time for the dirt to be extracted from Harry's smashed leg and only then could the surgeon commence a detailed examination of the injured limb. Gordon Irwin was appalled at the extent of the injury, and contemplated amputation.

Marjorie Wragg had arrived at the nursing home, and when the situation was explained to her, she told the hospital staff that if his leg was amputated, Harry would lose the will to live. For several hours an impasse developed, for Gordon Irwin believed that if the leg was not amputated Harry would die. The brilliant surgeon had the good fortune to have an equally brilliant anaesthetist, Dr William Seymour, as his assistant. Seymour suggested that one possible way — even if an unorthodox one — in which the leg might be saved was by constantly rubbing ether into it. Although the situation seemed hopeless, Irwin agreed that nothing should be left undone in the effort to restore Harry so that he could eventually ride again. Dr Seymour's suggestion was acted upon, and miraculously the leg was saved.

Nevertheless, Harry was in the nursing home for nearly three months, during which time he struck up a great personal friendship with Gordon Irwin, who was a marvellous raconteur, could play any tune on the piano without reading a note of music and could draw and paint with consummate skill. Marjorie Wragg gave Gordon Irwin's daughter a baby doll whose pink outfit she had knitted whilst at Harry's bedside, and was amused when the surgeon's young son exclaimed, 'Why has that lady got red nails?'

Harry's superb fitness was the key to his recovery and once he was able to walk with the aid of crutches he would go down to the local gardens where many of Newcastle's unemployed gathered each day. They did not recognise him, but found that he was a fund of sound advice on football, boxing, golf, racing and even upon the philosophy of life. Only when the subject of fishing was mentioned was he at a loss, for he knew nothing of the science of angling.

He was allowed home for Christmas. Marjorie collected him from Newcastle and drove him to Newmarket, where he spent ten days with her and the children before returning to Newcastle for further leg massage treatment. It was another two months before he could walk without crutches, but happily he was fit enough to return to the saddle soon after the commencement of the 1933 Flat Season and won a .race for Lord Rosebery at the Craven meeting at Newmarket.

Few other than the doctors and nurses realised his critical condition in the hours following his horrific crash, when his life was in danger. Understandably he was immensely grateful to Dr Basham, Mr Gordon Irwin and Dr Seymour, who became two of his closest friends in future years. Until his accident he had never smoked cigarettes, but the doctors persuaded him to smoke the occasional one in order to help him relax.

5

Life at Bedford Lodge

While Harry's racing career had been prospering, there had also been many changes in his private life. By the time of the accident in 1932 the Wraggs had three children — Peter, who had been born in October 1927, Geoffrey, three years younger, who was known as Buster as a child, and baby Susan, born in August 1932.

In the autumn of 1930 Harry, Madge and Peter had left Glenavis, on the Bury Road in Newmarket, where they had been living for two years since moving from North Lodge. They moved to Bedford Lodge, a far larger house also on the Bury Road. The house had a long history since being built by a Duke of Bedford in the early years of the nineteenth century. Sir Joseph Hawley, who won the 1851 Derby with Beadsman, had lived there, and so had Joseph Dawson, the trainer, before the property was acquired by the reprobate 'Abington' Baird, known as 'The Squire'. Subsequently the Hon. George Lambton took over the house and stables while Stanley House was being built, and he was followed by Bob Colling, who had moved to Bedford Lodge from Waterwich House. Eventually the house became the property of Lord Beaverbrook, who considered renaming it Calvin Lodge after the reformer and theologian whom he so admired. Lord Beaverbrook paid about £5,000 for the property, spent about £12,000 on it, and Harry purchased it for a sum reputed to be £5,000. He had intimated to a Newmarket estate agent that he was 'looking for a property' because Glenavis was becoming too small for the family.

When Marjorie Wragg learned that Bedford Lodge was on

the market she felt that the house would be the answer to all her dreams — and so it proved, for she rapidly made Bedford Lodge one of the centres of Newmarket hospitality. Known to everyone except Harry as 'Madge', she was generous almost to a fault, and an excellent hostess, having learned much of the art of running a home whilst on holiday with friends in France.

Witty and invariably well-dressed — having her hats created by Edell and her shoes made by Rayne — she loved London and would frequently drive to town, lunch at The Ritz and shop at Fortnum and Mason's. Admittedly she relished being a 'Queen Bee', but nevertheless she was kind-hearted, played the piano with zest, was an excellent dancer, had the latest books sent down by Hatchard's and collected antique furniture. She enjoyed gambling in modest amounts, with the Tote Double her favourite wager. Curiously she hated being alone, and when she and Harry were first married, she would insist on Millie Robinson, daughter of Alfred Sadler's head man, coming to stay with her if Harry's racing necessitated his absence for the night.

At Bedford Lodge she employed a cook, scullery maids, a nanny for the children and gardeners, one of whom had the task of collecting parcels from Newmarket station. Harry was content to give her free rein in the running of the house, a task which she accomplished with ease. Her efficiency was so renowned that some of the bachelor jockeys, including 'Rufus' Beasley, would ask her to organise dinner parties for them. It could be claimed that Harry pandered to her, but equally it is understandable that he was prepared to finance the cost and expense of maintaining an exceptionally comfortable house. He was expected to dress for dinner even if he and Madge were on their own, but his attitude may have been 'anything for a quiet life' and 'what is wrong with living in a style demanded by the wife you love if you can afford it?'

Frequently Harry would leave home at 5.00 am to drive to Lambourn to work. He had acquired a Rolls-Royce which was his pride and joy. In June 1934 he was fined fifteen shillings for not having a licence for his chauffeur. Jack Jarvis was fined a similar sum for an identical offence, and wrote to the court stating that he did not know that a licence was required, and added that he thought it hard, when he was paying thousands of pounds in income tax, that he should be summoned for so trivial an offence.

Usually, after riding at Lambourn, Harry would be back at Bedford Lodge by 11.00 am. If the weather was fine and there was racing at Newmarket, the family and house guests would assemble for pre-lunch drinks in the garden. Harry would disappear down the garden with a small sandwich. He would sit in a chair silently and methodically studying all the newspapers and calculating the form of all the horses which were running in the races in which he had a mount.

When time permitted Harry would spend hours deciding the correct distance for each horse, but such decisions often resulted in restless nights. Intelligent when planning his race tactics, he had radically altered the concept and theory of how to be successful on the undulating Epsom track and, by his victory on Felstead, totally dispelled the illusion that if one was not in the front rank at the top of Tattenham Corner all chance of success had vanished. One critic suggested that his style of riding would not have succeeded in America where catapulting from the start was the order of the day, but such criticism was dubious for he proved on countless occasions that he was perfectly capable of adopting tactics to suit prevailing conditions. It was claimed, however, that he kept a photograph of Danny Maher — three times Derby winner in the early years of the century — on his dressing room table to remind him of his 'won by waiting' tactics, and an ample supply of cotton wool to put in his ears to deafen the appalling language of grandstand critics when his late challenge just failed in its attempt.

In private Harry was punctual, precise, logical and well-organised, and carried these characteristics into his life as a jockey. He was always convinced that he was better than 'the next chap' and as an apprentice had once even sent a telegram to the absent trainer 'Won cleverly by a short head.' His self-confidence reached its zenith on the big occasion when that of some of his contemporaries was at its nadir. At Bedford Lodge he frequently discussed the question of whether or not jockeys were born or merely became great, but invariably ended up by stating that although strength, balance, good hands and good seat were vital ingredients for success, in the ultimate degree there was a mysterious unknown quantity which enabled some jockeys to have greater rapprochement with their horses than other men enjoyed. He was an expert dancer with a rhythmic sense of timing which was an infinite pleasure to watch, and employed similar style in his riding. There was never any flourish, never any display of exhibitionism or ostentation, yet onlookers felt as though he had a computer in his head working quietly, efficiently and non-stop. To many people who did not come into close contact with Harry, he seemed too serious-minded, but his friends knew he had a first-class sense of humour.

During the summer there were tennis parties at Bedford Lodge on Sunday afternoons. Harry always looking finely drawn, enjoyed playing, and it was in keeping with his character that he invariably worked out his opponent's weakness and planned how to take advantage of it. Bobby Jones and Harry's brother Arthur were regular players, and they seldom allowed a set to be played without being participants. It was not that they were selfish, but rather that they had to sweat as much as possible to keep their weight down. Bobby often played wearing a rubber suit, with rubber bands around the wrists, neck and ankles!

When riding at York, Harry would frequently take a suite at the Station Hotel which he would share with Dick Perryman, Bobby Jones and Gordon Richards. For Royal Ascot they and Fred Winter, Sam Long and Brownie Carslake would rent a house near Windsor, and insist that the house party comprised at least eight people so that they could have two tables of bridge in the evening. These Ascot 'house-parties' were also appreciated for the high teas served on their return from the races and which consisted almost entirely of prawns freshly delivered each day from a friendly fisherman!

Harry took a delight in playing practical jokes on Gordon Richards, whom he thought to be superstitious where his clothes were concerned if he was hopeful of riding a big-race winner. On these occasions he liked to wear a particular tie and pair of braces. One morning he came downstairs fussing that he could not find either and muttering that it probably meant he would not ride a winner that afternoon. Later in the morning he and Harry were walking around the garden when Harry suddenly said, 'What's that hanging on the wall?' pointing to a pair of braces and a tie that earlier he had deliberately put there. Gordon, always a man both big-hearted and with a sense of fun, took such pranks in the right spirit and accepted them.

One of the guests at Windsor each year was Phil Lancaster, the popular Newmarket bookmaker, who was saved from death due to the bridge table in the summer of 1933. He had planned to return to Newmarket with Fred Leader, the brother of Colledge and Harvey Leader, but was persuaded to remain so that bridge could be played. Tragically, Fred Leader and his wife were killed in a car crash near Stevenage on their way home.

Phil Lancaster, Harry and Bobby Jones had a great triumph in 1934 when their coursing greyhound, Little June Weather, won the Norfolk Stakes at Hockwold. They owned two other greyhounds, Large Johnny Walker and Little Johnny Wild — all named after the initials of Lancaster, Jones and Wragg. After the semi-final their dog was so exhausted that the trainer said, 'Offer the other finalist the Cup and we'll take the money.' The offer was refused, and in the event Little June Weather won the final, Harry and Bobby took the money and Phil the Cup.

Harry and Bobby Jones also played a great deal of golf together, often in the morning before racing. Harry played off a handicap of ten but Bobby was so good that he could give him nine shots! At Fulford, the golf course near York, Harry twice won the coveted Turfites Trophy. In the final of the first of these tournaments he was warned by a future amateur champion, Alex Kyle, that his bookmaker opponent, who played off a low handicap, would attempt to 'talk him out of it'. However,

Harry was immune to such comments as, 'that was a good drive for a ten-handicap player' or 'I'll just come across and watch you play that bunker shot' and won by seven and six over eighteen holes! He was imperturbable throughout the match and won at the twelfth when his frustrated opponent drove out of bounds. Three times in the course of his golfing career Harry did a hole in one (twice at Newmarket and once at Doncaster) and highlighted his prowess when defeating Wanda Morgan in a Racing Charity golf match in December 1935. Bobby Jones beat Joyce Wethered in the same match. However, the terrible fall that Harry had suffered at Newcastle in 1932 curtailed his golf to some extent, and he played only infrequently for the next fifteen years. Less golf resulted in the necessity to watch his weight and to diet.

Once Harry became acknowledged as one of the leading jockeys, he attempted to avoid the press as much as possible, and in consequence was unfairly accused of trying to antagonise them. One exception was Clive Graham, who joined the *Daily Express* team in 1931. He was very popular with Harry and his jockey 'cronies' but they were wary of him as a racing correspondent, for they thought that he might give the wrong interpretation to their remarks about horses and races. On many occasions they deliberately made fatuous comments to try to discourage him, but Clive was sufficiently clever to make the comments into amusing stories and consequently was always a welcome guest at Bedford Lodge.

Madge's sister Lily Leach was a much-loved member of the family, full of fun and a wonderful guest. She had married 'Chubb' Leach on 6 January 1932. Younger son of Felix Leach, who had been head man to Richard Marsh at Egerton House before setting up on his own at Graham Place, Newmarket, where one of his patrons was Sir Hugo Cunliffe-Owen, Chubb had been apprenticed to his father. Increasing weight necessitated that he gave up riding in 1930 and he took over the licence to train which had been held by his elder brother, who had died after an operation for appendicitis in November of that year. Chubb had more than fifty horses at Queensberry Lodge and saddled his first winner at Thirsk early the following season. His other brother, Jack, had been first jockey to H.L. Cottrill, and had ridden Adam's Apple to win the 1927 Two Thousand Guineas. In October 1928 Jack had married Betty, eldest daughter of Sam Darling, thus uniting two famous racing families.

Lily had had considerable experience as a singer in Leeds before her marriage, and could always be relied upon to get a party going by singing and dancing. Such parties often went on all night. Chubb Leach and Harry were great pals, and in the most unostentatious manner Harry helped Chubb and Lily if times were hard.

One morning Harry was riding out for Chubb and towards the end of a gallop Chubb called out, 'How are you going?' 'Not half as well as that thing you are riding. What is it?' was Harry's reply. Chubb told him that the gelding was called Doch-an-Doris, that he was an absolute rogue, and that the owners had given him to him as a present on the condition that he did not sell him. Harry asked to ride Doch-an-Doris if Chubb would send the string down the gallops again. After riding him Harry decided that the gelding hated working alongside other horses, but in fact was far from useless. He advised Chubb to use him as a hack, and told him that he would be happy to ride him whenever possible. Doch-an-Doris did them proud; he was brought out whenever Chubb was short of cash and in 1932, as an aged gelding, won six times!

Chubb was fond of a gamble and on one occasion he took Menado, a two-year-old, to Newcastle to run in a seller. Harry, Madge, Chubb and Lily were all staying with Dr and Mrs William Seymour for the races. The ever-hospitable Mrs Seymour provided salmon for lunch. Harry watched in silence as the others relished the delicious fish. Suddenly he grabbed a plate, said, 'I can't stand it any longer,' and took a large helping. Menado was fully expected to win the seller, but to everyone's consternation, a complete outsider shot to the front as the tapes went up. At half-way the wretched horse was lengths ahead whilst in the grandstand the Seymour party was moaning 'Oh my God, why did Harry have to eat that salmon!' Luckily the outsider stopped to nothing, and Harry got up to win by three-quarters of a length so that the episode of eating salmon and putting on weight was quickly overlooked.

Harry paid less attention to his weight in the winter, when he and Madge would holiday in Madeira, but for Harry the rest would often be interrupted by having to take the children back to school. Peter and Geoffrey would holiday with them but, when term-time beckoned, Harry would take them back to Southampton, give them into the care of his sister and return on the next boat to Madeira. It was no hardship for he enjoyed sea-voyages.

An interesting man I met on my travels was Lord Beaver-brook. I was coming back one day from Madeira on this boat and one of the first fellers that came up to me was Lord Castleross. He said, 'You'd be very interested to know that I'd like you to meet Lord Beaverbrook, he's on the ship.' I agreed. He said, 'Well, come down about seven o'clock to the bar and we'll have a cocktail.' Lord Castleross said to Lord Beaverbrook, 'This is Harry Wragg, I want to introduce him to you. He bought your place.' Lord Beaverbrook said, 'I know he acquired my place, but he didn't buy it, he stole it!' So I talked to him about Bedford Lodge. I loved it, and I was having a lovely time there. And I talked about his racing and he wasn't too happy about it. So I said I noticed that he had not been in the racing business very long and that because he hadn't had many winners, all he'd done was get rid of his horses. He told me he had to do that because his advisors had told him he ought to go into racing to take a lot of the burden off his mind — he'd got to have some relaxation and that was the way to do it. So first of all they made him buy some race horses and the next thing was they made him buy a stud — and then he'd got to entertain people like Lord Castleross. And so he found that instead of easing his work they'd given him ten times more to do, so he'd had to get rid of these people, he'd got to sell the horses. And that's what he'd done. I said, 'That's a pity because there's no doubt about it, you'll be coming back one day into this racing business and you'll see how good it is for you, and you'll be enjoying yourself.' But he never did come back.

During the winter of 1934-5, Harry and Marjorie sailed to New York on the *Aquitania* before holidaying in Barbados. They both loved dancing, and the song 'We could have danced all night' almost became their signature tune. On arrival in New York, accompanied by fellow jockey Jackie Sirett and his wife, they read in the paper that there was a dinner-dance at the Pennsylvania Rooms, and decided to go there. The Rooms were jammed solid and the head waiter regretfully told them that there was no chance of a table. Nevertheless, Harry stayed for a few moments, entranced by the music. Small wonder, for it was Benny Goodman giving a farewell concert. The next night Harry and Marjorie returned to find the Rooms far less crowded, with Bob Crosby and his band entertaining the dancers. Harry had expected Benny Goodman, for he had not realised that the previous evening had been a gala occasion. When he eventually arrived back at Bedford Lodge after his holiday, he bought all Benny Goodman's gramophone records and also many by Bing Crosby. He had heard some of Crosby's songs whilst in America and from the outset was smitten by the crooner's style.

6

Rockfel and Mickey the Greek

The year 1933 commenced ominously when news was received that Herr Hitler had been appointed German Chancellor despite the long resistance from President Hindenburg. However the majority of Englishmen were more perturbed by the news from Australia that Larwood's body-line bowling was causing the Australian Board of Control to complain bitterly to the M.C.C. Harry, who was still recovering from his leg injuries, felt that the Board was not justified in claiming that Larwood's bowling was unsporting. He did not ride at Lincoln or Liverpool, and by the time that he had his first ride of the season at the Craven meeting at Newmarket the nation was rejoicing that two specially-equipped planes of the Houston expedition had flown their pilots, observers and cameras over the top of Mount Everest. At the Craven meeting Harry won on Isadora, a filly owned by Lord Rosebery, being awarded the race after finishing second and successfully lodging an objection for bumping and boring. He showed that he had returned to his best form by riding three winners, including Foxhunter, at Kempton on Easter Monday.

In the Two Thousand Guineas Harry finished second on Sir Hugo Cunliffe-Owen's King Salmon to the French colt Rodosto, beaten a head. King Salmon, a half-brother to Blenheim, did not lose any of his high reputation in his next race, the Newmarket Stakes, when second to Young Lover, for in the course of the race he lost a plate and consequently emphasised his Derby chance. However, events were to prove that Hyperion was an exceptional colt and in finishing second to him in The

Derby King Salmon showed himself to be the second-best three-year-old in England.

A fortnight later the St James's Palace Stakes at Ascot proved yet again a graveyard for horses who had run creditably in The Derby, for King Salmon was unplaced to Canon Law. Nevertheless, Harry again had a profitable Royal Ascot — winning the Gold Cup on Mr Edward Esmond's Foxhunter, the Britannia Stakes on Lord Rosebery's Tartan and the Wokingham Stakes for the second year on Sir Hugo Cunliffe-Owen's Concerto. In addition he finished second to his brother Sam in the two-mile Churchill Stakes on Foxhunter. who was having a pipe-opener before his Gold Cup bid. Sam Wragg was enjoying a successful season and a fortnight earlier had won The Oaks on Chatelaine.

The Ascot Gold Cup brought out one of the best fields in living memory for it included Orpen, Nitsichin, winner of the Cesarewitch the previous autumn, Firdaussi, hero of the St Leger; Brulette who had won the 1931 Oaks, Hill Song, winner of the Irish St Leger, and Gainslaw, who had scored a victory in the Gold Vase forty-eight hours earlier. Foxhunter, beautifully ridden by Harry, challenged Orpen, ridden by Dick Perryman, at the distance and gradually forged ahead to win by a length with Nitsichin five lengths away third.

Although King Salmon was beaten at Ascot he was expected to make amends at Goodwood in the Gordon Stakes, but he could only finish second — ridden by Sam Wragg in the enforced absence of Harry who had been injured at the second July meeting at Newmarket when riding Talos in the July Handicap. After coming under starter's orders, Talos charged the tapes, fell and threw Harry to the ground. His left leg was cracked and he was unable to ride for several weeks.

However, the season belonged entirely to Gordon Richards, who equalled Fred Archer's record of 246 winners, rode his 247th winner, Golden King, at Liverpool on November 8th, and ended the season with 259 victories to his credit. Another happy occasion, a little earlier, was when Harry returned to the saddle on 2 October, winning the Selling Plate at Nottingham for eighteen-year-old Vivien Jarvis, daughter of Jack Jarvis. Vivien was not present to see the victory as she was in Paris at a finishing academy.

1934   Harry began the 1934 season by riding a winner owned and trained by Jack Jarvis on the first day of the Lincoln meeting, and two more on the second afternoon to become leading jockey. In the Two Thousand Guineas he rode Umidwar, who was unplaced, for H.H. Aga Khan, but rode Campanula to win the One Thousand Guineas for her owner and breeder, Sir George Bullough, who was a popular member of the Jockey Club.

Campanula, trained by Jack Jarvis, had been a brilliant two-year-old, winning the Windsor Castle Stakes at Ascot ridden by Eph Smith and the Moulton Stakes at the Newmarket Houghton meeting ridden by Harry. She had been allotted second place on 9st in the Free Handicap — only 7 lbs below Colombo.

One Thousand Guineas Day was fine and warm, and the ground firm — with Campanula installed an odds-on favourite. At the start she delayed proceedings by refusing again and again to go up to the tapes — a reluctance that she had also shown as a two-year-old. However, Harry's patience and that of the starter were rewarded and at 'The Off' she lost only a length. Going into the Dip it was obvious that the race lay between her and Light Brocade and inside the final fifty yards Harry urged his mount into the lead. Some critics claimed that he had won 'cleverly', others 'decisively' and Campanula's detractors 'all out'. A great credit to her sire, Blandford, and her dam, Vesper Bell, she had come into the possession of Sir George Bullough fortuitously. Lord Manton had bought Vesper Bell as a foal, but a few weeks later he was killed in the hunting field. When his yearlings were sold, Sir George Bullough bought Vesper Bell for 1,100 guineas.

In The Oaks Light Brocade took her revenge on Campanula who could only finish fourth. A curious fact about the two fillies is that they were both reared at the Ashley Heath stud at Newmarket where they were inseparable companions until they went into training — Campanula to Jack Jarvis at Park Lodge and Light Brocade to Frank Butters at Fitzroy House.

In The Derby Harry rode Umidwar, who failed to gain a place in one of the most dramatic 'Blue Ribands' on record, with Colombo being beaten by Windsor Lad and Easton. However, the meeting brought a triumph for Harry when he won the Coronation Cup on Sir Richard Brooke's King Salmon. Although it had been planned to run Hyperion, he was an absentee and King Salmon only had two rivals, Mate and Chatelaine, on whom Sam Wragg had won The Oaks the previous year.

At Ascot Harry took the St James's Palace Stakes in sensational style on Lord Rosebery's Flamenco, beating Colombo on whom odds of 5-1 on had been laid. He had walked the course in the morning and found that near the rails it was naturally softer than the hard surface in the centre of the course. He knew that Flamenco could act on the hard, and he laid his plans accordingly. He set the pace from the start and as the turn into the straight was met, swept very wide into the centre of the track. It was evident to those in the packed grandstands that it was neither a swerve, nor a case of Flamenco hanging to his left. Shouts of, 'Oh Harry, what are you doing?' were heard as Colombo moved up on the rails. He never reached Flamenco, who held on tenaciously for a half-length victory, with six lengths separating Colombo from the third horse. It was a brilliant but typical exhibition of tactical riding on the part of Harry. Later in the week he scored on Sir Hugo Cunliffe-Owen's Maid of Essex in the Granville Stakes.

King Salmon did not run at Ascot due to having pricked his foot after wrenching off a shoe on the Sunday after Epson Derby week, but contested the Eclipse — the most valuable weight-for-age race in the Calendar. His nine rivals included the Derby hero, Windsor Lad, and Umidwar. King Salmon had originally raced in the colours of his breeder, Lord Carnarvon, before being bought by Sir Hugo Cunliffe-Owen who sold him to Sir Richard Brooke, another patron of Ossie Bell's stable, shortly after the 1933 Derby.

The record book shows that King Salmon won by half a length from Umidwar, with Windsor Lad the same distance away third — but such a result gives no indication of the drama. Charlie Smirke was over-confident that his Derby hero could gobble up his rivals, had allowed himself to be boxed in and was unable to challenge until too late. He was furious with himself and more furious when he heard that the Maharajah of Raj-pipla had suggested that he had allowed himself to be trapped on purpose. In any event seeds of doubt were sown, and weeks later Windsor Lad was sold to Mr Martin Benson for £50,000.

A week before the Eclipse Harry had ridden Caithness, a moderate three-year-old owned by Lord Rosebery, in the Dullingham Stakes at the Newmarket Second July meeting. He beat his solitary opponent by a short head. The name of the opponent was Hyperion! There were no excuses for the great horse, on whom Tommy Weston appeared to be cruising in the early stages of the race. Suddenly it was realised that Harry was playing a 'cat and mouse' game and was waiting to pounce. Weston began riding for dear life — but to no avail. Hyperion saw and felt the whip and pulled out a bit extra but, sadly, in his final race he was beaten.

> I tailed him to the last two or three strides and only then did I challenge him. I just got up and beat him on the line. If it had been a proper sort of race I would have been well beaten.

Lord Derby was not present to witness the defeat of his champion as he was in Lancashire where King George V was opening the Mersey Tunnel.

Harry ended the 1934 season on a top note when he rode three winners on the final day at Manchester. In the last race Harry, who was described as looking 'rather tired, pinched and ascetic', beat his brother Arthur by six lengths, with Sam unplaced. On two previous occasions the three brothers had shared the honours of a race, for at Newcastle in June 1933 Harry had ridden the winner whilst Arthur had been second and Sam third; and in March 1934 at Doncaster the first three had been ridden by Arthur followed by Sam and Harry.

Harry had always had a great affection for Manchester racecourse and thought that he had discovered the secret of how to ride the track:

> There were occasions when I've benefited by discovering the difference of the ground on different parts of many racecourses. I used to regularly walk them and one of the racecourses where I had a lot of success due to this same sort of thing — picking out the best part on which to race — was Manchester. I think probably I won more races there than any jockey at that period of time and I was pretty certain if I was allowed to go — get exactly where I wanted to go — on this particular track no one would beat me. One small strip of the track made so much difference. The difference was that when they first built that track, when they put the rails in, they used something like cement to fix them — at any rate this is what I thought in my own mind. I examined the little strip very closely and it was a firm sort of surface close to where the post was put in. So long as you went down there you'd got a strip about two feet wide just by the rails and if you could keep on that bit you were going to run on faster ground. That's what I thought, and anyhow it used to sort of come off all the time.
>
> I remember one particular race on that track which was run at Manchester the very last meeting of the year, 1931. I was talking the night before, at the Midland Hotel, to one of the press fellers that I liked — Jimmy Parks, the only man of his era to carry a stop-watch on a racecourse — and he was telling me that he was very near going to be champion tipster of the year with his nap selections. So I said 'What are you going for tomorrow?' He said, 'I haven't made up my mind yet.' I said, 'I'll tell you this — I ride a horse called Tetraset and if I can get where I want to get, this feller will about win.' So he said, 'OK, I'll go for him.'
>
> So he went for him and the race came along and I got exactly where I wanted to go — I squeezed through on the inside and I got the last bit out of him and won at 10-1. When I came into the winning enclosure I could see Jim Parks coming towards me and I gave him a wave and he waved back and then I said, 'That was marvellous, did you

nap that?' He says, 'Yes, but — it's a very sad story — you
see I did nap it but the feller who was just one or two points
in front of me on the nap table works in the office and when
he saw my nap come through he deliberately napped
exactly the same horse. He reasoned that if he did the same
nap as me, then I could not possibly beat him. So although
I got Tetraset napped, he did it also. So really it was a bit
unfortunate.'*

You've got to realise that Manchester's ground was
always on the wet side — and they even have a lot of rain in
the summer time. Anyhow, as soon as the jockeys realised
that I was winning races on the stand side they all crowded
over and did the same sort of thing, making it very difficult
to get where I wanted to. In actual fact, although they
thought the stand side was the best place to race it didn't
make the slightest bit of difference really — there's only
one spot to race and that was where I discovered right
underneath the rails. You could do that on both sides of
the course, and at the last meeting of the season I proved it
again by winning a couple of races on the other side.
Because of the traffic jam caused by huge fields, I switched
sides and came up the other rails and won two races on the
far side of the course. I won three altogether on that day,
on Adriatic, Light Tackle and Stop Press, and I was also
third on Free Fare in the November handicap.

Harry also referred to his waiting style:

I did not deliberately set out to develop a waiting style, but
I did try to become a judge of pace. That is how I got the
reputation of riding waiting races.

All I did was to suit the capabilities of my horse to the
pace at which the leader was going. If it was a strong pace,
then I let my horse drop back and conserve his energy until
we neared the point where it really mattered to be in front.
If I found the pace was moderate, then I let my mount go
on, and make the running at the pace which I thought
suited him best.

I think I first received the name 'Head Waiter' after I
had got up on the post to win a race at Salisbury. A
spectator who had put his last fiver on my mount said,

---

*Curiously Tetraset won the identical race the next year, ridden by Arthur Wragg, and
again starting at 10-1.

'They ought to make him Head Waiter at the Café de Paris.'

Not everyone sort of greeted me with a name like the Head Waiter. There were two fellows in particular, Brownie Carslake and Colonel Dick Warden. Whenever I came in and had done anything these two would say, 'Well done, boy, how's brains — hiya brains.' And they would always give me a 'hi there' sort of business with the word brains. That was their way of congratulating me.

At the final meeting of the season at Manchester the feud between Harry and Michael Beary reached boiling point:

Naturally Michael Beary was very annoyed about me riding first of all his Derby winner and then after that, taking the ride away from him in the Eclipse Stakes. Well, I'd got nothing to do with it. I was doing what I was told to do, for the trainer said he wanted me to ride and that was that. Anyhow, Michael was always throwing digs at me and I could see something was brewing. One day at Manchester, where we had two weighing rooms, I was in a different room to my younger brother. Somebody came in and told me that there was an argument going on between my younger brother and Michael Beary and I thought, by jingo he's a bit rough is Arthur my brother, if he goes and belts Michael one there'll be real trouble. So I'd better go and see to it. So I go inside and I break them up and I say to Michael, 'I know what you want Arthur to do. You want the kid to hit you and the moment he hits you, you'll take him in front of the Stewards and you'll get him stood down, that's what you'll do.' And he said, 'Oh no, I don't want you telling me what to do,' and began pushing me away and poking at me, so I slammed a right and hit Michael and put him on the ground. I've been telling the kid not to do anything like that and then of course I do it, and I said to Arthur, 'Hard luck, I've done it to him now.' So then I said to Michael, 'Now you've got what you want, I suppose you'll go and tell the Stewards.' He said, 'Oh no, I won't go and tell the Stewards. I'll see you later on. We'll have it out later.' So I thought after that everyone was going away peaceful. However, before I left the races he said, 'I'll wait for you to come round to my room and I'll give you a ring when I'm ready for you.'

We stayed at the same hotel in Manchester and so all the

jockeys were in little groups — we played cards and we had a sitting room there. The telephone rings after we'd been there about an hour and it's Michael. He wants to speak to me. He said, 'I've got my room ready for you and I just want you to come up and we'll settle that little argument.' So I said, 'OK.' I told all the other boys — old Joe Childs says, 'You can't go,' and Freddy Fox says, 'Now, we'd better stop this nonsense.'

So they get on the telephone to Michael and tell him what a fool he's making of himself. I said to Bobby Jones, 'I'd better just prepare myself and go and sort him out. I think that's what I must do because I don't know what he knows about fighting but I think I can soon take him.'

So Charlie Smirke and Bobby Jones and I march round to his room. Of course the bed's been taken away from the room. He's made it into a proper little ring all ready set up and so immediately I said, 'Whenever you're ready.' And he said, 'What are you doing there?' because I'm wearing a pair of kid gloves. He said, 'What you doing with those on?' I said, 'I just don't want to hurt my hands too much, that's all, you can do the same if you want to.' Anyway, then we began and of course he knew nothing at all about fighting. I belted him and after five minutes I kept waiting for somebody to stop the fight because he didn't know anything at all about it. He was wrestling with me and doing anything, pushing me. So I walked away and then slammed a right, caught him full on the jaw and floored him. But he got up again, racing at me totally mad, so I belted him again but he still kept coming back for more. Eventually they did stop it — he was a right mess in a very short time. Everybody went to his aid and started doing things for him — putting a steak on his cheeks and his eyes.

Anyhow, the next day when he goes to the races Frank Butters, his trainer, was there and he said, 'What happened to you, did you run into a bus? Where have you been, what happened?' 'Oh,' Michael said, 'I had a little bit of trouble, just had a little bit of trouble last night, but I'm alright now, I'm alright to ride.' But he really looked a mess. My right hand was swollen but it didn't stop me from riding, although it did interfere with me a little bit, but fortunately it was the end of the season and I was alright the next week. But Michael said afterwards he'd been holding a grudge ever since those rides on Blenheim and Rustom Pasha. I thought probably it was something like that and he said he was happy it was all over. But we had a terrific job keeping it out of the newspapers.

Harry had given up boxing in 1920, but never lost interest in the sport and gave some exhibition fights. One of these was against Teddy Baldock, bantamweight champion of the world:

> I boxed him in London and it was a very enjoyable evening and I got quite a lot of praise for it, too. He kept poking his nose out to give me every chance to score some points and every time he did poke it out I kept just tapping him, which pleased the crowd and brought up a cheer or two. This happened until eventually towards the end of the round I was leading with my left, he chopped that down, hit me one in the tummy and one on the chin and then I was on the floor. They rang the bell, put me in the corner and it could be seen that he really caught me. If it had been a proper fight I would have been out there for five or ten minutes. Anyhow there was a long time before they rang the bell to come out for the second round and Sam Russell, a feller we knew well from old-time fighters, he was in my corner, he said 'Now look, don't take any liberties, just box like you have been boxing but don't do any more than that,' and of course everything finished very happy afterwards. I just did as I was told to do.

It was reported in the papers the next day that the boxing had been a riotous burlesque at Sam Russell's testimonial tournament party. Teddy Baldock protested that Harry was 'doped' but the referee overruled the protest. Ringside supporters told Harry to kick Teddy, and during the first round Harry's second hastily dropped his towel into the ring as Teddy, grinning in mock ferocity, prepared a left hook which deliberately he never delivered. Then someone threw a red rubber sponge into the ring, and Teddy and Harry joined forces to kick it away. When Harry slapped Teddy's face, the champion apologised for putting it in the way, much to everyone's delight.

It was announced in January 1935 that there would be a change **1935** in the riding plans of Jack Jarvis's stable in the forthcoming season, with Harry no longer retained on a 'definite' basis. Instead Eph Smith, a nineteen-year-old son of a Berkshire farmer who was apprenticed to Major F.B. Sneyd, was engaged, and Harry was only to be given mounts when suitable occasions arose and his other engagements permitted. It has never been made explicitly clear why the services of Harry were virtually swept aside, although the misunderstandings, if they existed at all, between Harry and Jack Jarvis may have originated when Sandwich was a three-year-old.

Misunderstandings between Harry and Lord Rosebery might have been more recent, particularly since Lord Rosebery was convinced, with no justification, that H.H. Aga Khan wanted Harry to ride for him. Lord Rosebery was paying Harry a retainer of £2,000 a year, and seemed to believe, on hearsay, that the Aga Khan was willing to offer £6,000 and that Lord Astor was prepared to pay a similar sum for Harry's services. Harry, however, was more content with retainers from Sir Hugo Cunliffe-Owen and Lord Rosebery and repeatedly stated that he was not intending to sign any contract with the Aga Khan.

Somehow Lord Rosebery got to know about these offers and he came and challenged me about them. I said, 'Oh no, I'm not thinking of that.' So he said, 'Why don't you contradict the rumours?' I said, 'I've no need to contradict them, I'm happy to do what I'm doing, riding for you and Sir Hugo. That's good enough for me, I don't have to tell the press. I don't have to tell anybody else. It doesn't make the slightest bit of difference so long as you know.' Anyhow, later on in the year, we went to Scotland. We always had a lot of runners there, particularly at Edinburgh and Ayr, and we didn't have a very good meeting but a terrific lot of runners. We won three or four races but we expected to win a lot more.

So when we came back after that meeting, about a week later, Jack Jarvis told me that in 1935 they weren't going to go through with my retainer, they didn't want me. I thought that's bloody funny. They'd already got E. Smith, who was a lightweight jockey at the time, riding one or two of our horses — Jack Jarvis obviously thought he could ride them all. I said, 'That's alright by me but it's rather strange. Lord Rosebery's been attacking me about my going to ride for the Aga Khan and Lord Astor. I've told him I wasn't but then suddenly he says he doesn't want me. Who is it that doesn't want me?' Jack Jarvis said, 'I don't know, that's what Lord Rosebery says, anyhow.' So I thought the best thing I could do was to talk to Sir Hugo Cunliffe-Owen and I told him that I didn't mind two hoots really. And I said to him 'Don't you think there's something funny — they must think I've done something wrong to be chasing me for the last two months to fix up a contract to ride again, like I was always going to do it anyhow, and then suddenly say they don't want me? It doesn't look good.'

I went to see Lord Rosebery too and ask what it was all about and he said I hadn't done anything wrong. I explained, 'I don't want you to try to shield me in any way if you think I've done something wrong. I want you to tell me because I haven't done anything wrong in my life, and especially not for people I'm riding for. I haven't let anybody down in my life either.' He said, 'It's a bit cheaper, easier, to engage Eph Smith as a lightweight, and then you whenever you're available.' I said, 'Well, that doesn't make sense to me but anyhow it doesn't make the slightest bit of difference either.' The press made quite a good lot of show about it when I beat Lord Rosebery's horses several times.

The unhappy affair blew over eventually and it was proved afterwards that they were probably wrong in getting rid of me really because later on I beat them in several Classics when I was riding for Lord Derby.

Perhaps the fact that hurt Harry the most concerning the parting of the ways was that he had done so much to encourage Jack Jarvis to bring in Eph Smith as the lightweight jockey of the stable. When Smith had ridden Whiteplains to win the 1934 Northumberland Plate, Harry had told Jack Jarvis, 'Watch that boy, he's a good rider and obeys instructions. I told him to keep driving the horse as soon as he reached the straight, and he did exactly as I told him.' Harry had ridden Whiteplains in the Great Metropolitan at Epsom and realised the ability and limitations of the horse — but Jack Jarvis may not have been best pleased that Harry had told Eph Smith what to do, believing that it was his prerogative as the trainer to instruct Smith. If Harry had retained a manager this state of affairs might never have been reached.

At the outset of the 1935 season Harry must have been despondent when Flamenco, ridden by Eph Smith, won the first leg of the Spring Double — for Lord Rosebery's colt carried 9 stone, a weight that he could have made without any difficulty. Ironically Harry finished third, only beaten three lengths and one and a half lengths, so he had a reasonable view of the 'primrose and rose hoops' as they flashed into the lead. In the Two Thousand Guineas he was unplaced on Miss Dorothy Paget's Desert Cloud behind Bahram but in the One Thousand Guineas finished second on Hyndford Bridge to the French filly Mesa. Hyndford Bridge was a sister to Portlaw who had started favourite for the 1931 Two Thousand Guineas.

In The Derby he rode H.H. Aga Khan's Theft into fourth place, and was promptly interviewed by the Stewards who were dissatisfied that he had pulled out on Theft to allow his far more fancied stable companion, Bahram, a clear run. They drew his attention to Rule 139 which stated: 'Every horse that runs in a race shall be run on its merit, whether his owner runs another horse in the race or not.' Sensibly Harry admitted that he had contravened the Rule, was cautioned, and warned that if he or any other jockey disregarded the Rule in future they would be severely dealt with.

In the press it was pointed out that when Harry won The Derby on the Aga Khan's Blenheim, the same owner also ran the more fancied Rustom Pasha. It was also emphasised that until a few years previously, when the rule was altered, an owner could make a declaration to win with one horse and any other could be pulled aside provided that the first choice could win. The rule was changed partly because the Aga Khan and a few other owners were keen on having more than one representative and disliked a declaration, whether optional or not. Finally it was stressed that every owner's horses now had to race on their merits; a horse put in solely as a pacemaker was against the written rules of racing.

A fortnight before The Derby Theft had been very heavily backed as one of the certainties for a place. There was no doubt that if Theft had come in third the bookmakers would have lost something like £100,000. Some of the small bookmakers, who scarcely laid Bahram at all, would have been very badly hit.

In conversation with Ajax of the *Evening Standard* after the race Harry explained:

> I had a lovely position going up the hill. I had intended to go along just behind the leaders and not wait as so many people thought that I would do. Before we reached the top of the hill I heard somebody shout. I had a glance over my shoulder and found that it was Freddie Fox trying to squeeze through. There was not room for him to do so, but when I realised it was Bahram, and I was also riding for the Aga Khan, I gave way and he was able to take the position which might have been mine.

Harry added that if he had not given way Theft, a son of Tetratema, would probably have finished second because he had an abundance of stamina and was running on strongly in the closing stages. Nevertheless his subsequent victory in the seven-furlong Jersey Stakes at Ascot when he was ridden by Gordon Richards proved that he also had the speed to win over a shorter distance. Theft added further to his reputation in July by being second to Windsor Lad in the Eclipse. At Ascot Harry won the Britannia Stakes on Finalist but otherwise had a dismal meeting. Goodwood proved better, for after finishing second on Almond Hill in the Stewards Cup to his brother Sam on Greenore in a desperate finish with less than a length covering the first four, he won the Goodwood Stakes on Hoplite and the Rous Memorial Stakes on Baber Shah. He was third on Lord Glanely's Buckleigh behind the Triple Crown hero Bahram in the St Leger. The season ended yet again on a successful note at Manchester for on the final afternoon Sam Wragg won the Manchester November Handicap on Free Fare and Harry rode three winners to make it a family occasion, and bringing his total to 102 winners, slightly less than half the number of victories achieved by Gordon Richards.

1936 In 1936 Harry was somewhat in the doldrums, and his Classic mount, His Grace, was unplaced in the Two Thousand Guineas and fifth to Mahmoud in The Derby. Ascot brought him victories in the Granville Stakes on Sir Hugo Cunliffe-Owen's Constellate and in the Jersey Stakes on Thankerton who had been third in The Derby, but Goodwood, York and Doncaster brought him little luck.

1937 1937 proved hardly better. He was unplaced on the Aga Khan's second string, Sultan Mahomed, in the Two Thousand Guineas, and was also unplaced on Colonel Giles Loder's Field Fare in both the One Thousand Guineas and The Oaks. He had no greater luck on Sir John Jarvis's Gainsborough Lass in The Derby and had only one success at Ascot when he won the Britannia Stakes for Mr James Rank on Azam Pasha. He won the Chesterfield Cup at Goodwood on Lady Ralli's Finalist and an hour later took the Nassau Stakes on First Flight, trained by Ossie Bell for Lord Londonderry to complete a stable double. He drew a blank at York but at Doncaster won the Great Yorkshire Handicap on Columcille for Lord Londonderry, the Tattersall Sale Stakes on Stafaralla for Prince Aly Khan, the seller on a colt of Harry Peacock's, the Princess Mary Stakes for Lady Cunliffe-Owen on Tamasha, the Scarborough Stakes on First Flight, a filly sired by Felstead, and on the final day the seller on Portulack and the Park Hill on Nadushka. In the autumn his brother Sam took the Cesarewitch on Punch and at the Cambridgeshire meeting Harry won the Cheveley Park Stakes on Stafaralla, trained by Frank Butters. In future years Stafarella was to become the dam of Tehran.

1938 1938 was Rockfel's year. Sixteen years earlier, in December 1922, her grand-dam Sweet Rocket had been bought by Cecil Boyd-Rochfort for Lord Londonderry who had asked him to find a filly foal to run with another that he had acquired. Boyd-

Rochfort bought Sweet Rocket for £250 and as a two-year-old she won three races including the Caterham Stakes at Epsom on Derby Day less than an hour after Harry Wragg had ridden in The Derby for the first time. Sweet Rocket's first foal was Rockcliffe, who made her debut on Monday 30 June 1930 at Wolverhampton in a selling plate, ridden by Harry. She started at 10-1 and won by two lengths.

> The Sweet Rocket filly, she was called Rockcliffe eventually, was a very little filly, nothing to look at really, and with no scope. The head man said, 'The guv'nor's not coming but he gave me the orders to tell you to get as near as you can, win if you can, because we've got to get rid of her, we've got to sell her.' I said, 'OK.' Away we go, but I could tell even going to post, this thing, although she's small, there's something about her that gave me a bloody good feel. In the race coming back she ran marvellously. I knew all the way through the race she was going to win. I'd never seen her race before, but she was running like an experienced animal — and I didn't appear until the very last moment and just gave a little back-hander, she went on and won on the bridle — very impressive. So when I pulled up I said to the head man, 'What did the guv'nor say about this thing?' 'Get rid of her.' I said, 'Look, no matter what happens, you buy this in and I'll be responsible for it — I'll tell the guv'nor afterwards what has happened and what we've done.' So very luckily he did what I said and he bought her back for 210 guineas.
>
> I went back home to Newmarket and Captain Bell rang me that night. He was furious about me buying this thing back. I said, 'Now look, you'll be very pleased one day about what I did. I tell you that this filly has got something, although she hasn't got scope, that could develop, I'm pretty certain. She's so intelligent — she's really brainy, and she knows all about it, she's got to be something a little better than selling-plate class.' As a matter of fact a selling plater would be worth thousands of pounds to a fellow like Stanley Wootton who dealt in selling plates — she'd win any selling race in the country and she could win it by a head, neck, anything like that, she needn't win by three or four lengths. She could manage it so well. However, Captain Bell said, 'The thing is this, she belongs to

Lord Londonderry and he doesn't have selling platers and
this is the idea of selling her.' I said, 'Then if that's the case,
you've got to buy her back from him.'

She appeared again three months later in a selling race
at Chepstow. I said, 'Good gracious me, you're not going
to dare run that thing again in a selling race, the odds are
somebody will pinch her, somebody will buy her. You
have got to realise she's better than a plater.' But he said he
didn't think so and so I replied, 'Now if she wins, don't
forget you must buy her back. I tell you what I'll do, you
watch me very carefully, I'll just drop in behind these
things and I'll appear about fifty yards from home — I'll
make it really very short and I'll just pull on the outside
and I'll show you this thing can win on the bridle.' Of
course I did exactly that and when I pulled up I said,
'Didn't I tell you? Now don't forget, don't let her go, don't
sell her — buy her back.'

I went and got dressed for other races and that sort of
thing, and asked afterwards what the filly had fetched. He
said £380, so I said good. 'Oh,' he said, 'I sold her.' I said, 'I
don't believe it — you'll regret that, I know you will.'
Anyhow he said, 'Well, she's gone and I told you that Lord
Londonderry doesn't like owning selling platers.' I told
him, 'I don't mind what Lord Londonderry thinks — I
wanted you to have her, you buy her yourself.' Anyhow,
that was that.

Now Tom Rimell — he had been head man when I was
an apprentice with Bob Colling — was the trainer who
bought her and he came to me afterwards and said, 'I've
just bought that thing of yours, Harry, do you think she
would suit my kids to ride?' I said, 'Just the job, anybody
could ride her — lovely little thing.'

But Rockcliffe did not achieve any more success. She ran in a
seller at Liverpool early in November and finished second, with
Harry riding the hot favourite who finished third. Rockcliffe's
jockey objected to the winner, but the objection was over-
ruled. The following week she ran again at Derby, ridden by
Harry and finished second — beaten two lengths. The hard-
working filly was brought out for the third time in a fortnight
when Harry again rode her in a Seller at Manchester. She
started favourite and finished third. Harry now knew her better

than anyone, and still held her in high regard. He learned that
she was to be sold at the Ascot Sales in December and promptly
told Ossie Bell that he should buy her back. Bell insisted that he
was not interested.

I said, 'Now don't be silly, you've got to buy her.' Anyhow,
we discussed this for a long time and he said he wasn't very
interested. So I then thought very much about this and I
mentioned it to Freddy Winter — this animal was going to
be sold and I told him how good I thought she was and he
ought to buy her. And I said I was still going to chase up
the Captain and see if he'll go and buy her — she was going
to be sold on December 8th, the next day. So I said, 'Now if
for instance he's there or he bids for this thing, then don't
interfere with him, but if he doesn't want her, then you
buy her and you'll do very very well with her. Anyhow the
Captain did go to the sale and he bought the filly for 250
guineas. I felt that was really marvellous.

When I went down to ride work the following March he
said, 'That's that thing you made me buy,' and I saw she
had grown and she looked a much better animal. I said,
'This filly will win several races and what I want you to do
is to promise me that you will not give her back to Lord
Londonderry the moment she starts winning some nice
races.' It wasn't long before she was winning, and the first
race she won was at Newcastle. My brother Sam rode her
and I told him what type of animal she was and she could
do anything really, she was so intelligent, but to get her
handicapped you've got to win just a short distance so I
warned him not to win a long way.

When the filly ran I was down south riding at Brighton
and I looked at the paper that night and I saw that she had
won by five lengths. I thought, good gracious me. I rang
Sam and said, 'What the dickens are you doing?' He said,
'Look, I didn't hit the front till about twenty yards from
home and she really spurted by then — she is brilliant!'
After two more races we won four times in five starts: at
Wolverhampton, Newmarket, Stockton and Leicester.

All these races were won in the colours of Lord Londonderry —
so Harry's advice regarding ownership had been overlooked!
Lord Londonderry, a member of the Jockey Club, had married
Edith Chaplin, daughter of Viscount Chaplin, owner of the

1867 Derby winner Hermit. As a boy he had hunted with the South Durham from Wynyard Park in the 'Lambton' country and as a young soldier had won regimental point-to-points. He often expressed his belief that racing should be organised so that it did not prohibit all but the very rich from owning thorough-breds, and invariably encouraged small owners whom he re-garded as the backbone of the sport. Curiously he disliked black horses although he believed that black fillies became the best broodmares.

In 1932 Rockcliffe, ridden by Harry, won at Epsom on the eve of The Derby, was unplaced in the Newbury Summer Cup carrying 8 st 5 lbs and in the Bessborough Stakes at Ascot, before winning the Trundle Stakes at Goodwood to prove she was a gold mine! She ended her racing career by wining at New-castle in October after failing in the Ebor Handicap and at the Doncaster St Leger meeting. Ironically her victory was Harry's final ride before his appalling accident, for the Northumberland Autumn Handicap Plate was the race immediately preceding the Astley Nursery Handicap in which he rode Donatia. Rock-cliffe was then retired to stud and in 1934 was bought from Lord Londonderry by Sir Hugo Cunliffe-Owen. Her first foal, by Felstead, was the filly Rockfoil who, as a three-year-old, even-tually won one modest race at the Worcester summer meeting.

Her second foal, also by Felstead, was the lop-eared Rockfel. Rockfel had not the constitution to match her big frame, and it was hard to build her up. As an unnamed plain two-year-old filly who was very long in the leg, she made her debut at Sandown in the Ditton Selling Plate. She was not fully fit, and after running 'very green' Harry dropped her out of contention.

In those days there was a shorter period of time between making the entry for a Seller and the day of the race than that between entry and race day for Maidens at starting. Once Rockfel had shown that she needed a race, to enter her in a Seller was the best plan, particularly as Sir Hugo had made it clear that he wanted it believed that she was as useless as Rockfoil. Ossie Bell was horrified. However, as her full sister had already run six times unplaced, it was not surprising that no one put in a bid for her, although if they had done so and acquired her they would have gained one of the greatest bargains in bloodstock history.

Six weeks later she was unplaced at Salisbury in a five-furlong race ridden by Harry. There must have been some slight stable confidence for she started fifth favourite in a field of twenty-three. Going under the four-furlong starting gate she ducked and lost a considerable amount of ground. Harry gave her one slap and she flew, making up an immense amount of the lost ground. When he dismounted he told Captain Bell that she was the fastest horse that he had ever ridden. Ossie was not really a true horseman, and if anything was not sufficiently hard on his horses. Sensibly he took much notice of Harry's opinion and shrewd comments for he appreciated that his common-sense and ability to assess the merit of every horse he rode was far greater than that of the majority of his contemporary jockeys, and realised that the wise advice and counsel shown by Harry after trial gallops was of inestimable advantage to the stable.

At the first October meeting at Newmarket Rockfel started favourite in the six-furlong race, showed much more promise and may have been somewhat unlucky. The race finished at the winning post in The Dip, and once again Harry was perturbed that she might duck as she went under the five-furlong starting gate at the end of the first furlong. This was a possibility he wished to avoid for he knew that her owner, Sir Hugo Cunliffe-Owen, intended to wager heavily. He explained his worry to the starter before the commencement of the afternoon's racing. To his delight and amazement the starter agreed to have the strands of the five-furlong starting gate tapes removed! Nevertheless Harry did not win. There were thirty runners, split into two groups on either side of the track, and the judge placed him third, beaten a head and a short head. Harry was convinced that he had won by a length and Sir Hugo Cunliffe-Owen was furious! Until the advent of the photo-finish it is probable that many incorrect verdicts were given inadvertently by judges, but no one could demand that the verdict was altered. The first judge had been appointed in 1772, possibly as a result of six judges acting for one race at Durham the previous year and all giving a different result.

Rockfel made no mistake a fortnight later at York. She started at 5-2 on and won with insolent ease.

Rockfel was described as a 'dark brown filly, with a rather plain head and lightish neck; wide deep quarters; and perhaps lacking a little in quality'. Ridden by Sam Wragg, she had her first race of the 1938 season when she finished third in the Free Handicap to Lapel, trained by George Lambton. After the race Sam told Harry that he would have won if he had not held her up. She then won the Princess Elizabeth Stakes at Epsom's spring meeting, again ridden by Sam Wragg. Her next race was the One Thousand Guineas, which she won by one and a half lengths from her nineteen rivals — with Harry riding the favourite Stafaralla for Prince Aly Khan, having begged off Rockfel to ride the Frank Butters-trained filly. There was little doubt that Frank Butters was very hard on his horses and Stafaralla was not enjoying such training. Nevertheless Harry thought that she had the ability to win the One Thousand Guineas, but his opinion was proved wrong.

Harry made no similar error in The Oaks and elected to ride Rockfel, who started a short-priced favourite and won in faster time than that of Bois Roussel who had won The Derby forty-eight hours earlier. For once Harry did not employ his 'Head Waiter' tactics and allowed Rockfel to lead from the start to finish. She was never off the bridle and ran home like a scalded cat. Harry had great difficulty in pulling her up, and in fact collided with the starter's hack on the bend leading to the paddock, more than a hundred yards past the winning post. The starter had been sedately making his way back to the grandstand across the Downs and had just reached the paddock when the incident occurred. As Rockfel had also won the One Thousand Guineas in faster time than Pasch, hero of the Two Thousand Guineas, she was entitled to be considered the best of the Classic winners of the year. Generously Sir Hugo Cunliffe-

Owen gave a similar present to Sam Wragg as he gave to Harry for winning The Oaks.

At Ascot Rockfel was set to carry 9st 10lbs in the Coronation Stakes, but the task of giving 14lbs to Solar Flower proved beyond her. However when they renewed their rivalry at Hurst Park in August Rockfel, affectionately known in her stables as 'The Old Lady', again asserted her supremacy. In the autumn she showed her brilliance by beating Pasch in the Champion Stakes. Her final race of the season was the Aintree Derby which she won easily. When the Free Handicap weights were published she received 9st 9lbs — the same weight as Bois Roussel — and Sir Hugo Cunliffe-Owen indicated that he hoped Rockfel would remain in training as a four-year-old with the Ascot Gold Cup her objective.

Another very popular horse during this era with whom Harry was associated was Mickey The Greek, sired by Apple Sammy, winner of the Two Thousand Guineas. His owner, Nat Frieze, was a great friend of Chubb Leach who persuaded him to buy the horse as a yearling for £150 in partnership with another of Chubb's friends. To everyone's consternation this friend departed the country in a hurry and was eventually found to have joined the Foreign Legion! Needless to say he departed without settling his share of the purchase of Mickey The Greek or the outstanding training fees! Nat Frieze therefore had no option but to take over the entire ownership. As a three-year-old in 1937 Mickey The Greek ran twelve times in the course of an arduous season and proved a rare money-spinner for his connections. He needed to be held up for one short sharp burst and if this was not possible then he did not win. Harry won on him at the Craven meeting, was unplaced at Epsom and Kempton, third at Newmarket, second at York, unplaced at Newbury and second at Sandown before winning the July Cup by a head from Daytona. This triumph was his only other victory of the season, for he failed at Nottingham and Doncaster — on neither occasion ridden by Harry — but was second to Daytona in the Ayr Gold Cup, ridden by Dick Perryman, before he finally ran third to the dead-heaters Shalfleet and Willow Knight at the Newmarket first October Meeting.

1938 proved an equally busy year for Mickey the Greek who ran ten times. Once again Harry rode him to victory in his first race of the season when he won at Chester — beating the hot favourite Ipsden, ridden by Sam Wragg. He failed at York before Ipsden took his revenge in the Cork and Orrery Stakes at Ascot. Mickey the Greek was second in the Gosforth Park Cup, ridden by Brownie Carslake; second to Shalfleet in the July Cup; unplaced when again ridden by Carslake in the Nottingham Stewards Cup, before Harry rode him to a neck victory in the Nunthorpe Stakes at York — the Sprint Championship — over his old rival Shalfleet. He was unplaced at the Doncaster St Leger meeting when set to hump 9st 7lbs in the Portland Handicap, ran badly in Newmarket in October, and ended the season by once again being beaten by Shalfleet in the October Stakes at the Houghton meeting.

Mickey the Greek was now acknowledged to be one of the general public's favourite sprinters and once again he did not disappoint them during his 1939 campaign, even though he failed in his first race at Chester. At Ascot he ran in the Cork and Orrery Stakes for which Miss Dorothy Paget had backed her colt Colonel Payne to win a fortune. Colonel Payne, named after an immensely affluent American relative of Dorothy Paget, was a half-brother to Orwell. Originally trained by Frank Butters, he was eventually sent to Fred Darling. He showed such speed on the Beckhampton gallops that Darling unwisely told Dorothy Paget that he thought the colt was a certainty for his Ascot engagement. Such information was manna from heaven to the gambling-obsessed Dorothy Paget, whose greatest joy in life was a huge tilt at the Ring. Before the Cork and Orrery Stakes she started backing Colonel Payne as if settling day was not a consideration. In the paddock before the race Chubb Leach told Harry that he had little chance of beating Colonel Payne, ridden by Gordon Richards, but Harry had other ideas. He believed that the Jack Jarvis-trained Old Reliance was Mickey the Greek's biggest danger and decided that he would follow him in the early stages of the six-furlong race:

> So I went into the paddock to get my orders and to discuss with the owner and trainer about this. I said what I would do was come to the stand side as we'd be sure to split up into two groups and I thought Old Reliance, who had drawn a small number, was the one that'd carry me home, he's the one to follow. So Chubb Leach said, 'Look, I can tell you something a little bit different. I think your danger is going to be Colonel Payne, one of Dorothy Paget's, it's said she's got a fortune on it. Gordon rides him and he's on the other side of the course.' I said, 'Well, I don't want to be doing that,' but he replied he was certain Colonel Payne was going to be the danger. Reluctantly I accepted that so when I left the gate I started to follow Colonel Payne. I didn't like it really but anyhow all through the race I just dropped in behind him — I'm going like a bomb — and Colonel Payne was making the running. I could run over him anytime I like.
>
> We've got about a furlong to go and I look across the course and on the stand side I can see Old Reliance almost drawn level with us and going on and I can see Colonel Payne starting to tire. I look again — we're level — and I've still got a furlong to go and I want a little bit less. I wait and wait and wait till I can't wait any longer because Old Reliance is getting away, so I switched round Colonel Payne and ran past him by about four lengths. Mickey the Greek is carrying me to the front but I made the front a little too soon and he starts to tire, begins to pull up. It's no good me hitting him because he was so intelligent he would have said if you don't know where the winning post is, I don't. So Old Reliance came back at me and got up and beat me. But I would have won a minute if I had been following those on the other side. I was really furious. After I came in, I was really wild. I said, 'We've just thrown a big race away.'

Harry was disgusted, although his fury was nothing compared to that of Dorothy Paget whose rage was only mollified when Gordon Richards told her, 'I think Mr Darling is on the top of the grandstand cutting his throat.' However good came out of evil. Chubb Leach decided to saddle Mickey the Greek in the

Kings Stand Stakes the next afternoon with Harry again in the
saddle. Admittedly Harry had to beg off riding a horse for Frank
Hartigan, who was promised the odds to a sizeable sum — re-
putedly £200, but nevertheless his judgement that Mickey the
Greek was a champion sprinter was vindicated.

> Next day came along and they let me do just what I
> wanted and I rode him my own way. I was going with two
> handfuls all through the race just like Mickey the Greek
> always is, and I pulled him out the last bit and won very
> cleverly by three lengths. He started at 20-1 which was a
> bit of a shock to the punters. I had a terrific lot of success
> with him. I won nearly all the big sprint races — we lost a
> few — but we only lost them when for instance I wasn't
> able to track what I considered my most dangerous horse.
> If we were on different sides of the course and I had to pull
> out at a different time — then that's the only time we got
> beaten.

In mid summer Mickey the Greek was unplaced in the July
Cup and the Molyneux Cup at Liverpool, won the King George
Stakes at Goodwood beating Old Reliance, was third in the
Nunthorpe Stakes to Portobello ridden by Gordon Richards,
and unplaced at the Newmarket October meeting. Understandably there was great rivalry, but not animosity, between
Harry and Gordon, and Harry derived immense pleasure from
'putting a fast one' over the champion, particularly at the start
of a race:

> We often had a new starter, from the Army or the Navy.
> And this day at Leicester we had a Commander — I think
> he'd been starting battleships — he was a new feller but
> there were only a few runners over five furlongs — and
> Gordon Richards was my only danger. I was pretty certain
> that the connections of my horse had gone for a 'touch'.
> We had a talk with the starter before the race and he said
> how we would start — what we would do. We would walk
> in and hope we got a very good start.
> We're going in the first time nicely and Gordon's flying,
> he's galloping, and I saw this happening so I went straight
> across the field, put them all up in the air, otherwise he
> would have got about six lengths start. Anyway the starter

screams, 'No, no, no,' so we go back. It happened again the second time so again I rushed across the field — I was going right underneath the starter, it was very easy for me to ride across the other horses — and I said to Gordon, 'Look, don't take liberties. I mean, I don't mind you getting a good start providing I start with you.' So as we go back this next time the starter said, 'I'll tell you what I want you to do. I want you to all walk back about ten yards, turn round to me and walk in quietly.' Well, I'm drawn right underneath him so what I did was just take a small turn round and as they started to walk in from about ten yards back the started called out, 'Are you alright, Gordon?' I cried, 'Yes sir,' — and before you could say Jack Robinson, I was in The Dip before they started. When we pulled up after I had won very easy, Gordon said to me: 'You've done a few things in your time, but now you've become a starter — what's it all about?'

Mickey the Greek's greatest rival, Old Reliance, was owned by **1939** Sir John Jarvis. Another very useful horse that he owned in 1939 was the three-year-old Admiral's Walk, a Hyperion colt, who suffered from the fact that he was over-shadowed by his stable companion Blue Peter. In the Two Thousand Guineas Harry finished second on Admiral's Walk to Blue Peter, ridden by Eph Smith, and was unplaced to them in The Derby. When Admiral's Walk won the St James's Palace Stakes at Ascot, Eph Smith rode him as he was the stable jockey. In the One Thousand Guineas Harry was unplaced on Sir Hugo Cunliffe-Owen's Flyolley — but was delighted that Bobby Jones won on Galatea II — on whom he also won The Oaks.

7

War-time experiences

Throughout the summer of 1939 the nation had far more significant matters than horse-racing on its mind, with war against Germany being declared at 5.00 pm on Sunday, 3 September. Racing had taken place at Manchester on the previous two afternoons, but there were to be no more fixtures until the Newmarket October meeting seven weeks later. Harry returned to Bedford Lodge from Manchester and to the realities of war:

> The very first night we had an air raid for Newmarket was surrounded with airfields. There were so many in East Anglia and the Germans were going to try and put all these places out of action. We got an air-raid siren and the Germans dropped a stack of bombs straight across the Limekilns by the seven-furlong post — they'd stupidly taken them as being an aerodrome although they couldn't see any planes but they knew that on the left were Snailwell, and Mildenhall. Lakenheath was not very far away but within striking distance — that's what they were aiming at.
>
> So the very next day we had to start to dig trenches, and all the trainers formed groups and made a local defence company. I don't know who was in charge of them but we had to have different posts all over Newmarket. I know they gave me a post at the bottom of Long Hill. As I was living at Bedford Lodge it wasn't very far to go. So the moment an air-raid siren went we had to go to this dug-out affair. In my group there were three others: Mr Jimmy Dewar, the whisky magnate, who lived next door to the Hon. George Lambton at Mesnil Warren: the vicar, who lived just across the road in St Agnes's church; and there

108

was another feller called Parker — I think he was an old soldier. We were told what we'd got to do — the moment the siren went we had to go to this place and stay there until the all clear went. We just sat there and talked — nothing special.

But one night the air-raid siren went and I was going from Bedford Lodge on duty, all of a sudden somebody jumped out in front of me just before I got to Long Hill and said, 'Halt, who goes there?' Frightened the bloody life out of me. It was a soldier with a rifle and a bayonet on it almost sticking into me. I said, 'What's all this about?' 'Well,' he said, 'who are you and what are you doing?' I told him what it was all about and he said he came to inform each little company what was happening. There was a possible chance there could be a landing. The Germans might send parachutists onto the areas like Long Hill, so we'd got to be on the alert.

When I got to my post I was the first to arrive. When the other two arrived I frightened the life out of them. I didn't have a rifle with a bayonet, I had a sixteen-bore shotgun but I frightened them just the same. I told them what might be happening and it was a bit scarey really. When I'm giving them the orders, the vicar kept coughing away. I said, 'Listen, I'll tell you what you want to do. I think you must go and take up a position by Mr H.J. Joel's in that ditch. I don't want you near me coughing because if a German is going to land I want to have a chance of shooting him before he shoots me. If you cough like that beside me, the buggers are going to get me, not you.' So I made a plan for him and I said to Mr Jimmy Dewar, 'We've got a sand gallop just by the side of Long Hill — you can go and lie on that and then we'll meet,' and to the other feller I said, 'You can go round by Warren Hill Road and cover that part. And we'll meet the moment the all clear goes.' After about an hour the all clear went and off we marched home — nothing had happened.

A couple of nights later the Army altered their tactics a little bit. They were pretty certain that the Germans were going to drop some troops so we had to cover a bigger area — and Newmarket is a large place. I was on top of Long Hill and Bury Hill where they join together towards Moulton Paddocks, resting with my back to the rails. We'd been there a hell of a long time — nothing had happened — and then from out of the blue there was a rustle just behind me and a bloody hare jumped through the fence within two yards. I could have shot it with my sixteen-bore shotgun. I thought, I daren't shoot because it'll probably disturb everybody and they'll think I'm shooting at Germans, so I didn't. Then the all clear went.

A few days later I started to have some practice with a Lewis machine gun because the Germans were really taking liberties. They were flying very low over Newmarket and I spotted a Heinkel one day coming over my house. I could have thrown an orange and hit the pilot. He was just above the garden and I thought, by heck I've got my Lewis gun, it's just the job to shoot down a plane. So I got the gun nicely placed. The next day was a misty sort of morning and it wasn't very long before the air-raid warning went — and a German plane flew down no distance at all from me. I saw the pilot as plain as anything, but although I was by the side of my machine gun there was no way that I could shoot him because there was a big tree in my way. I thought, this is ridiculous. I've got to do something about it. That morning passed and the next day I got a ladder and I went up the tree and started cutting down the branches to give me a better view in case the same thing happened again. I'd only probably done about two branches when another plane came and I could have thrown a stone and hit him he was so low. He was then going straight to Newmarket where we had a lot of aircraft on the side of the racecourse. I climbed down and said to my wife, 'Of all the things, I missed a sitter this morning.' She said, 'What do you mean?' I said, 'A German plane came and I'd got my gun all ready down below but I'm up in this tree sawing off some branches. If I hadn't been there I certainly could have got him.' 'You could have got nothing,' she said, 'I think you're making a mistake. Say for instance you'd hit him, you couldn't have brought him down anyhow, and he would have gone back home and said, do you remember that big white house as you flew over Newmarket? We'd better give that a sorting out tomorrow.' I think probably she might have been right.

Life in Newmarket was really disturbing because of these air raids. I'd got a shelter built downstairs for the children and for the family, but it was very worrying. So I decided to take them away because we were getting a hell of a lot of air raids in East Anglia. I thought they would be better to go down to the Lambourn area, particularly as Peter and Geoffrey's school had been evacuated to Wool-hampton near Newbury. It would be more peaceful there. So I took them down and we'd only been there about a week when they rang up from home to say there had been another air raid and the Germans had dropped a bomb in the paddock by the side of Bedford Lodge. The windows had been blown in and there was lots of damage, so I had to go back and see what it was all about. On my return I found that two or three parts of the roof had fallen in, the kitchen quarters had been badly damaged and all the windows had been smashed. In Geoffrey's room the ceiling had fallen in so he would have been badly hurt if he'd have been in bed. Obviously we were doing a good thing by being away. I decided to stay and have the house fixed up and while I was getting it fixed I thought, I'm not doing a lot of good really with my little machine gun. Probably I'll get a lot more practice against the Germans if I join the Army, even though the Jockey Club are thinking about putting on a bit of racing.

The manner in which Harry and his pals carried out their Home Guard duties would have made 'Dad's Army' seem like selling platers. His idea that to bring down a German aeroplane would have been the treat of his life was on a par with the remark of the elderly Earl of Leicester who had armed his staff and servants at Holkham Hall with antiquated weapons in-cluding pikes and swords. On learning that the expected in-vasion was not likely to bring crack Panzer divisions onto the Norfolk coastline near his home he said, 'I am very disap-pointed.' It was rumoured that Harry was becoming interested in 'food for Britain' gardening at Bedford Lodge, but the notion that his vegetables were being trained to come with a late rush was not based upon truth.

During the remaining weeks of the season the majority of the leading jockeys were able to ride, and the names of Harry, Gordon Richards, Charlie Smirke, Tommy Weston, P. Beasley and R. Perryman were seen on the number-boards. Harry rode three winners and two seconds at Newbury one Thursday

afternoon when there were more than 150 runners. By mid-
October racing had been resumed. The St Leger had been
abandoned but meetings were held at Newmarket, Newbury,
Thirsk and Manchester, because the Jockey Club thought that
they should keep something open just for the troops to go to.

Harry spent the winter of 1939-40 chopping down trees, and
enjoying his new found hobby of carpentry. He made a wheel-
barrow, a chicken shed and a green house. By April 1940 the
newspapers were blazoning headlines concerning the Nazi
invasion of Norway, and little space was given to the opening of
the new Flat Season. However huge crowds flocked to Aintree
and Lincoln for the 'Spring Double' won by Bogskar and
Quartier Maitre, and equally large crowds attended Newmarket on 1 May when the Two Thousand Guineas was
contested. Harry finished second on H.H. Aga Khan's Stardust
to M. Marcel Boussac's Djebel, who won easily by two lengths.
The fact that Stardust dwelt at the start had no effect upon the
result. Forty-eight hours later, Harry rode Sir Hugo Cunliffe-
Owen's Thyrse into fourth place behind Godiva in the One
Thousand Guineas.

Harry again rode Stardust in the New Derby Stakes at
Newmarket — the race was moved from Epsom for the duration
of the war, and run over the July course. He was sixth behind
Pont l'Evêque, ridden by his brother Sam. On Derby Day the
majority of racegoers came by motor coach whilst two 'Race
Specials' ran from King's Cross. The July course was more
crowded than on any other raceday in its history, with many
spectators in service uniform paying five shillings and one
shilling tax to gain admission to the Silver Ring. The next
afternoon Harry was unplaced behind Godiva in the New Oaks.

Harry again had to settle for being runner-up on Stardust in
the Yorkshire St Leger won by Turkhan once racing was
resumed after a period of almost three months. However,
Stardust was one of the best colts of his generation and went on
to win the Champion Stakes by three lengths, with Harry
confident of victory throughout the entire race. Unfortunately
in the course of the final half-mile he had swerved in front of

Lord Rosebery's Hippius, ridden by Eph Smith, who lodged an objection for crossing a furlong from the winning post. The objection was sustained even though the luckless Stardust was three lengths clear at the winning post. The incident did nothing to enhance the friendship of Harry with either Eph Smith or Jack Jarvis.

During the autumn Bahram and Mahmoud left England for Ireland en route for America, and in July the Racing Calendar had consisted of one page only — the smallest publication in its long history. The *Daily Mail* campaigned for race meetings to be held, but although the reasons put forward were plausible, their clamour fell on deaf ears. In some quarters there was widespread resentment that racing continued in war-time and many letters were published in *The Times* claiming that the sport, described as 'an insane and unseemly spectacle', should cease for the duration of hostilities, whilst those who condemned its continuance were legion. Ranged against them was the Hon. George Lambton, who was one of the chief advocates of war-time racing and who spiked the guns of many critics when he wrote a long letter to *The Times* '. . . my job is racing and I am not ashamed to carry on, and if when we have won this war I have left something for a younger generation to build up again, I shall be content . . .' Nevertheless, the Stewards did all in their power to meet stringent war-time requirements whilst at the same time keeping racing alive. They suggested to owners that they should not attempt to keep horses, especially geldings, of limited ability in training and tried to enforce the edict of the Ministry of Agriculture that the number of broodmares be reduced by twenty-five per cent.

In an afternoon raid in February 1941 Newmarket was badly bombed, with many people believing that spies had provided the German Air Force with information that it was a vital moment for a raid to be carried out. An important military meeting was being held in the Doric Cinema, and the cars of almost the entire South Eastern Command, including many top brass, lined each side of the High Street. A lone German raider came down low over the Bury Road with the rear gunner firing indiscriminately. The plane flew over the High Street, dropping sticks of bombs whilst the gunner fired at any moving target that he could see. Luckily the plane turned off course just before the final bombs left the bomb bay. If it had not done so a direct hit on the cinema would have been inevitable. The White Hart hotel, the Post Office and the Marlborough Club were demolished but the town had a lucky escape, for if the bombs, instead of falling plumb onto the buildings, had fallen into the middle of the street — which was crammed with people attending the market — many lives would have been lost including those of troops who packed the town.

At this period of the war, the future of the racecourse was seriously in jeopardy due to the proposed call-up of men under the age of forty-five. On the racecourse side eighteen men were employed, of whom twelve were under the age of forty-five, whilst on the Bury side the nine men included three liable for call-up. As the Clerk of the Course pointed out, 'It will be impossible to carry on the present racing programme in 1942 should the twelve men under the age of forty-five be taken from us.' One argument for allowing the men to remain was that the Jockey Club had agreed to plough up eighty-four acres on the Heath and if they had no staff it would not be feasible for them to carry out this task. Another problem was that Tindall, the Newmarket printer, had only one man for the printing of racecards and was perturbed that if his printing plant, which was of foreign manufacture, was put out of action due to the bombing then he would not be able to produce racecards for the Newmarket meetings. To make matters worse, the Royal Air Force, who already had all the back of the Flat and Southfields for an aerodrome, were considering increasing the area of ground required for aeroplanes between the Rowley Mile grandstand and the Ditch and were contemplating requisitioning this ground for ten years, as it could provide suitable runways for the heavy bombers coming in ever-increasing numbers from America. The Jockey Club were worried that if such requisition became reality the future of Newmarket would be at risk, and appreciated that it might result in a massive reduction in the number of horses that could be trained at racing's headquarters for at least two decades.

In July 1941 Harry joined the Army serving as a bombardier with an Ack-Ack regiment. He had been graded C.3 because his leg had never fully recovered from his Newcastle accident. His poor recovery meant that he always had to wear a pad under his breeches when riding to protect a small piece of bone which had never mended properly. If he did not wear this pad the bone broke through his skin. Consequently the Army thought that he could not be expected to undertake long route-marches and gave him a clerical task. Before the end of the Flat Season he managed twenty days' racing out of a possible thirty, and rode twenty-eight winners from the time he put on battle dress. Madge, when asked how Harry had been able to get away from his Army duties for so much racing, replied, 'Harry has had no special privileges, but he does get a twenty-four hours' leave fairly often because his work often keeps him up all night. Often he has gone straight from his battery to meetings, and we have not seen him at all. Sometimes he goes racing when he has been at his post all night. He rides when he would normally be sleeping. Another thing is that he has the advantage of being stationed near a racing centre.' Indeed, the War Office were unhelpful to racing soldiers and stated, 'In no circumstances is special leave granted for taking part in professional sports, including racing. Leave out of normal turn is granted only to men forming a team or a side for sports approved by the Army Control Board.'

Madge invited Harry's C.O. to breakfast at Bedford Lodge where several members of the Leach family had made their wartime headquarters, and where evacuees had been billeted in the rear quarters. There was a pet parrot in the hall at Bedford Lodge who greeted everyone with the words, 'I'm a pretty polly.' On one occasion when Chubb Leach came home on leave, he was so pestered by the parrot that he told it to 'Shut up, you silly bugger.' From that moment the parrot greeted all visitors with these newly-learned words and eventually was

banished to the kitchen by Madge. Chubb's young daughter,
Felicity, was nicknamed 'Flopper Flipper' by Harry and the
name remained for years. She and her brother, Bill, were told by
'Aunt Madge' that as hot water was in scarce supply they must
empty their hot-water bottles in the morning and use the water
for washing! One day the Leach children and Peter and
Geoffrey were discovered by Madge playing strip-poker in a
tent in the garden. As Felicity had lost all her clothes the boys
were smartly taken indoors and suitably punished.

After a few months of Army life Harry described his
impressions:

> I find Army life has a beneficial effect on my riding. I keep
> very fit by my activities on the gun, and do not suffer from
> lack of riding practice. They put me in charge of a Bofer
> gun. I was stationed first of all at R.A.F. Mildenhall. The
> R.A.F. had soldiers to guard them when the German
> bombers came to raid. Sometimes these raids were very
> near but they didn't drop any bombs on us. I suppose they
> were finding out the different places. However I com-
> plained. I said, 'Look, we're in a good position, we have a
> very good chance to attack these 'planes.' When I was
> making my report I said we were at action stations and yet
> we weren't allowed to open fire. My C.O. said, 'No, you
> mustn't do that, because if you did you're going to give
> your position away — the Germans will know exactly
> where we are if you open fire. They'll know that you're
> guarding something.' But I thought, I'm still not going to
> do much good if we're not going to be able to fire unless
> they drop bombs on us. If they drop bombs on us they've
> gone before we can get a crack at them. So I said I would
> like to get a bit closer to some action and so they arranged
> for me to go to Gorleston near Great Yarmouth. See some
> action — I never stopped for I was working in the Guns
> Operations Room, where we tracked the German planes
> and gave advance warning as they approached the coast.
> They didn't just have one raid, it was all night and every
> night. The guns were firing for periods of three-quarters of
> an hour at a time without stopping and it went on for one
> or two hours every night. I got more than I was bargaining
> for because I never got any sleep.

One day I was coming out of my billet going to the

operations room where my work was, plotting away the different aircraft coming over and reporting to other gun sights the position of the enemy coming in and which way they were coming. As I came out there was a German 'plane shooting shells down the road and I ran zig-zagging up the road thinking he was after me. When I got to the operations room I stopped and looked round, he was going the opposite way to me while I was running up it he was running down it. I thought he was after me.

I'd placed myself in an awkward position now that I was stationed near Great Yarmouth because I'd got no car. I had sold a Pontiac which did about ten or twelve miles to the gallon. As you could not get any petrol coupons there was no point in me having it so I sold it, but I got nothing for it, about £50. I was in a bad way if I wanted to get off any time to the races, for I had to hitch-hike. I could only do that on a Saturday but I wanted to ride work occasionally too. So I had to arrange for somebody who had got some petrol to come and pick me up and I would go off every Saturday to ride work, and also on Wednesdays if I could get away, but if I was riding on Saturday I was not allowed to get another day off to ride work in the same week unless I did extra duties and swapped hours of work with other soldiers. However I was lucky for I often gave them tips, and they thought it worth their while to oblige me and make money backing my selections.

In the spring of 1941 Harry had ridden Morogoro, trained by **1941** Fred Darling, to win the New Craven Stakes. A fortnight later he finished second on Morogoro to Lambert Simnel in the Two Thousand Guineas, and was considered unlucky by some onlookers. He also finished second in the One Thousand Guineas on Mrs Arthur James's Beausite.

Ten days after the first two Classics had been contested, Gordon Richards was kicked on the leg by a fractious filly who lashed out whilst at the start of a race at Salisbury. He fell to the ground, fearing that his left leg was broken. His worst fears proved correct and doctors at Salisbury Infirmary had the unpleasant duty of explaining to him that he would not be able to ride again before the end of the season. Harry was at Salisbury and Fred Darling immediately invited him to ride for

Beckhampton in the enforced absence of Gordon. As a result Harry won on Big Game later in the afternoon and had the good fortune to be associated with some of the best Beckhampton horses during the remainder of the season.

He finished second on Morogoro in the New Derby to Owen Tudor, also trained by Fred Darling. After the Two Thousand Guineas Fred Darling asked Harry which colt he wished to ride in the New Derby. He had ridden Owen Tudor at the Salisbury Whitsun meeting, and although starting odds-on had been beaten. Harry was certain that Darling's desire that his horses were 'always up with the leaders' was wrong, and believed that Owen Tudor was a far better colt if held up for a late run. Consequently he told Darling that he would like to ride Owen Tudor in The Derby. When asked who should ride Morogoro he suggested Billy Nevett. The suggestion was acted upon, but to his annoyance Harry was suddenly informed by Darling that he had changed his mind and that Nevett would ride Owen Tudor whilst he rode Morogoro at Newmarket. Understandably Harry was not amused, but felt he could do nothing about it other than to warn Billy Nevett not to listen to Darling's riding orders. He told Billy to hold up Owen Tudor until the final furlong was reached, and his instructions were carried out exactly, with Mrs Macdonald-Buchanan's colt cutting down Morogoro to win by one and a half lengths. Harry always believed that Morogoro would have won if the race had been run at Epsom.

Twenty-four hours later Harry stormed home on Commotion, owned by Mr J.A. Dewar. Captain Ossie Bell had no three-year-old colts or fillies of sufficient merit to run in The Derby or The Oaks, so there were no hard feelings that Harry rode Beckhampton horses in the Classics.

A month later four of Ascot's principal races — the Gold Cup, the St James's Palace Stakes, the Coventry Stakes and the Queen Mary Stakes, were run at the first July meeting at Newmarket. Harry scored a notable success on Sir Hugo Cunliffe-Owen's six-year-old Finis in the Gold Cup, beating Tommy Carey on Dorothy Paget's Olidon by a head. There had been no rain for three weeks and the ground was exceptionally firm. Harry rode one of his most typical races, delaying his challenge until the last possible moment, before getting up to win in the last strides. Finis acquired his name as he was the final foal of his dam Felkington, also the dam of Felstead. Later in the season Sam Wragg won the Cesarewitch on Filator, whose dam Filastic was also out of Felkington.

Gold Cup Day was a marvellous afternoon for Harry for he rode two of the most brilliant two-year-olds of the era; Big Game and Sun Chariot, both of whom raced in the Royal colours. Harry scored an easy victory on Big Game in the Coventry Stakes, defeating a colt named Watling Street, owned by Lord Derby, by four lengths, and an hour later took the Queen Mary Stakes by a head on Sun Chariot who was racing at Newmarket for the first time, and who did not truly find her action until the rising ground was met. Big Game was named after his sire, Bahram, who was renowned as 'the mighty hunter' whilst Sun Chariot's name was a reference to both her dam, Clarence, and her dam's sire Diligence, for a Clarence and a Diligence were types of carriage. Diligence had been exported to Russia in 1935.

Luckily, Harry had struck up a very good relationship with the temperamental Sun Chariot. Early in the season she had caused Fred Darling many anxious moments on the gallops and at one point he had contemplated taking her out of training. The first time that Harry rode her at Beckhampton she proved stubborn and a furious Darling came up, intending to thrash her. Harry, who had not been told of her foibles and idiosyncrasies, pleaded that she be given another chance. He began to humour Sun Chariot, showed endless patience, and eventually persuaded her to behave properly:

Halfway through the work she ducked to the left down into a little plantation and when they caught up with us they told me she was a little bit scatty and that she'd got a funny temperament. Anyhow, as I started coming out of this plantation Fred Darling came down in his little car with his Long Tom whip. He was going to thrash the life out of her. He was playing hell and said he thought he would

send her back home. I said, 'Well now, if you'd told me this
sort of thing might happen I could have avoided it. For
instance, let's go and start again and I'll show you I'll get
her past there.' 'Oh,' he said, 'she's done this before, she's
ducked down there before.' I said, 'Well, she won't do it
the next time. Let me just give it another try now, I'll have
some horses on the inside of me when I come up to that
plantation so that I'll have to knock them over for her to
get down there.' So then we repeated the gallop. We went
back and did the same thing again and I kept her covered
up with two horses on my left and we went straight by,
right as rain. She went very very well. She had a lot of
ability so she was worth really persevering with. I went
there several times after that and I liked her a lot.

The next thing was Fred Darling asked me to come
down and ride Sun Chariot at the starting gate because she
wasn't too happy about leaving it. They were having a lot
of bother. So I went down and rode her and she started
being very awkward, whipping round every time we were
going to jump off. So I said, 'Let's try something different.
I'll tell you what I'm going to do — I'm going to put my
tail to the gate and when I say "Right" just pull the gate.
I'll just have half a turn and I'll get her.' We did that and it
worked beautifully. So we do it again. I put her with her
tail to the gate and we did exactly the same thing.

She did it well so Fred Darling was rather pleased with
me because he really wanted to get her running in a race at
Newbury. Unfortunately we were drawn one, which
meant we were furthest away from the starter. We did talk
to the starter about her and explained how difficult she
was. We planned that I would put her tail to the gate but
the moment that I thought the field were in line I would
turn, hoping the starter would release the gate. That's
what we talked about, but unfortunately the starter was a
long way away from me. However everything worked out
all right and Sun Chariot broke nicely and won by two
lengths — but she wasn't very keen in her finish although
she had a lot in hand. She was a little bit of a madam and
she wanted her own way so we had to get round her.

I rode her several times after that and each time I went
to the start and did exactly the same thing she broke well,
so we were really getting her out of that bother about being
awkward at the gate. But I was more worried about the

manner in which she raced. When she was making her run in a race, although she was very good, she didn't want to be in front too long as she started to pull up. So I told Fred Darling, 'We'll have to be careful in future, when we're racing with her, what we are going to do.' Later on in the season we were running in the Middle Park Stakes at Newmarket and I'd got the race well won coming into the Dip. I was going to win nicely but as I hit the front she started to pull up. Immediately I sat still, took her back again, we hadn't got very far to go but I did, I dropped her back and then pulled her out very near home and she won cleverly. So I said to Fred Darling afterwards, 'She nearly threw it away.' I told him what had happened and I said, 'Always remember this with this filly, whenever she's racing, even when I'm not riding her next year, never, never let her hit the front too soon. She'll throw the race away.'

Sun Chariot's Middle Park victory by three lengths from Ujiji and Gold Nib, with Watling Street fourth, was the first time that a filly had won the race since Mr Marshall Field's Golden Corn had triumphed in 1921. On the same afternoon Harry also won the Newmarket St Leger on Owen Tudor. As six weeks earlier he had taken the Champagne Stakes on Big Game, again relegating Watling Street to second place, it was understandable that he felt he had enjoyed a wonderful season. At the end of it he was Champion Jockey for the first time. He had ridden in 259 races and won 71 of them. In addition he had finished second in 53 races and third in 30 races. His nearest rival was Eph Smith with 61 winning mounts. Perhaps the outward recognition of his success that brought him the most pleasure was a letter from King George VI enclosing a pair of gold cufflinks, whilst the news which depressed him the most was learning of the death of Rockfel, who died from a twisted gut in November. Her loss was irreparable, especially as she was carrying a filly foal by Hyperion.

8

Riding for Lord Derby

1942 The final five seasons of Harry's riding career found him inseparably linked with the racing fortunes of Lord Derby, by whom he was retained in 1942 as jockey to the powerful Stanley House stables. For more than thirty years Lord Derby's 'black, white cap' had been carried with distinction on both the English and the French Turf, and the Hon. George Lambton had trained such champions as Swynford, Tranquil, Sansovino, Colorado, Fairway and Hyperion for him. His trainer since 1939 had been Walter Earl, with whom Harry had first struck up a friendship when he was training for Solly Joel in the 1920s and who was confident that the 1942 season would bring much success to the stable.

Earl knew that Watling Street was a potential Classic winner even though he had proved inferior to Big Game and Sun Chariot in 1941. Sired by Fairway out of the French-bred mare Ranai, whom Lord Derby had purchased at the 1926 Deauville sales, Watling Street had run six times as a two-year-old, and won twice. Described as a well-made bay colt, with good clean legs and a lovely length from hip to hock, he was no easy horse to train and undoubtedly a colt with his own ideas about life in general, and being trained in particular.

Nevertheless he proved no match for Harry and Walter Earl, who had been born in Bohemia in 1890 where his father was riding for Mr Baltazzi. In 1924, having been apprenticed to Willie Waugh and ridden with some success under both Rules, he was appointed private trainer to Solly Joel, who died in 1931. Earl remained at Moulton Paddocks until 1939 when he went to

122

Stanley House on the death of Colledge Leader. Because Earl had been a jockey before becoming established as a trainer, Harry found it easy to communicate with him. Earl was a first-class horseman, who never liked to delegate work to others, and a man with very strong ideas as to how to train his horses. Harry approved of these ideas which were in contrast to those held by Ossie Bell and Jack Jarvis. He had found that Ossie Bell was inclined to be too easy on his horses and hated over-doing them on the gallops, and had rapidly realised that although Jack Jarvis got his horses 'as fit as fleas', they could seldom act on a firm surface, needing soft ground to show their best form. Walter Earl believed in the dictum 'no feet no horse', had his own blacksmith and was one of the first Newmarket trainers to time gallops, all of which delighted Harry.

Watling Street was thought to be somewhat of a handful at Stanley House and several of the stable lads were frightened of him, considering him an utter bastard. However Harry knew that he was an exceptional colt, provided he was properly trained. One morning in early May, Walter Earl confided to Harry that he was at his wits' end to know the best way to train the colt, on whom he had a very substantial bet for The Derby. Days earlier in the Two Thousand Guineas, Watling Street, ridden by S. Ellis, had finished second to Big Game, being beaten four lengths. In that race Umballa, by Umidwar out of Fara, a sister to Fairway and Pharos, had been more fancied at Stanley House, and consequently had been Harry's mount, but although he was a useful colt he failed to gain a place. Lord Derby had always hoped that Watling Street would prove better than Umballa because he was entirely home-bred, whilst Umballa's sire was the property of H.H. Aga Khan. Nevertheless he was pleased that Big Game won, for he thought it was a good thing for racing that the King should have a Classic winner. However he too was of the opinion that Watling Street might be an exceptional colt, and discussed him with Harry who reiterated his confidence in Walter Earl:

Walter Earl was a horseman. I remember that coming up

to The Derby I used to get over and ride Watling Street whenever I could. It wasn't far away where I was stationed so I would get off to ride him work and when I did so the boy that was riding him at the time was always very pleased to see me because he was a little bit scared about him. Watling Street was rough, almost a crazy sort of horse, but he was manageable if you rode him with confidence and gave him a bit of rein — he'd fool around, but he wasn't all that difficult. I went to ride him one morning and as the horses pulled up on top of Bury Hill where I was standing by the chalk pit about two hundred yards away, I saw this boy get off him. He was going to lead him to me because he thought he could lead him better than he could ride him. I told him when he came down never to do that: 'This horse will begin to know you and you won't be able to ride him at all if you do things like that, because horses understand. He'll think he's boss.' So I got on the horse and just sat on him talking to the lad. As I was sitting I knew any moment that Watling Street was going to jump, kick and do something stupid, but I threw the reins on his neck and just acting the goat a little bit trying to cheer the boy. I told him the horse couldn't eat him. 'You see, this feller's all right if you don't take any notice of him.' As I said that Watling Street whipped round with a jump and kick, but I was ready for it. So I said, 'Well, that's just it. You've got to think all the time ahead of him and while I'm talking to you I'm thinking all the time what this feller's going to do.' On the way down the Plantation going to work at the Limekilns he kicked about four or five trees. That's the sort of horse he was.

So I said to Walter Earl after the work, 'You know, this horse has got a big chance in The Derby although I can only get over here once a week to ride him. I don't fancy the boy that you've got riding him. He's a little scared. Now do you know what I would do — I imagine you've backed him to win The Derby? — now look, he's not going to get to the post if you don't ride him yourself.' Walter said, 'I couldn't ride him.' I said, 'I know you could eat him, let alone ride him. But I'm just telling you — if you are concerned about where your money is — if he gets to the post you've got a big chance of winning a nice bet but you won't have any if you leave that boy on him. So what I want you to do is whenever possible you ride him out. Ride

him yourself and I'll get down on work days as many days
as I can — I'll arrange it somehow.' Walter did exactly
what I said and he rode that horse. He was a bit of a
handful but Walter was a horseman, he could manage
him. Anyhow, things went sweetly and I got back on the
weekends to ride and exercise him. We won The Derby,
but without Walter riding him at exercise I don't think
that we would have done so.

As Derby Day approached, the confidence behind Big Game
had grown ever stronger and on the form book his success
seemed assured, even if those at Beckhampton who saw him on
the gallops had doubts as to his stamina. On Derby Day King
George VI, wearing khaki, and the Queen travelled to Newmarket to be joined by tens of thousands who had wended their
way by train, car and taxi, defying the austerity of war-time
conditions. The sky was dull and overcast, with intermittent
rain falling throughout the morning, much to the discomfort of
spectators. Seventy-seven-year-old Lord Derby, who had not
been well for many months, was not at Newmarket for he had
made up his mind that for the duration of the war he would not
visit a racecourse. He believed that the instant he did so people
would demand to know from where he received the necessary
petrol coupons for his motor car.

Big Game was the centre of attraction in the paddock before
the race and was installed as the odds-on favourite, with Lord
Rosebery's Hyperides, who had slaughtered Umballa in his
previous race, at 9-2, and Watling Street, with an eye 'bold
enough and with plenty of expression but not kind expression' at
6-1. There seemed little confidence behind any of the remaining
ten runners. Once the tapes went up Lord Rosebery's second
string, Seasick, made the running, but at the distance it was
evident that Big Game was beaten and that the race lay between
Hyperides and Watling Street. Harry rode a superbly-judged
race, collared Eph Smith's mount fifty yards from the post and
went on to win by a neck with Ujiji two lengths away third.
After the race Harry explained:

  I thought it all out carefully many times before the race,

and came to the conclusion that my own mount, Watling Street, and Hyperides were the best stayers in the field. I did not believe in the stamina of Big Game, and decided that if I had the choice I should follow Hyperides in preference to Big Game. I had complete faith in the ability of Watling Street to last every yard of the journey no matter how fast the pace might be. I was hoping Big Game and Hyperides would have a tussle for supremacy before I wanted to make my run; it so happened that they did so. I did not want to come on the scene too early, because, from the experience I gained in the home gallops, I thought my colt might want to pull up after hitting the front. So I let him go out of the gate at his own pace, and was one of the backmarkers for the first half-mile.

As we made the turn into the straight I was last but two, but shortly afterwards went to the outside so that I could take up whatever position I wanted without meeting with interference. I moved up a little, and when they started to race in earnest about three furlongs from the finish I had the option of going over to the right to follow Big Game or staying on the outside and having Hyperides as a pace-maker. I decided to stay where I was, and though I was about four lengths behind with only a quarter of a mile to go, I felt fairly sure of winning. I could see Big Game was wavering and Hyperides was being ridden right out. At the top of the hill I gave my colt one tap with the whip just to liven him up. That was the only time I hit him and it had the desired effect. He closed a bit, but I was still a couple of lengths in arrears as we started the climb to the winning post. I knew I would win at that point, because Watling Street had lengthened his stride and was laying himself down to his work in the style which made me feel he had the necessary reserve. I collared Hyperides fifty yards from the winning post and won by a neck. I have no doubt I could have made it a bit more if I had hit him again, but I did not want to take any risk and just pushed him through with the hands. It was more or less what I had planned to do and it all came off as I had anticipated.

Eph Smith also described the race: 'It was bad luck being caught close to home. But I must say I had a perfect run all the way, and so far as that is concerned I have no excuse to make. I did feel that I was going to win when I went into the lead and started the rise to the winning post with an advantage. But when we struck the rise my colt hung a bit and that may have made all the difference.'

Lady Derby was present to see Watling Street's victory and was accompanied by her two grand-daughters, Ruth and Priscilla (now Ruth, Countess of Halifax and Mrs Priscilla Hastings). Priscilla had the added excitement that her own colt, Solway, who had been given to her by her grandfather, ran a respectable fifth, while it did not escape her attention that the name of the dam of Hyperides was Priscilla!

In a letter to Lord Derby shortly after the race George Lambton remarked, 'I saw Walter Earl riding Watling Street as a hack this morning. It really was a very great feat to win The Derby with such a very difficult horse to train. I take my hat off to him. No horse could have run gamer, no jockey could have ridden better than Harry Wragg!'

On the afternoon before The Derby the King had seen Sun Chariot win The Oaks. It was the first time in Turf history that the race had been run before The Derby, but the authorities thought that if The Derby was contested on a Saturday it would be possible for many war-workers to be present. Harry rode Payroll for Lord Derby, but was unplaced.

With the exception of the Classics, racing at Newmarket was comparatively humdrum, with the same horses meeting in handicaps over and over again:

Racing became very dreary especially as every two weeks we would race at Newmarket for a day and the same horses ran against each other. So naturally when you ran in handicaps you were constantly meeting the same horses, and as the handicapper would put you up in the weights you couldn't win too far in any of these races. I remember I'd won three times on a horse called Paper Boy. I kept winning but I was only just winning heads and necks but in reality each time I was winning with about 7 lbs in hand and just scrubbing along.

And it got to the time that I was racing against Gordon. Now Gordon is a feller that everybody thinks is belting away at his horse, but he's not really, he's just flapping

about. I can't have him flapping about and coming out
and beat me so I've got to beat him. But I've got to beat
him as short a distance as I possibly can. Going into The
Dip at Newmarket, I know I'm going to beat him but I'm
not quite certain how much he's got in hand. So I drew
upsides of him, I only just wanted to beat him a head or
neck, and I shouted if you don't hit that horse I will and the
next second he went bang-bang, and that was alright and I
went up and beat him about a neck.

You had to do that sort of thing because otherwise the
handicapper would ensure that instead of going up 5 lbs
the horse would probably be put up 8 or 10 lbs, and you
won't win the next time. That's why I won three or four
times with both Paper Boy and Paper Weight — by just
winning short distances.

Travelling was not easy during the War. One day I went
to Pontefract for Ernie Davy, a trainer I liked. I can't
remember how I got there, but I know he arranged
transport for me. I think it was my only ride, anyhow the
horse won and after the race Ernie came in the weighing
room and took me out to meet the owner. Ernie was right
down to earth and he said, 'Here's your jockey — he's just
ridden a brilliant race for you. You couldn't have won
without him, so put your hand in your pocket and look
after him.' The owner put his hand in his pocket as Ernie
said and started peeling off fivers and putting them in my
hand. 'Go on, keep going, keep going,' Ernie kept saying.
Eventually ten fivers had changed hands and I really felt
very embarrassed at receiving fifty pounds, so I stopped
him. Ernie interrupted, 'I told you keep going because you
wouldn't have won without him.' I said, 'Now thank you
very much, you've done me very well and I'm very pleased
to come up to ride for you. Now I've got to try and work it
out how I'm going to get back.' Ernie said, 'We'll see to
that, we'll look after you.'

Throughout the war the two men who above all others were
responsible for racing being maintained were the Earl of Sefton
and Mr Francis Weatherby, known to his friends as 'Guggs'. At
Oxford Guggs, whom many thought to be a better cricketer
than Douglas Jardine, ought to have earned a 'blue' but he
often lunched too well and thus dissipated his chances. Throughout the 1920s racing had been on a comparatively minor scale

and Guggs would think nothing of drifting into Weatherby's offices in Cavendish Square with a murmured apology that he had been scoring a century at Lords for the M.C.C. or the Free Foresters. The outbreak of World War II found him virtually in control of racing's secretariat. He received a letter from the Clerk of the Course at Newmarket suggesting that Weatherby's moved out of London and took over the Jockey Club Rooms, and telling him that the whole of the Rowley Mile grandstands had been handed over to the Royal Air Force. However Guggs continued to work in London and on one occasion ordered the contents of the strongroom safe to be cleared out. To his surprise amongst the contents was a magnificent gold and bejewelled snuff-box given by the Czar of Russia to James Weatherby in the nineteenth century as a token of his gratitude for bloodstock bought by James on behalf of the Imperial Stud. On many occasions during the war Guggs dined at the Cavalry Club with Lord Willoughby de Broke and Sir Edward Hanmer and discussed plans for racing in post-war Britain. Sometimes they were joined by Lord Sefton, who was Senior Steward for much of the war years, and who enjoyed his reputation for being aristocratic, autocratic and unbending. In reality he was a wise administrator who had much in common with Guggs Weatherby. He loved debunking pomposity, and when asked by a 'nouveau riche' social climber if he would like to dine with him at his house in Eaton Square hautily replied: 'Has the tarmacadam reached there yet?'

After The Derby, Watling Street did not run again until the St Leger in which Sun Chariot beat him three lengths, with Hyperides third. The race proved a battle of wits between Gordon and Harry, who had calculated that the only way to beat the brilliant filly was to track her. Consequently he dropped Lord Derby's colt to the rear of the field in the early stages of the race, hoping that Gordon would take Sun Chariot past him, but assuming that Darling had instructed him not to challenge Watling Street until the last possible moment.

So I thought whatever happens I've got to get Sun Chariot

in front of me somewhere, somehow, during the race and attack her late because I know jolly well that if she hits the front too soon, she'll pull up and I'll go and beat her. Anyhow I dropped my horse out just a little bit keeping him about six to eight lengths off the pace but I can't find Gordon, he's nowhere. And of course, he's behind me, he's tracking me, for it was obvious that Fred Darling had told him to stay behind me at all costs. Well I thought the only thing I can do is to make it as difficult as I can for him and I take Watling Street back, allowing the rest of the field to get away from me, giving my horse plenty to do. Of course I know I'm giving Watling Street plenty to do and also giving Gordon plenty to do, but I also know that I'll be worrying him quite a bit. So things went on like this. We got to the mile post, I'm very far behind now, and realise that I'd better start increasing my pace a little bit. I started to increase a little bit here, a little bit there, during the last mile. Each furlong a little bit more, a little bit more, till eventually when I got to about four furlongs from home I thought I'd got plenty to do now to be able to catch the leaders in The Dip. However I worked it out that I was going to just catch them. As I got into The Dip I hit the front and was winning my race when, bingo, the filly came by me and ran over me. After the race Gordon called me every name under the sun. He said, 'All you did in that race was try and beat me.' I said, 'Correct, that's exactly what I was trying to do. You've won the race, so what are you worried about?' Gordon remarked that I and Fred Darling, the pair of us ought to be put in a bottle and thrown in the ocean, or words to that effect, and I remembered then that he wasn't on the same wave length as I was with Fred Darling.

In retrospect Harry told the press:

When I went into the lead Watling Street was going like a train. But when Sun Chariot came at me I realised that it was she who was the real express. I kept going in the hope that she might shorten her stride, but she carried through much too strongly for me.

1943 Although it was decreed by the Jockey Club that there would be no Free Handicap run in the spring of 1943, a handicap was produced which put Lady Sybil and Nasrullah at the top of the

two-year-old handicap, followed by Umiddad and Ribbon.
There was no mention of Lord Derby's filly Herringbone even
though she had made a winning debut ridden by Harry at the
end of April, had finished third to Cincture and Lady Sybil in
June, had won at Newmarket in July, and had ended her two-
year-old career by finishing third to Open Warfare a fortnight
later. Walter Earl decided that she had done enough for the
season, whilst Harry thought she was potentially a high-class
filly.

In the spring of 1943 she made her season's debut in the
Upwell Stakes, running third to Lord Rosebery's Ribbon (out
of the mare Bongrace) and Open Warfare before winning the
One Thousand Guineas. Originally she had not been entered
for the Classics but when the entry list was re-opened her name
was included, even though there was still a possibility that she
would be sold. In the One Thousand Guineas she ran on
strongly, challenged Ribbon inside the final half-furlong and
won by a neck — precisely the same distance by which Watling
Street had defeated Hyperides. Lord Rosebery and Jack Jarvis
must have been aggrieved by these results and wistful at their
possible folly of dispensing with Harry's services. The Hon.
George Lambton had watched the race and told Lord Derby,
'The One Thousand Guineas was a beautiful race, both fillies
running very game and straight. I thought once that Herringbone was going to win cleverly but Ribbon hung on so well that
I should say that Herringbone was all out at the finish, but
Ribbon had a very hard race. Wragg rode beautifully.

'The Two Thousand Guineas was also a fine race,' Lambton
continued. 'I have no doubt myself that Pink Flower ought just
to have won. Nasrullah packed up in a stride. Frank Butters tells
me that Gordon Richards still says that he will win The Derby,
that he did not like the blinkers, and that he rode him the wrong
way. I doubt all this . . .' Harry had ridden Lord Derby's Booby
Trap and was never in contention.

In the New Oaks Herringbone disappointed behind Why
Hurry with the luckless Ribbon again beaten by a neck!
Herringbone then ran second to Umiddad, with Pink Flower

and Ribbon behind her on 1 September and three weeks later scored her greatest triumph when she beat Ribbon by a short head in the New St Leger Stakes. The field of twelve who contested the race was of the highest class and included the first three in The Derby — Straight Deal, Umiddad and Nasrullah; the first two in the Two Thousand Guineas, Kingsway and Pink Flower; and the first three in the New Oaks. Once again Harry timed his challenge to perfection to gain the mastery in the final strides and win by a short head. In retrospect he remarked:

> It was a nicely run race all the way and as they set off at quite a good gallop I dropped out and got the filly to settle down with only two behind me. When we reached the straight there was a general closing up without the positions being altered to any material extent. Just before reaching Plantation Corner I had a look round and decided nothing was going better than Umiddad. He was just in front of me on the inside. I made up my mind I could not do better than follow him. Umiddad was going through in fine style and I was tracking him in the hope that he would clear a path for me. But he ran into unexpected trouble. Rather more than a quarter of a mile from the finish Why Hurry came over and Umiddad caught a rare bump. I had to steady my filly to escape the trouble ... Elliott then set about pushing Umiddad through and I followed him. Once I got a clear run I realised it was time to get a move on. So I put Herringbone under a rally and got her going in earnest for the first time. She answered as I had expected. I sailed past Umiddad but Ribbon started the rise to the winning post with a considerable advantage. Fortunately my filly was able to produce a fine burst of speed but I had to ride for all I was worth to make up the leeway. It was touch and go but I just managed to catch Ribbon and beat her by a short head.

The Hon. George Lambton had never had a very high opinion of Herringbone, and disliked the manner in which she walked about with her head in the air, but he admitted that she had run a marvellous race, even though he was not positive that she had won. He told Lord Derby that many spectators thought that the judge had made a serious error in awarding her the race, but

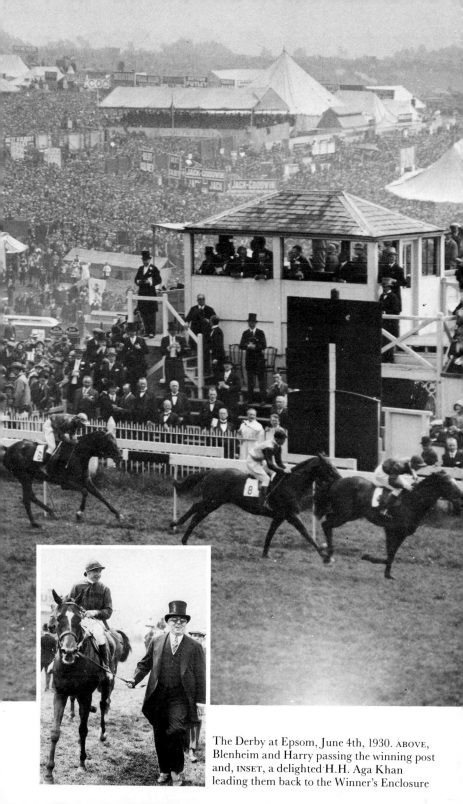

The Derby at Epsom, June 4th, 1930. ABOVE, Blenheim and Harry passing the winning post and, INSET, a delighted H.H. Aga Khan leading them back to the Winner's Enclosure

OSITE PAGE Harry and Marjorie
xing at Bedford Lodge

INSET A house party at Bedford Lodge,
left to right Dr and Mrs Seymour, Luke
mour, Charles and Betty Hodgson,
rry, Geoffrey; *front* Peter, Lily Leach
ding Susan

TOM INSET A convalescing Harry with
two young sons at Bedford Lodge,
ember 1932

PAGE RIGHT Lord Derby's Watling
et and Harry entering the Winner's
osure after their Derby victory,
market June 13th 1942

w The finish of the 1943 New St Leger
Harry forcing Herringbone into the
to defeat Ribbon (E. Smith) by a
t head, with the Derby winner,
ight Deal (T. Carey) three-quarters of
gth away third, Newmarket
ember 18th, 1943

LEFT Walter Earl with Garden Path and Harry after her victory in the Two Thousand Guineas, Newmarket May 17th 1944

CENTRE Harry scoring a comfortable three-quarter length victory on Monsieur L'Amiral over Ford Transport (T. Weston) and Geoffrey's Lady (A. Carson) in the 194 Cesarewitch, Newmarket

BELOW Harry winning the 1946 Manchester November Handicap from Delville Wood (G. Wells) on the final afternoon of his riding career

added, 'We have been racing on the July course for fifty years, and no one has ever been able to say what has won a close race except the judge.'

The race which immediately preceded the New St Leger was the Cheveley Park Stakes in which Harry rode Garden Path, a full sister to Watling Street. Earlier in the season she had made a winning debut, and ran third in the Cheveley Park behind another Fairway-sired filly, Fair Fame. Her final race of the season was the Middle Park Stakes in which she finished third to Orestes and Happy Landing. Walter Earl had not hurried her preparation, but was convinced that she was a top-class filly, an opinion which was shared by Harry, who ended the season by winning the Ascot Cambridgeshire on Fun Fair; the Newmarket Cesarewitch on Germanicus; and by being second on Lord Derby's Full Bloom in the Newmarket Cambridgeshire, beaten a head by Tommy Carey on Quartier Maitre.

Walter Earl was delighted with the physical progress made by **1944** Garden Path throughout the winter months, and at the back of his mind sensed that he ought to challenge the colts whom he did not think were a vintage crop. He discussed the subject with the Hon. George Lambton, who agreed with him, and who mentioned to Lord Derby, 'my information is that Happy Landing is not going well; that Frank Butters' three-year-olds are not up to Classic form . . . Gordon Richards told me that the three-year-olds at Beckhampton are not up to their usual standard, but I am not sure that he is a good judge of the unfinished article. I have seen Fair Fame moving — her action is splendid but she looks on the light side . . .' The views of 'the Honourable George', a man of sartorial elegance who was renowned for the length of time he took to adjust his hat to the correct tilt, influenced Walter Earl, who mentioned his ideas as to the future of Garden Path to Harry.

> He'd got a goodish filly in Garden Path. She was entered in the One Thousand Guineas and she looked as if she could win the race. She was also entered in the Two Thousand Guineas but you don't often run a filly against

a colt. But in this particular case Walter said he liked to have a bet, and in the ante-post betting she was a very big price. Naturally — the bookmakers were prepared to lay a big price because they assumed she wouldn't run in that race, she'll run in the fillies one. Walter spoke to me and asked me what did I think about the two races. I said, 'As a matter of fact the colts are not good. She'd win the fillies' race but she could also beat the colts — I'm pretty certain of that.' He said, 'I'm asking you because I think I could have a good bet.' Now, I don't bet, I've never backed a horse in my life and I've never done anything wrong, but I would always advise my trainer to the best of my ability whatever he wanted to do. I would go with him, help him. So when he said, 'Do you think it would be OK if I suggested to Lord Derby that Garden Path run in the colts' race?' I said, 'It doesn't make any difference to me. I've told you what I think about it and that the colts are just as easy to beat as the fillies are — there's nothing in it, nothing really between the two races.' So Walter Earl decided he was going to run in the Two Thousand Guineas against the colts. That caused a bit of an uproar, especially with all the connections with Lord Derby's team — so they came to ask me. I said, 'Now look, if the trainer thinks that's the best race, I must say I agree with him. I don't think he's done anything wrong in deciding to run in this race but you can criticise him if he gets beaten.'

Garden Path won her first race of the 1944 season by a comfortable three lengths, beating Merry Mark and Honeyway. Then came the Two Thousand Guineas which she won by a head from Growing Confidence. Significantly she started favourite to beat her twenty-five rivals who included Tehran, Ocean Swell, Fair Glint and Honeyway. The race was run in rain, but Harry was unperturbed and brought the filly with a devastating late challenge which swept her into the lead close to home. She became the first filly to win the Two Thousand Guineas since Sceptre in 1902 and her connections were overwhelmed with congratulations.

Lord Derby wrote to the Hon. George Lambton: 'Very many thanks for your congratulations about Garden Path. I should like to have seen the race but travel is now so impossible that neither Alice nor I in our old age would undertake the journey.

'I think Garden Path is a good filly and evidently stays well, but I don't really think she is as good as some of those that we had in the past. She is rather highly strung and I am afraid to over-run her, so whether I shall run her in The Derby or not I do not know. I have not made up my mind at all events at present.

'I think Sun Stream may develop into a really smashing good mare. At the present moment she is rather excitable, but I think both she and Hydrangea will be very useful additions to the Stud.

'Alice is very well and still extraordinarily energetic. At the same time, as with me, though not by any means to the same extent, Anno Domini is beginning to take its toll, and energetic though she is her energy is not quite what it was a year ago; nor could I expect it to be.

'As for myself, I cannot really walk 50 yards and I have to be wheeled from one room to another.'

Queen Nitrocis, Lord Derby's representative in the One Thousand Guineas, was known to be vastly inferior to Garden Path, and the fact that she finished fifth to Picture Play indicated that Garden Path would have won if she had contested the race.

Garden Path did not run again before The Derby in which she failed badly behind Ocean Swell. It transpired that she had been badly struck into the near hind suspensory, and as a result of her injury was virtually pulled up. She had a very sore leg for a long time, and it was agreed to retire her to her owner's stud. 'If' is a word of immense meaning, but 'if' it had been decided to run her in the New Oaks instead of The Derby she would probably have won comfortably, and gone on to take the St Leger.

Lord Derby's comment, 'I think Sun Stream may develop into a really smashing good mare' proved correct. A filly by Hyperion out of Drift — and thus a full sister to Heliopolis, who had been third in The Derby to Blue Peter — she won her first race by four lengths to give Harry an armchair ride. Then came the Queen Mary Stakes which she won comfortably from Sweet

Cygnet and Fille du Regiment. She started at 8-1 on for her next race which she won by five lengths before contesting the Cheveley Park Stakes on St Leger Day. In a desperately exciting finish she failed by a head and a short head to beat Sweet Cygnet and Neola. In many respects it was an unsatisfactory race, for only Neola was smartly into her stride, and many critics considered that the start was a fiasco, with Sun Stream the chief sufferer. However Harry had her in the lead by the time the distance was reached where she appeared to falter. It subsequently was announced that she had put out a stifle, and there were thoughts that she might be taken out of training.

Due to his military duties Harry had less rides than in previous years, and at the end of the 1944 season had only ridden eighteen winners from a hundred and eleven mounts. Understandably he began to consider retirement:

> I think the army slowed me down a bit and it really was the start of me thinking about ending my riding career. I was riding as well as ever I had ridden in the past but I was getting tired. Of course I think it had got to do with the late nights I was keeping with the work I was doing in the army. I was trying to come out and ride and then do night duties in the army. However it helped me to make up my mind and start thinking I'd got to start training.

1945 In the spring of 1945 Sun Stream was becoming 'cussed' and difficult to train, but nevertheless won the One Thousand Guineas by three lengths, beating her thirteen rivals with the utmost ease. Second was Blue Smoke, owned by Lord Rosebery, trained by Jack Jarvis and ridden by Eph Smith, who must have thought that Harry was a thorn in their flesh.

> Now this filly, she didn't work with you at all. All she wanted to do was make every post a winning post and you had a terrific job controlling her and I should say her best distance might be six or seven furlongs. But we won two Classic races with her over a mile, and a mile and a half, which just shows that if you can make them do something you want them to do, how much better it turns out. When I say she was brilliant, she was, and very fast, but she had no idea of wanting to go and get her distance, and I had a

hell of a job trying to make her get these distances. After she'd won the One Thousand Guineas then we'd got to come up for The Oaks, which is a mile and a half. There was no chance she was going to get that distance the way she tried to perform in her work, and so we arranged some work for her and I ran her into the heels and back of different horses and I'd leave it till very close to home before I pulled her out and she went and beat them. She'd only got a run of about a hundred yards but if I brought her out close to home she looked very impressive. I said I wasn't confident, but fortunately The Oaks was going to be run at Newmarket, so we'd got a big chance of getting the distance because it's a wide course and following horses you can go from one to another, which is impossible to do on an ordinary racecourse, especially Epsom.

I was giving her work one day and her lad was complaining about how difficult she was to settle and she won't do this and won't do that, so this day I was a bit fed up with her. She was pulling away but a furlong from home I went and hit the front after I had four or five horses leading me. I ran over them. But by the time I reached Walter Earl they'd run back over me. She'd finished her run and she was exhausted. So when we pulled up Walter comes round, has a look at her and says, 'You know, these Hyperion fillies are funny, Harry.' I said, 'What do you mean?' He said, 'Well, today she hasn't done anything at all.' I said, 'You've got to think again. Stand by the side of her quite a while, she's had the hardest bloody gallop she's ever had in her life. I brought her out of it a bit too soon because I was getting fed up with her.' She had to alter her mind to have any chance of winning The Oaks. So her next work was much better and I kept her back to the very last moment and that pleased him, that pleased him much more.

So we come along to Oaks day. I remember Raymond Glendenning — he was the BBC Radio broadcaster — came and had a drink before the races at Bedford Lodge. In those days they only had one commentator and he had to do the entire race. You can't see a mile and a half at Newmarket anyhow and so he was going to have a hard job and he asked me if I could give him some idea of how the race would be run, especially in the early stages. I said, 'I can't help you, because I won't be taking any part in that. I'll be waiting until the very last moment on my filly and I can tell you this, that as you are reading the race, whatever's in front close to home, I'm hoping that I'm just behind them. So if you look behind the two fillies that are leading you'll probably find me just in there — I'm hoping to be on the bit just on their heels — if I haven't been exhausted by then.' It so happened that coming into the Dip that day I'd been from one filly to another all the way through the race, never off the bridle and I'm running behind four horses coming out of the Dip, four in a line challenging going to the winning post. So I gradually work my way to the outside of those four and about fifty yards from home I just produced her. However, she was really spent, but I got my head in front just before the line. I know I passed the winning post in front but two strides past the post I was running about fourth and I believe that Raymond Glendenning said at the time, 'Here comes Sun Stream, I think she's got up.' Anyhow the distances were all heads and necks. I'd got the verdict but she was the most difficult animal to ride, and never raced again. I've ridden one or two like her but she was the worst of the lot because she didn't give way anytime. If she'd have been raced in America she'd have been up there with the leaders all the way, but she wouldn't have got more than seven furlongs going that way. In England the best races are over a mile, and a mile and a half so you've got to try and make horses relax to try and make them get those distances.

Despite his admitted tiredness Harry was enjoying a marvellous season. He won the Coronation Cup and the Great Yorkshire Cup for Lord Derby on Borealis, he triumphed in the Ebor Handicap on Wayside Inn, and continued his superlative run of success on Lord Derby's two-year-olds Gulf Stream, Neapolitan, Downrush and Sky High. Gulf Stream had three outings and retired unbeaten, having won the June Stakes, the Chesterfield Stakes and the Gimcrack Stakes. No surprise was shown, therefore, when he headed the two-year-old Free Handicap.

Neapolitan, who raced in the colours of Lord Derby's grand-daughter, Priscilla Bullock, contested five races and won three of them. Harry always believed that if Neapolitan had been trained in a different manner and ridden up front he would have been the best colt of his generation. He had a lovely action and really bounced along over the turf, but Walter Earl tried to make him settle in his work gallops. The colt resented this policy and if he had been allowed to bowl along in front from the start he might have won more races as a three-year-old.

Downrush won five of his seven races, whilst Sky High made a winning debut before finishing second to Khaled in the Coventry Stakes at Ascot, and to Rivaz in the July Stakes. Before Sky High's first race Harry had told Walter Earl that the colt was a 'smasher' and would win easily. He suggested that Walter could indulge in a massive gamble, but that if he wished to keep the price as long as possible he must not gallop the horse when the Newmarket touts were watching. Walter funked this plan of campaign and gave Sky High several gallops before the ever-observant eyes of the Heath watchers, with the result that Sky High started favourite on his debut. As predicted by Harry he won decisively by five lengths.

It was an *annus mirabilis* for Lord Derby and for Harry who was so closely associated with all his winners. To add to Lord Derby's delight, five of the first six in the leading two-year-old list were sired by Hyperion.

Harry also scored on the very fast two-year-old Vilmorin, and was second in the Cheveley Park Stakes on another exceptionally fast filly, Rivaz. In addition he won the Milford Follies Plate (Div II) at Pontefract on Horama, owned by Mr Eric Moller. This minor success was to prove of immense significance for he asked if he might train for Mr Moller and his brother once his riding days were over.

In the Cambridgeshire Harry rode Paper Weight, who was unplaced behind Esquire, trained by Bob Colling, to whom he had been apprenticed, and whose retirement was imminent.

The year 1946 was to be Harry's final year as a jockey. The **1946** Second World War was over, the trial of war criminals had commenced and Britain was beginning the long, arduous haul back to peacetime conditions. The Flat racing season opened at

Lincoln, and at the end of the week Harry won the Union Jack Stakes at Liverpool on Sky High, whilst on the day of the Grand National family honour was maintained when both Sam and Arthur rode a winner at Aintree.

At the Craven meeting Harry won the Craven Stakes comfortably on Gulf Stream, who failed to reproduce his form in the Two Thousand Guineas for which he started favourite, but could only manage to finish a remote fourth to Happy Knight ridden by Tommy Weston from Bobby Jones on Khaled. This result showed, if nothing else, that the 'old brigade of jockeys' were still a force with which to be reckoned. Harry rode four winners at Chester, including taking the Dee Stakes on Neapolitan. He took the Hurst Park Great Jubilee on Sir Alfred Butt's Paper Weight by a short head, and the Great Northern Stakes at the York spring meeting on Neapolitan, before the Epsom Derby meeting where he was confident that Gulf Stream had a very bright chance of glory.

It may have been an austere Epsom with the grandstands in need of paint, but at least the 'Blue Riband' was being held at its spiritual home for the first time since 1939. There were seventeen runners for the one hundred and sixty-third renewal of The Derby Stakes, with Happy Knight the favourite at 5-1 and Gulf Stream sharing second favouritism with Khaled and Fast and Fair. Harry rode a copybook race, taking Gulf Stream into the lead at the distance and momentarily he looked assured of victory. Radiotherapy could make no impression upon him; Khaled was dropping out of contention, and Fast and Fair was faltering. Harry was sitting motionless for Gulf Stream was giving his best, and to those in the grandstands interested in Turf history it seemed that Lord Derby was to be credited with another 'Blue Riband' victory to add to those of Sansovino and Hyperion. Suddenly the unconsidered outsider Airborne came storming up the centre of the course, passing horse after horse and it was realised that the grey colt might even reach and challenge Gulf Stream. The two horses were wide apart but at the winning post Airborne was a length ahead, with Gulf Stream two lengths clear of the third horse, Radiotherapy.

For Harry the result was bitterly disappointing, but:

> I had no excuse. I had a lovely run, did everything right and came to win my race with a furlong to go. I'd given Gulf Stream a back hander, I wasn't very hard on him but just pushing him out. The last hundred yards I saw something come up on my right, not near me but away from me, right in the middle of the course. It flashed by me and I knew he got up and beat me. I just couldn't understand it, but anyhow I've got no excuses. I know all the people on the stands thought I'd won then this thing finished so fast.
>
> It turned out he was a very good staying horse although at the time I didn't know the first thing about him. As we were going into the paddock I said to Tommy Lowrey, 'What the hell is that, what's the name of that?' He said Airborne. I said I'd never heard of him. That's how funny it was, to think there's a horse running in the race that I'd never heard of. Anyhow he beat me, beat me well and afterwards he turned out to be a nice sort of staying horse. He won a race at Ascot and went on to take the St Leger.

Airborne was trained by Dick Perryman, one of Harry's greatest friends. He had served his apprenticeship with Fred Leader, and in 1925 married Ellen Beadle, daughter of R. Sherwood's head-lad. He rode his first Classic winner in 1926 when he had the mount on Mr A. de Rothschild's Pillion in the One Thousand Guineas. At the end of 1934 he was appointed stable jockey to Lord Derby and won the 1936 One Thousand Guineas on Tideway for his patron. Later in the season he rode Quashed to win an epic Gold Cup at Ascot. Harry succeeded him as first jockey to Stanley House.

Three days after The Derby Harry won The Oaks for Sir Alfred Butt on his filly Steady Aim whom he had ridden into third place behind Neolight and Hypericum at Hurst Park on Easter Saturday. For Harry the most satisfying factor about Steady Aim's Epsom success was that her sire was Felstead, on whom he had scored his first Derby victory eighteen years previously.

Perhaps the second most satisfying thing from his point of view was that the runner-up, Iona, was owned by Lord

Rosebery, trained by Jack Jarvis and ridden by Eph Smith! Quick Arrow, the dam of Steady Aim, had been bred in France by M. Leon Volterra who sent her to England in 1940 where she won two races. Two years later she was put up for compulsory sale as the property of a citizen of an enemy occupied country. Sir Alfred Butt bought her for 700 guineas and sent her to Felstead. Alfred Butt had commenced his business career as a clerk at Harrods, but his love of the theatre, allied to flair and showmanship, brought him renown and wealth as Chairman and Managing Director of the Drury Lane Theatre where he produced such musical spectaculars as *Rose Marie*, *Showboat* and *The Desert Song*, all of which were smash hits.

In The Oaks the unfortunate Eph Smith must have believed that victory was in his grasp as he passed the toiling leaders once Tattenham Corner was reached, but Harry had other ideas and calmly swooped down on Iona and went on to win by three lengths to prove that Steady Aim possessed an abundance of stamina.

Harry now seemed to be riding on the crest of the wave and three days after celebrating his forty-fourth birthday scored a hat-trick at Manchester's Whitsuntide meeting. His only winner at Ascot was Sir Alfred Butt's Petition, who had no difficulty in defeating his nine rivals in the New Stakes. Petition, a half-brother to Paper Boy and Paper Weight, gave Harry further triumphs when winning the Richmond Stakes at Goodwood, the Gimcrack Stakes at York and the Champagne Stakes at Doncaster. There were no clashes with Tudor Minstrel, the other brilliantly fast two-year-old, because he was retired in mid-July due to the ill-health of Fred Darling. Goodwood proved more lucrative for Harry than Ascot for in addition to his success on Petition, he won the Chesterfield Cup on Signalman, the Drayton Handicap on Vicinity and the Molecomb Stakes on Lord Derby's Rule Britannia. A fortnight earlier he had won the Eclipse, which was run at Ascot, on Gulf Stream who beat Edward Tudor by three lengths. A notable feature of this race was that the first four were all sired by Hyperion. Gulf Stream made no show behind Airborne in the

St Leger and neither did he shine in his final race of the season, the Champion Stakes. After two races in 1947 he was exported to the Argentine.

Meanwhile Harry was continuing to ride a stack of winners, including the ever-popular sprinter Sugar Palm, and Chipchase in the colours of Sir Percy Loraine. He also rode winners for Noel Murless. There followed a notable triumph in the Cesarewitch on Mr H. Barnard Hankey's Monsieur l'Amiral, a result which shook the Ring and achieved a very considerable betting coup:

> I had lots of fans in the final years of my riding career, who included trainers as well as the press. Many times they wanted to know what I was riding in big races. I would try and help them whenever I could. Anyway, one day Jack Leach came along and said, 'What do you ride in the Cesarewitch?' I said, 'I ride a French horse, I think it's some name like Simallon.' Charlie Elliot overheard the conversation and said, 'They've got two in the race but this'll be the one, the other one isn't much good.' I knew jolly well that Jack wanted to have a bit on, so did his brother Chubb and Nat Frieze, the owner of Mickey the Greek, he liked to do the same. So I told them all that this horse has got a fairly good chance. I had a word with Charlie Elliot, he's not the best judge in the world, mind you, but he said of the two the other one's had no chance, this had a great chance. So they all had a bit on it at long odds and one or two of the press fellers did the same sort of thing after I told them.
>
> About two days before the race, the horse arrived in Newmarket and Charlie Elliott asked me to come down and have a ride on him. He had not yet told me what the name of the horse was, so I go down and have a ride on him. I liked him, I was impressed. I said, 'What's his name?' He said, 'Monsieur l'Amiral,' a name nothing like the one I've told these fellers. I asked about Simallon and was told, 'Oh no, that doesn't run, you ride this horse.' So I thought, thank you very much.
>
> I said to Jack Leach and Chubb and Nat and one or two others and the press people too, 'This horse I told you I'm riding, it's got nothing at all to do with the race, I'm riding a horse called Monsieur l'Amiral.' They'd lost their bets

on Simallon, but luckily Monsieur l'Amiral was a 25-1 chance. So they were alright. On the day we're going to post, and I was talking to Charlie Elliot, who was riding Star Lover. I often asked him for his judgement, for instance when he was riding horses in races when we used to go about as apprentices, I'd say, you're riding so and so, what do you think about this Charlie? I don't think he was right once, so you couldn't respect his judgement. As I was going to post, I liked the way Monsieur l'Amiral was going, he felt something, there was a bit of class about him. I thought, this feller's going to give me a good ride. So I went up to Charlie — we'd got a long way to go for the Cesarewitch across Newmarket Heath — and as I was going towards the Ditch I said, 'Charlie, this feller is the one you said that's not got any chance. The way he's carrying me to post now, he's giving me such a feel that I'm confident.'

Once the tapes were up I was content to stay well back all through the race going very comfortably, until I decided to make my challenge. I won by three-quarters of a length. The following day a feller came up to me at the races and gave me a brown paper parcel. He threw it at me and when I opened it, it was full of cash. I was only getting such presents towards the end of my career, but I suppose that the huge amount of cash floating about in post-war Britain had something to do with it. I wasn't a grafter and I wasn't really after money, that's why I wasn't sort of getting all the perks probably that I should have been. Anyhow, it suited me because I didn't like to put the pressure onto anybody. I liked to get on with trainers especially, and that's how I've been all through my life.

Monsieur l'Amiral was owned in partnership by Mr Barnard Hankey and Mr Ian Henderson. Emile Charlier, the trainer, had been asked by them on the eve of the Grand Prix de Paris in June to buy them a horse capable of winning the Cesarewitch. He told them that the ideal horse was running at Longchamp the next afternoon and bought it for them. He knew that Monsieur l'Amiral was a true stayer for he had seen him win over two miles the previous year. In addition he had trained his sire, Admiral Drake. `

Before the season ended Harry had won the Aintree Derby on

Turkish Tune, and was to have his final rides in public at the three-day November meeting at Manchester, the course for which he had so much affection. On the first afternoon he had three mounts and finished second on two of them. On Nat Frieze's Bosco he was beaten a neck, and frustratingly lost the Delamere Handicap by three-quarters of a length to Lord Rosebery's Tregor ridden by Eph Smith. On the second afternoon he won the Seller on a colt trained by Chubb Leach, whilst the third afternoon proved a fairy tale come true.

Harry did not have a mount in the first race on Saturday 16 November, but won the second race on Tiffin Bell, an Irish-trained two-year-old owned by Roderic More O'Ferrall. Tiffin Bell was drawn on the far side of the course, a position from which the experts claimed no horse won over five furlongs in Manchester mud. Harry remained on the far side throughout, and won by a mere four lengths! Next came the Farewell Handicap, in which his mount was the 7-4 favourite Aprolon, trained by Noel Murless. Harry reminded the huge crowd that he deserved his title of 'The Head Waiter' by bringing Aprolon with a strong burst to win by a short head in the last stride. Harry had now achieved a double, which he was to turn into a treble when triumphing on the 20-1 shot Las Vegas in the Manchester November Handicap. The four-year-old, whose sire was a brother to Blenheim, was owned by Sir William Chaytor and trained by A. Boyd. He had not been seen on a racecourse for two months but he won cleverly by three-quarters of a length. Harry knew he had the race in safe-keeping a furlong from home, but he may have been lucky that the favourite, Dornot, broke down before the straight was reached. 'I heard his fetlock go when he was no more than cantering,' said his jockey, Rae Johnstone, who always considered Harry to be the greatest jockey of the era. Harry's victory was very popular everywhere, but particularly in Northumberland where Las Vegas was the hope of miners in the coal fields owned by Sir William Chaytor.

The fifth race of the afternoon did not work out exactly as Harry had hoped. He could have ridden by putting up a few pounds overweight, for in his entire career his weight had seldom fluctuated other than between 7 st 12 lbs and 8 st 4 lbs, and he had hardly ever needed to take a Turkish bath. However, he decided to give up the mount on Billet, a two-year-old owned by Lord Derby, to Doug Smith. Harry had ridden Billet earlier in the season and knew that he had some ability. He also knew that there was a fair chance that he might train Billet in 1947. Therefore, with an eye on future handicapping, he was not terribly anxious for Billet to win. Doug Smith, who had been appointed to succeed Harry as first jockey to the 17th Earl of Derby and the horses trained at Stanley House, had other ideas. He asked Harry if he should stick to the rails, and Harry advised him to do so, whilst hoping indirectly that Doug Smith would get beaten. His hope was dashed, for Billet won by half-a-length with the third horse six lengths away, giving a clue to the handicappers of his merits.

Then came Harry's final mount, on Viva, a six-year-old mare trained by C. Pratt, in the Consolation Stakes. Viva led momentarily but faded out of contention and was unplaced to Phebus, ridden by Michael Beary. Nevertheless Harry was almost mobbed as he came back to the unsaddling enclosure. He had graced the Turf for twenty-eight years, and throughout his career had combined dignity with his artistry in the saddle. No wonder, therefore, that racegoers at far-away Lingfield Park had cheered as they received the news of his Manchester winners, whilst Harry commented to a friend, 'It is all too wonderful. What a grand finish to my career.' Statistically, this career which had begun in 1919, brought him 1,762 winners from 11,658 races ridden in Great Britain.

The sporting pages of the morning papers were full of news concerning his retirement from the saddle, and added that two other retiring jockeys were Bobby Jones and Tommy Carey. It was stated that all three intended to set up as trainers and that Harry had been promised horses by Lord Derby, Sir Hugo Cunliffe-Owen, Mr Charles Sweeney, Mr Ben Hilliard, Sir Percy Loraine and the Aga Khan.

The week after his retirement he, Tommy Carey and Bobby

Jones were guests of honour at a Farewell Dinner presided over by Lord Rosebery at the Albany Club. The guests drank three cocktails before dinner — 'Watling Street', 'Royal Lancer' and 'Straight Deal' — before sitting down to 'Huitres Albany' or 'Saumon d'Ecosse Harry Wragg' or 'Homard Cocktail Watling Street', 'Faisan T. H. Carey' and 'Ananas Glace Bobby Jones.' Amongst other gifts, the ex-jockeys were each presented with a pair of binoculars subscribed by readers of the *Sporting Record*, whose donation was limited to sixpence a head. One Swindon reader, who admired Harry above all other jockeys sent stamps to the value of five shillings, explaining that he had a family of ten!

References to Harry's retirement appeared in all the national papers, and in the *Daily Express* a cartoon appeared of a woman knocking on the door of Bedford Lodge and when her knock was answered saying, 'I wonder if Mr Wragg has any old racing silks coupon free?'

9

The move to Abington Place

The major upheaval in Harry's change-over from jockey to trainer was the move from Bedford Lodge to Abington Place, the massive red brick house and stables built by Martin Gurry after he had abandoned the virtually-impossible task of training for the dissolute Scottish millionaire Mr 'Abington' Baird. Baird had owed him a considerable sum of money and paid up after he had been threatened with court proceedings. When Gurry had secured payment he built his new training establishment, which was completed in 1890. With a twist of ironic humour he named them after his ex-employer. On Gurry's death in 1923 Alfred Sadler moved to Abington Place whilst Cecil Boyd-Rochfort took over Freemason's Lodge. Sadler died in 1940, but ill-health had compelled him to give up training in 1932. Subsequently Sam Darling, who had been training for the Maharajah of Baroda at Warren Place, bought Abington Place, which he sold to Harry after he had lived there for six years.

When Harry and Madge moved into Abington Place their son Peter was at veterinary college in Edinburgh, Geoffrey was at Fettes school and Susan still a schoolgirl. The property, wittily referred to as 'Abington Palace', needed much work done to restore it to its former glory. A kitchen garden surrounded by a privet hedge which had been created in the quadrangle formed by the stable yard needed to be dug up and lawn-seed sown in its stead, and the entire premises required repainting. A headache concerned labour and accommodation. Initially Harry wanted six stable lads although he had not got suitable accommodation for them. He had to make do with four, all of whom received a minimum wage — fixed by the union — of £4 a week. Accommodation in Newmarket town was like gold dust, almost impossible to procure, so that one of Harry's priorities became the provision of a dormitory at Abington Place. The other obvious priority was the acquisition of horses to train.

Harry had begun his stable by buying Madge a yearling as a birthday present. He said that when inspecting a yearling prior to possible purchase he remembered its breeding and looked for flaws. He also believed that it was useless to buy a yearling unless its conformation was perfect. Panorama was a stallion of whose stock he approved, for he sired fast, tough two-year-olds.

At first the pride of the stable was a Fair Trial-Rosy Legend colt who was a half-brother to Dante and Sayajirao and who had been bought by Harry at Tattersalls October Sales for 9,500 guineas. The colt was looked after by twenty-seven-year-old Leslie Smith, who had been one of Captain Ossie Bell's apprentices before the war and who had ridden five winners.

Those who had admired Harry as a jockey were convinced that he would make an immense success of training, for they believed that mentally and temperamentally he was ideally equipped for the task ahead. They were also convinced that it was in his nature to reduce the art of training to an exact science.

Harry saddled his first winner within a month of the **1947** commencement of the 1947 Flat season. The victor was Sir Percy Loraine's Chipchase, who won the Severals Stakes at the Craven meeting, ridden by Gordon Richards, but the colt may have been lucky to keep the race. The Stewards interviewed Gordon and asked him why he started from the middle of the field instead of his proper draw which was seventeen out of the nineteen runners. After hearing his explanation they severely cautioned him. Harry, naturally, was delighted, especially as he had ridden Chipchase to victory the previous autumn. Sixty-six-year-old Sir Percy Loraine had entered ownership in 1932, but until the end of World War Two his horses were trained in

Ireland. A member of the Jockey Club, he had been Chairman
of a Committee set up in 1945 to report on the most suitable
method of introducing the photo-finish, and on the formation of
the Race Finish Recording Company became its Chairman.

On the day after the victory of Chipchase, Billet, now owned
by Mr B. J. Hilliard and trained by Harry, was unplaced in an
Apprentice Plate. Billet was to prove the most successful horse in
Harry's yard during 1947 and won the Cecil Frail Handicap at
Haydock, the Claremont Stakes at Sandown and the Grandstand Handicap at Lewes, to bring three victories to the score of
twenty-five races won by sixteen of Harry's horses in his first
season.

1948   Billet was to be one leg of a training double for Harry the
following spring when he won the Gosforth Park Handicap at
the Newcastle Easter meeting on the same afternoon as Harry's
own gelding Tit Willow won a three-year-old Maiden Plate. In
his next outing Billet gave Harry his most important victory to
date when winning the Chester Cup by five lengths. The official
handicappers were now beginning to assess the merit of Billet
and he did not win again during the season, although he
finished second in the Goodwood Stakes and second in the
Northumberland Plate, beaten a short head. However, Harry
enjoyed another successful season and had trained eighteen
horses to win twenty-nine races.

Harry quickly realised that training was no picnic:

> There's a bit more to it than there is to riding and in fact I
> found out that the moment I started to train. Riding horses
> is a damn sight easier — it's a piece of cake compared to
> training. I never worked as hard in my life as I did when I
> began training. I got a lot of surprises. I didn't realise
> much until I started having runners and listening to what
> the jockeys said when they came back after a race. I felt
> they would tell me more than they did and I was really
> very surprised that some of them didn't know where they'd
> been and I had to gather the facts together myself. I found
> I had to make up my own mind when I wanted to know
> how a horse ran. It was no good listening to what the

jockeys had to say. They weren't giving me any advice. When I'd been riding, when I came back after a race, I would tell the trainer all kinds of things about a horse, but this never happened to me. Jockeys were never telling me anything that I didn't already know myself and I had to start thinking out what was the best thing for each horse and I got into the habit of not asking too much after a race and forming my own opinion.

At the outset of the 1949 season Harry had thirty-five horses in his care, headed by the five-year-old Billet and the four-year-old Riding Mill, who had only lost the St George's Stakes at Liverpool by a head to Alycidon. The two-year-olds included fashionably bred colts by Bois Roussel and Dastur, and fillies by Nearco and Dante. Lord Londonderry had sent him horses, and so had Sir Eric Ohlson, the owner of Dante: **1949**

> One four-year-old colt that disappointed me was Drakkar, who had been sent to me from France. He belonged to Baron R. de Nexon and the intention was that he would be trained for the Lincoln. He was a bit of a savage, I had to take him out early by himself away from the string. If he got loose there was hell to pay so I made sure that he didn't come across much when he was out. One day I took him out for one of his last works before the Lincoln, for which he was much fancied, and we went over Water Hall. We trotted across the middle walking ground, passed the plantation to canter down the gallop.
>
> We were just going to canter down and his rider Leslie Smith jumped off to take off his sheet. As he did so the horse turned round, grabbed him and shook him like a dog shakes a rat. Then Drakkar knelt on him. I jumped off my pony, Paddy, and started belting him to get him off. Then Drakkar spotted my pony, who had seen the disturbance and was careering off towards home. He coursed Paddy right across the middle of Water Hall taking bites out of him, just like a dog coursing a hare. In the end my pony came back towards us hoping that we might be able to help him. As he got near to us, Captain Boyd-Rochfort was coming round the corner towards us with his string. Paddy spotted them and ran for cover, zigzagging in between them, but when he got to the other side of the string, Drakkar was waiting for him, so off he went back through

them, but Drakkar was again waiting for him. By this time
Boyd-Rochfort's head lad had grabbed the reins of
Drakkar and caught him, so I shouted to Leslie Smith to
get on him quick and take him off home, he'd done his
work. Drakkar did run in the Lincoln and I was a bit
disappointed with his run, he finished fifth, it looked as if
Rae Johnstone who was riding him was a bit scared about
him. I sent him home to France, I didn't want any more to
do with him.

There were also rumours that Johnstone had not tried to win,
but such rumours seemed unjust.

The 1950s   The first outstanding colts that Harry trained were Royal
Serenade and Fraise du Bois II, both of whom were foaled in
1948. The purchase of Royal Serenade, for 1,600 guineas on the
first morning of the Doncaster Yearling Sales, was an astute
acquisition on Harry's part, for prices rose steeply during the
remainder of the week for fashionably-bred stock. Racing in the
colours of Mrs Geoffrey Kohn, Royal Serenade made a winning
debut at the Easter meeting at Birmingham, and then showed
his ability and brilliant speed by winning at Chester's May
meeting. At Epsom he won the Caterham Stakes on Derby Day
before suffering his first defeat when he was runner up to Stokes
in the Windsor Castle Stakes at Royal Ascot, where Harry
saddled Ben Hilliard's Bay Meadows, ridden by Arthur Wragg,
to win the New Stakes, and Bakshishi to win the Chesham
Stakes for the Begum Aga Khan. All three colts had clocked
very fast times on the gallops and Harry was confident of success.

Royal Serenade was again runner up in the valuable
National Breeders Produce Stakes at Sandown in July. The field
was one of the strongest for many years and included Belle of
All, who was receiving 12 lbs and who defeated Royal Serenade
followed by Grey Sovereign, Verdura, Arcot, Chinese Cracker
and Zucchero. At the Doncaster St Leger meeting, Royal
Serenade showed that he had retained his form by winning the
Rous Stakes, and ended the season by winning the Prendergast
Stakes at the second Newmarket October meeting. It was
assumed that Royal Serenade, whose dam Pasquinade was one

of the few foals from Pasch's only season at stud and who never raced, would become one of the top sprinters of 1951.

At the Newmarket July Sales held two months before the Doncaster Sales where Royal Serenade was bought, Harry paid the huge price of 14,000 guineas for Master Boatman, a superbly bred colt by Big Game out of the dam of Steady Aim. He was acting on behalf of the Begum Aga Khan. The next lot into the ring was a colt by Bois Roussel out of Sugar Hills, a mare belonging to Major Lionel Holliday. Harry also wished to buy this colt, but when no higher bid than 6,300 guineas was forthcoming, the yearling was withdrawn. A month later the Begum was talking to Sir Alfred Butt at Deauville and he mentioned to her that his stud groom had a very high opinion of the Bois Roussel colt, who had been named Fraise du Bois II. As a result the Begum agreed to buy him privately. Ironically Master Boatman proved a failure, whilst Fraise du Bois II was a great success.

Harry did not hurry the colt, who ran for the first time at the Ascot Heath on the Saturday of Royal Ascot week. His reputation had preceded him for he started favourite, and ridden by Gordon Richards won by three-quarters of a length. An hour later Harry saddled Jai Mahal to win the Churchill Stakes, to round off a memorable week. Charlie Smirke rode Fraise du Bois II at Goodwood where he was beaten by Llanstephan in the Rous Memorial Stakes, but the combination scored a decisive victory over Stokes in the Royal Lodge Stakes at Ascot in September, and in doing so avenged Stokes's Royal Ascot defeat of Royal Serenade. In consequence of his fluent Ascot success Fraise du Bois II started odds-on for his final race of the season, the valuable Gainsborough Stakes at Hurst Park. He was totally outpointed by M. Marcel Boussac's Nyangal, but held on to second place over the fast finishing Medway. Excuses were made that the pace was slow and the race no more than a three-furlong sprint, and the handicapper was content to allot Fraise du Bois II the weight of 9 st 2 lbs in the Free Handicap.

He gave Royal Serenade 8 st 13 lbs, Bay Meadows 8 st 11 lbs

and Bakshishi 8st 10lbs, so that Harry had the distinction of training four colts in the top fourteen in the Handicap. Bay Meadows was unbeaten in his four races but as he was bred on sprinting lines he had no Classic engagements. Bakshishi, a grandson of Blenheim, won two races and was runner-up to Big Dipper in the July Stakes at Newmarket and third to Grey Sovereign in the Richmond Stakes at Goodwood.

At the end of 1950 it was announced that Harry was to train horses for M. Marcel Boussac. The news was disclosed at the Gimcrack Dinner where M. Boussac was the guest of honour, his colt Cortil having won the Gimcrack Stakes in August, and where one topic of conversation was the worry that in some stables training fees had risen to seven guineas a week!

Harry was accustomed to stay at Ye Old Bell at Barnby Moor for the St Leger meeting. In 1950:

> Bloodstock agent Frankie More O'Ferrall asked me if I could book into the hotel two Californian clients, named Rex Ellsworth and Ellwood Johnston, that they'd got down for the sales week, which I did. I asked Frank how I would know them. He said, 'If you go into the sales paddocks and see two fellers wearing big cowboy hats, they're the ones you're looking for.' I couldn't miss them when I got there, and I walked up and introduced myself. One was a tall, thin six-foot feller, he was Rex Ellsworth, and the short thick-set feller was Ellwood Johnston. I arranged to pick them up and take them to the hotel after the last race. We got back to the hotel, I asked them would they like a drink. It was about 6 o'clock. They didn't want a drink so I said we'll have some dinner round about 7.30. While we were having dinner they explained that their wives were staying in London, they were starving as they'd had nothing to eat. At that time we were on rations. My wife said to them, 'You can't judge England by how you're getting treated in London, you must bring your wives down to Newmarket, come and stay with us the weekend.' So they rang back and arranged to bring their wives down to stay with us at Newmarket. Also during the dinner I asked what they would like to drink and Ellwood Johnston said he would like a glass of milk. I thought that a bit of a joke because we were finding it difficult to get anything

like that, but I called over a waitress and said, 'My friend would like a glass of milk if possible.' She said 'I'll see what I can do.' I'd got my young daughter, Susan, staying with us, so she said, 'Daddy, if you can get a glass of milk I'd like one too.' The milk duly arrived. I thought this was funny at the time but I must admit it was a start of a wonderful friendship.

Every winter since 1950 I've either stayed with one or the other for a short while in America. I have learnt quite a lot about horses from Rex Ellsworth and also from Ray Bell, who had been a cowboy and who owned those two very fast horses, Windy City and The Pie King.

I particularly liked staying with Ellwood Johnston because he started me off playing golf again. I hadn't played for fifteen years and I had slipped from the ten handicap from which I played in the thirties to an eighteen handicap in the fifties. Mind you, I couldn't beat Ellwood with an eighteen handicap. I couldn't because he didn't believe in giving me my strokes, and he was a hard nut to crack. Years later, when I was in my seventies still playing golf, I would play off the same tees as his daughter-in-law, Judy, but Ellwood couldn't bear giving me such an advantage, so he would creep up behind or he might start off a yard behind me on the tee. We did not play for money, but the loser paid for dinner if we went out to a restaurant.

Rex Ellsworth was a very good judge and I learned a lot from him even though I thought he spent far too long inspecting and checking horses that he was considering buying. When I looked at a horse I first examined its outline and if that attracted me I would go through all the different points that the horse should have: good body, depth through the heart and a good hind leg. I knew the type of horse that Rex liked and was often on the look-out for him. One day he wanted to buy Khaled, bred and owned by the Aga Khan. We went to see him at stud in Ireland. He had performed marvellously on the race-course, being second to Happy Knight in the Two Thousand Guineas and winning the St James's Palace Stakes. As we inspected Khaled I said, 'Rex, you can't buy him, he makes a noise.' However, Rex was determined and bought him for $160,000. He proved a tremendous success and Rex founded his stud upon him. Before Khaled died he had been rated the best horse ever to stand in California and had sired Swaps, winner of the Kentucky Derby.

Another horse that Rex tried to buy was Aristophanes. I bid £21,000 for him, but a higher bid was received. The horse became a very successful stallion in South America. Rex did not have a terrific amount of money but he kept buying horses. He was a very successful trainer and perhaps he should have been selling some of the horses and bringing some money in, but he never wanted to sell anything, so the only money coming in was his winnings at the races. He did not deal and sell as he should have done.

Harry elected that the Dee Stakes at Chester should be Fraise du Bois II's first race of the 1951 season. He disappointed everyone by falling badly behind Sybil's Nephew and Faux Pas, and Charlie Smirke's explanation that he had lost an iron in the backstraight caused eyebrows to be raised. Harry was still confident that the colt had a first-rate chance at Epsom, but decided that he should be fitted with blinkers. To Harry's chagrin, when Fraise du Bois II reached the start of The Derby, he would not face the tapes and kept whipping round, with the result that he was left almost a furlong. Critics took the view that no other horse was to blame for this failure, but it was obvious that the blinkers had been a mistake and he never wore them again.

Fraise du Bois II redeemed his tarnished reputation at Royal Ascot where he ran third to Supreme Court in the King Edward VII Stakes before being sent to Ireland to contest the Irish Sweeps Derby. The ground was very firm at The Curragh, but as neither Harry or the Begum Aga Khan were present it was left to Geoffrey Wragg to make the final decision to run — much against the advice of Charlie Smirke. Fraise du Bois II proved no easy ride, for his resolution was in doubt, but Smirke exerted all his skill to force him into the lead close to home to win by three-quarters of a length from Signal Box, who had been third in The Derby at Epsom.

He did not race again until the St Leger in which he finished second to M. Marcel Boussac's Talma II. Talma II won by ten lengths and was on an aeroplane back to France almost before the 'Weighed In' had been announced. As Fraise du Bois II defeated the third horse, Medway, by four lengths it is fair comment to consider that Harry's charge was the best three-year-old trained in England, and that Talma II's performance far exceeded his usual ability. Before the race, Charlie Smirke was utterly confident of victory and dropped out Fraise du Bois II a long way behind the leaders, but even if he had employed wiser tactics it is doubtful if he would have beaten the French invader.

Royal Serenade also added to Harry's growing reputation as a trainer. Unplaced in his debut at Hurst Park in April and in the Two Thousand Guineas, he made ample amends by taking the Jersey Stakes at Royal Ascot, ridden by Charlie Elliott. Subsequently, in an epic duel with Hard Sauce he lost the July Cup by a short head, before winning the Nunthorpe Stakes by four lengths with Charlie Elliott looking round for non-existent danger. At Birmingham he failed to give a stone to Lady Godiva in the Union Stakes, but turned the tables on Hard Sauce whom he beat by one-and-a-half lengths. After the race the Stewards cautioned Harry to ensure that in future his runners appeared in the parade ring a reasonable time before the race.

Royal Serenade's final race was at Ascot in the Diadem Stakes, run half an hour after Talma II had managed to scramble home by a neck from Eastern Emperor in the Cumberland Lodge Stakes. In the Diadem Royal Serenade only had one rival — the Two Thousand Guineas winner Ki Ming — who beat him by half a length. Harry's disappointment was diluted that night when he won a television set in a sweepstake at the Henley Polo Club Ball. Before the commencement of the next season Royal Serenade had been exported to California where he won six races including the ten-furlong Hollywood Gold Cup to emphasise that English-trained sprinters can win over longer distances in America.

Throughout the next three decades Harry was to train many horses bred at Kildangan in Co. Kildare, where Roderic More O'Ferrall laid the foundations of the stud in the early 1930s.

One autumn whilst shooting in Scotland he met Sir Percy Loraine who had been appointed High Commissioner in Egypt in 1929 and was to become British Ambassador to Turkey in 1933, a post he held with distinction for six years. Sir Percy Loraine earned the confidence of Kemal Ataturk, who shared his enjoyment of the game of poker and did much to improve Anglo-Turkish relations. He asked Roderic More O'Ferrall to buy him a couple of yearlings. The purchase of two yearlings at the 1932 Ballsbridge Sales resulted in initial success, for a chestnut colt by Beresford, bought for a paltry 75 guineas, won twice before leaving to race in Egypt, and a daughter of Blandford acquired from the Sledmere Stud for 520 guineas and given the name Kyloe won the 1934 Irish One Thousand Guineas after finishing third in the Irish Two Thousand Guineas to Cariff. Kyloe was sent to Epsom for The Oaks but failed to gain a place behind Light Brocade, but when she returned to England in October to contest the Atalanta Stakes at Sandown she was ridden by Harry, who quickly became a friend of Sir Percy and Roderic More O'Ferrall.

In the autumn of 1932 Frank More O'Ferrall, Roderic's bloodstock agent brother, made another acquisition for Sir Percy Loraine when he bought the three-year-old Straight Sequence out of training from Frank Butters at Fitzroy House for a mere 130 guineas. Straight Sequence had raced in the colours of Sir Alfred Butt who had recently bought Orpen to stand as a stallion. Unfortunately no suitable stud farm had come onto the market, so he decided to sell all his fillies out of training. His bad luck proved to be the good fortune of Sir Percy Loraine for Straight Sequence, who was virtually the first mare to arrive at Kildangan, became the foundation mare of the stud. In 1934 Kildangan Stud sold for the first time at the Doncaster September Sales, and in 1941 scored their first notable success when Khosro, whose dam was Straight Sequence, won the Irish Two Thousand Guineas and went on to be second to Sol Oriens in the Irish Derby. Seven years later Sir Percy Loraine saw his colours again carried to a Classic victory when Queenpot, whose maternal granddam was Straight Sequence, won the One

Thousand Guineas at Newmarket, ridden by Gordon Richards and trained by Noel Murless. Five years later Nearula, who was bred at Kildangan, won the Two Thousand Guineas to give another triumph to the stud in which Sir Percy Loraine became an equal partner on the first day of 1953.

Harry was sent Kildangan yearlings to train and one which arrived in the late autumn of 1952 was a bay colt by Dante out of Yasna who was owned by Sir Percy Loraine, and to whom the name Darius was given. Harry had ridden Yasna in the Sceptre Stakes at Chester in May 1938. Darius ran for the first time at the Newmarket Second Spring meeting, being ridden by Sam Wragg to finish second to Cross Petition. Harry was pleased with this performance, and was confident that better things were to come. They did so ten days later when Darius, again ridden by Sam Wragg, won easily at Doncaster's Whitsuntide meeting. At Royal Ascot he finished second to Ray Bell's The Pie King in the Coventry Stakes before defeating Princely Gift by a short head in the July Stakes. He took the Rous Memorial Stakes at Goodwood by three lengths and the Champagne Stakes at Doncaster by a length and a half before being beaten into second place by Royal Challenger in the Middle Park Stakes. In the last four races he was ridden by E. Mercer, who was to win the Ayr Gold Cup a week later on Blue Butterfly, bred by Frank More O'Ferrall and B. J. Hilliard, and trained by Harry.

In March Harry and his family had been saddened by the death of his brother Arthur at the age of forty-one. Arthur had ridden in public for the first time at Lincoln in 1927 and the following year had suffered fractured ribs and internal injuries including ruptured kidneys in a serious fall at Windsor when riding Silver Sue at the May meeting. He did not resume riding until the beginning of the 1929 season, when he came back with a flourish by winning the Tathwell Auction Plate on Lillywhite. He lost his apprenticeship in August of that year but continued to ride for Stanley Wootton and other Epsom trainers. In 1932 he was retained by R. J. Colling and the Hon. George Lambton and rode forty-five winners, but increasing weight was beginning to become a problem. The following winter he holidayed with Harry in Jamaica and continued to ride with competence and skill throughout the next three seasons. He married Phyllis Georgina Wood at the beginning of 1936, and at Epsom on Oaks Day that year, he finished third on Holyrood in the Chipstead Handicap. In the Racing Calendar it was reported, 'The Stewards, enquired into the running of Holyrood. They were not satisfied with the explanation given by the jockey, A. Wragg, and reported him to the Stewards of the Jockey Club. The Stewards of the Jockey Club considered the report of the Epsom Stewards on Thursday June 4th and withdrew A. Wragg's licence'. His licence was not restored until 1940. Four years later he became associated with Sir Hugo Cunliffe-Owen's Rockefella, the superbly-bred colt by Hyperion out of Rockfel, who was trained by Ossie Bell. In the autumn he twice won on Rockefella at Windsor, having previously partnered Mehrali to win two races and Abbot's Fell to win three times, and ended the season with twenty-seven victories to his credit. In 1945 and 1946 he rode many more winners, including Fine Prospect and Golden Hackle, trained by Ossie Bell for Dorothy Paget. Ossie found her totally impossible as an owner, and even with his tact and diplomacy their association did not endure for long. Arthur Wragg relinquished his licence in 1947-8 in order to spend the summer months in Switzerland for he suffered from tuberculosis. Feeling that recovery was on the way he renewed his licence in 1949 and rode thirteen winners, but finally gave up riding at the end of the season. In July 1951 he was too ill to go into the witness box to give evidence in a case concerning a horse named Stella City and died less than a year later.

Harry trained his first English Classic winner when Darius won the Two Thousand Guineas in 1954. He had been given a 'pipe-opener' at the Easter meeting at Kempton when he was beaten one and a half lengths by Tudor Honey, but won convincingly by a length from French challenger Ferriol and Poona at

Newmarket. Ridden by Manny Mercer, Susan Wragg's husband and thus Harry's son-in-law, he had far too much speed on the hard ground for his rivals and was never headed after reaching the Bushes. In The Derby he ran gallantly to be third to Never Say Die but twelve furlongs showed up his stamina limitations, and Harry wisely reverted him to a mile for his next race, the St James's Palace Stakes at Royal Ascot. He only scrambled home by a short head from Umberto, and may have been feeling the affects of his race at Epsom. In the Eclipse he finished second to King of the Tudors, a race he should have won if Manny had carried out Harry's explicit instructions. Darius ended his three-year-old career by running third to Aureole and Vimy in the King George VI and the Queen Elizabeth Stakes a week later.

Harry and Sir Percy Loraine decided to keep Darius in training as a four-year-old and he showed his toughness by running seven times. Beaten a short head by Narrator in the March Stakes at the Craven meeting, he then won the Burwell Stakes in mid-May before Narrator again defeated him in the Coronation Cup, run half an hour after Meld had won The Oaks. Lester Piggott rode him to victory in the Eclipse, but he was not especially fancied when he again contested the King George VI and the Queen Elizabeth Stakes, and few were surprised when he was unplaced behind Vimy. He resumed his winning ways when scoring a short-head victory over the 33-1 outsider Immortal in the Rose of York Sweepstake at the York Ebor meeting. If he had been defeated there might have been some unfair remarks made by the huge crowd, for the owner of the four-year-old Immortal was Sir Percy Loraine and the trainer Harry Wragg! In fact Immortal was a superbly-bred colt by Dante out of Steady Aim who had won the Newbury Spring Cup in April. Darius only ran once more, when runner-up to Hafiz II in the Champion Stakes before being retired to stud where his best progeny were Pia, heroine of the 1967 Oaks, Pola Bella who won the French One Thousand Guineas, Derring-Do, Varano and Darling Boy.

The next outstanding colts that Harry trained were Lucero

and Talgo, both owned by Mr Gerry Oldham who was to prove both lucky and 'a marvellous owner. He just left you alone and let you get on with the training'. Educated at Eton and Trinity College, Cambridge he had spent several years working on studs in Newmarket and Kentucky in order to gain first-hand experience of bloodstock before setting out into the ranks of owners. His first purchase, the filly Rocquita, was bought as a yearling at the 1948 Newmarket September Sales and was sent to Harry to be trained. This filly, who was sired by Rockefella and bred by Mr J. A. C. Lilley, won a modest race at Beverley in the autumn of 1949 to credit Harry with his first winner on behalf of Mr Oldham. Initially the two men had been introduced by Walter Earl, who was a personal friend of both of them, but Harry did not know that he had been the jockey hero of Gerry Oldham ever since he had been a schoolboy.

Mr Oldham sold Rocquita in 1950 and did not acquire another racehorse until Harry bought a Mustang colt on his behalf at the 1953 Ballsbridge Yearling Sales for 2,200 guineas. Gerry Oldham had decided, as his initials were G. A. O., that the names of colts that he owned should end with the letter 'O' and fillies with the letter 'A'. Furthermore, if it was feasible, they would be named after a city, town or village in Europe with which he was acquainted. The Mustang colt was named Sombrero and ran three times as a two-year-old without winning. In 1955, however, he was considered good enough by his trainer to contest the Jersey Stakes at Royal Ascot. Although still backward he ran promisingly, and in his next race finished second to the Queen's Annie Oakley at Newmarket before winning a maiden race at Newbury in October.

Gerry Oldham's racing appetite was now whetted, and given a tremendous boost by the exploits of Talgo and Lucero in 1956. Talgo, who had failed to win from three starts as a two-year-old, made a winning debut at Birmingham at Easter before finishing unplaced to Pirate King and Cash and Courage in the Craven Stakes. He proceeded to win the Duke of York Handicap at Sandown before scoring a notable victory in the Irish Derby which he won by six lengths from Roistar. Harry did not race

Talgo again until the St Leger, in which he finished fourth to Cambremer. Subsequently he ran second in the Prix de l'Arc de Triomphe to Ribot. In 1957 Talgo was kept in training, but was not successful, although he ran creditably in both the 'King George VI' Stakes and the Prix de l'Arc de Triomphe won by Oroso.

During 1956 Harry was ill with prostate gland trouble and much of the day-to-day training was taken over by Geoffrey. However the season proved very successful, for the Irish Derby was only one of three Irish Classics that Harry took during 1956, for Lucero ridden by Manny Mercer won the Irish Two Thousand Guineas for Gerry Oldham and Harry's own filly Garden State took the Irish Oaks.

Lucero, bred at the Brownstown Stud, had not been hurried as a two-year-old, and after finishing second on his 1955 debut at Lingfield, second to Gilles de Retz at the Ascot Heath meeting, and third to Gratitude and Prince of Greine in the New Stakes at the Royal Ascot meeting — which was postponed until July on account of a railway strike — Harry decided to rest him for the remainder of the season. He was first past the post at Kempton's Easter meeting on his seasonal debut for 1956 but had to withstand an objection for bumping and boring before keeping the Coventry Three-Year-Old Stakes. Manny Mercer then rode him into third place in the Craven Stakes in which Harry also saddled the unplaced Talgo. He dead-heated for third place with Water Snake behind Adare and Following Breeze in the Jersey Stakes at Royal Ascot before winning the Sussex Stakes at Goodwood. In his final race he was unplaced in the Rose of York Handicap at York.

Meanwhile Garden State, who had been unplaced behind Honeylight in the One Thousand Guineas, second to No Pretender in the Lingfield Oaks Trial, and unplaced in The Oaks, upset the French 'hot pot' Janieri in the Irish Oaks to give Harry his first winner 'owned and trained by H. Wragg'.

As Harry was still in hospital Geoffrey Wragg went over to Ireland with Manny Mercer for the race. They stayed with Maxie Cosgrove, the well-known veterinary surgeon who was a life-long friend of Harry's and who always stayed at Abington Place when he came to Newmarket. Geoffrey and Manny shared a bedroom at Maxie's and lay awake most of the night thinking how marvellous a tonic it would be for Harry if they could win The Oaks the next day. They planned how Garden State should be ridden, but the big snag was that the French filly, Janieri, looked a certainty. Eventually they decided upon a plan which had been used before but did not always work out, to track the French filly all through the race come hell or high water, and hope that in the final furlong her jockey, S. Boullenger, might think that he was winning so easily that he would ease up and allow Manny to pounce. Plans worked exactly as hoped, for inside the final furlong as Manny thought the moment for decisive action had arrived and urged Garden State to join issue on Janieri's left, Boullenger looked to his right. He saw no danger for there was none to see, and he was unaware of Manny until he looked in the opposite direction. By the time he had realised his folly the race was over with Garden State winning by a neck.

Harry was always on the look-out for new ideas, and had built an indoor riding school so that his horses could be exercised during wintry spells. When he was on winter holiday in California he invariably kept his ears and eyes open, and picked up hints regarding clocking gallops, and the value of installing a weighing machine for his horses. He was the first English trainer to acquire one, for he had been impressed by those he had seen in America and by details of the advantages to be derived from their use which had been given to him by M. Marcel Boussac, whose horses were weighed regularly. The idea was the horses should be weighed before and after each race, thus disclosing the amount of weight lost by the exertion.

Harry, never prepared to let 'the grass grow under his feet', also sent his apprentice, Peter Robinson, to California, where he was given a licence and had a few rides. Harry was convinced that the experience of riding on American race-tracks would be of great value to his apprentice, and so it proved. He never ceased in his efforts to reach perfection in his training methods, was always interested in any new device offered to him, and with justification deserved the reputation of having 'mechanised' the training of thoroughbreds to a greater extent than any other man in England.

In July 1957, H. H. Aga Khan, whose wife was one of Harry's principal owners, died in Geneva. He had been a significant influence on the English Turf for more than three decades, but had not always been respected for his attitude towards bloodstock breeding and the sale of his Classic winners. Lord Rosebery had made reference to the sale of Tulyar in his 1952 Gimcrack speech and stated, 'A leopard does not change his spots', and at times the Aga had been given an unkind press. However, he and Harry had always been on the best of terms. Harry and Madge had holidayed at the Aga's sumptuous villa, Château de l'Horizon, in the South of France, and the Aga and the Begum had stayed at Abington Place. One of these visits, made specifically to see Palestine run in the 1949 Middle Park Stakes, had occurred when the Aga was on a strict diet. Harry and Madge had been given instructions as to his food requirements, but these went overboard when he came downstairs for breakfast, demanded boiled eggs and with an almost schoolboy grin said, 'Please do not tell the Begum about this.'

One August when Harry was to meet the Aga Khan in Deauville he was requested to bring a brace of grouse with him. They were eaten with relish for dinner the same evening.

> The Aga was a lovable character and very amusing. He was a good doer, who loved his food. One night we went out to dinner at a small but smart restaurant. The Aga seemed intent on watching the food prepared for a man at the next table, and despite being told by the Begum, 'Yaki, let the man enjoy his food without watching him,' he told the head waiter to bring him a portion of the same thing. I thought it was ice-cream, but the Begum told me that it was a cheese dish, very fattening and that the Aga should not eat it.

In the mid-1950s two more owners who entered the stables were

Mr and Mrs Arpad Plesch. Mr Plesch, born in 1889, was a Hungarian financier who lived in Beaulieu, near Nice. He had been educated at the University of Budapest where he became a Doctor of Law, in Paris and at Oxford and Berlin, before becoming a Captain in the Hungarian army. Much of his wealth stemmed from his financial acumen, which made him appreciate the importance of gold following the depression of the 1930s and subsequently realise the money there was to be made in Cuban sugar and by large investment in post-Second World War Japan. An exceptionally knowledgeable gardener, he was renowned for possessing one of the finest horticultural libraries in the world. From his love of all things botanical he was prone to give the majority of his horses botanical names. He believed that a horse's measurements gave a vital clue to their racecourse ability and created his own system of assessing thoroughbreds based upon mathematical calculations involving height, girth and hip to hock measurements. His wife, known as Etti, was a granddaughter of the owner of the famous Hungarian horse, Kisber, who won the 1876 Derby and Grand Prix de Paris.

Mr Arpad Plesch, who was becoming known in English society by the 1950s, entered the ranks of owners in 1955 as a result of the purchase of the mare Dinarella. He and his wife were lunching at the Haras de Mesnil, owned by Madame Couturie, when understandably the conversation turned to the subject of bloodstock breeding. Madame Couturie mentioned that the mare Dinarella, bred by Federico Tesio at Dormello, was at her stud in foal to Tornado and might prove a sensible acquisition as she was from a top-class family. Mr Plesch bought Dinarella for about £3,000, and as he had no stud, sent her to be boarded at the Middleton Park Stud in Co. Westmeath.

His lack of a stud farm was quickly rectified as a result of a lunch with Mrs Aileen Plunkett. A fellow guest was Captain A. D. Rogers, who took the Plesches to see the Dollanstown Stud, which was on the market. The stud was the proud possessor of a long history, having been founded in 1906 by Peter Purcell Gilpin. The Plesches thought it enchanting and bought it. Immediately they began investing in yearlings, added one hundred acres to the property and commenced the task of making it one of the showpieces of Ireland.

The first colt that Harry trained for Mr Arpad Plesch was Nagami, by Nimbus out of the Hyperion mare Jennifer, who made his debut in the 1957 Gimcrack Stakes won by Pheidippedes. Harry also ran Lavandier, owned by H. H. Begum Aga Khan in the race, but neither colt was placed. At the Doncaster St Leger meeting Nagami won the Tattersall Sale Stakes by a head, and ended his two-year-old career by running second to the filly Torbella in the Dewhurst Stakes.

Harry elected to give Nagami his first run of the 1958 season in the Craven Stakes. He never hurried his colts and was perfectly satisfied when Nagami finished second to Bald Eagle. Nagami ran with credit to be third to Pall Mall in the Two Thousand Guineas and equally creditably in The Derby to run third to Hard Ridden and Paddy's Point. He maintained his consistent record by being third to Alcide in the St Leger in addition to being fourth in the Irish Derby and winning the Gran Premio del Jockey Club ridden by Lester Piggott.

In 1959, after a 'pipe-opener' in the Coronation Stakes at Sandown, he ran third in the Ormonde Stakes at Chester, before winning a sub-standard three horse race for the Coronation Cup, and the Grand Prix de Printemps at Saint Cloud. Considering his evident ability and class it surprised many critics that his final race in England was the Ebor Handicap at York in which he failed behind Primera. Further renown was brought to Harry throughout the season by Discorea, in the 'light blue, scarlet spots' of Mr and Mrs Plesch. Discorea's dam, Stella Polaris, had been a useful filly who had run third to Asmena and Plume II in the 1950 Oaks, ridden by Martin Molony. Sired by Borealis, a half-brother to Alycidon, she had already produced a winner in Cassiopeia. It was perfectly reasonable, therefore, that when Harry was marking up the Tattersalls Doncaster Sales Catalogue he should make a note of the Dante-Stella Polaris filly submitted by the Shadwell Stud and mention her to Mrs Plesch. In fact the filly, when inspected, proved bitterly disappointing in conformation, and was eliminated from Harry's list. However as she was being led around the sale ring it became evident that she would be sold for virtually nothing. After a quick conversation between Harry and his sons, Peter and Geoffrey, they decided to buy the filly on their own account, and were lucky enough to acquire her for 470 guineas. Harry telephoned Mrs Plesch and explained to her that the filly did not seem up to standard and that he had not bought the lot for either herself or her husband. Mrs Plesch replied, 'Never mind, I'll still take her.' Harry was too wise to argue with one of his patrons on such a matter.

The filly, named Discorea, ran three times as a two-year-old, running second on her debut at Newmarket in August, winning a modest race at Yarmouth, and finally being beaten a neck in the Warwick Autum Breeders Stakes. She proved her ability in 1959 by winning the April Handicap at Epsom, being runner-up to Mirnaya in a three-horse race for the Oaks Trial at Lingfield, and in the autumn taking third place behind Collyria and Cantelo in the Park Hill Stakes and again being third in the Newmarket Oaks. Sandwiched between these performances was her victory in the Irish Oaks which she won by three-quarters of a length from the odds-on favourite La Coquenne owned by Prince Aly Khan.

Her victory was a great triumph for Harry had already won the Irish Derby with Fidalgo in the colours of Mr Gerry Oldham. After failing to reach his reserve at the Ballsbridge Sales Fidalgo, a three-quarters brother to Talgo, had been bought privately by Peter Wragg for a sum reputed to be 3,000 guineas. Harry decided to give him only two races as a two-year-old, and delayed his debut until the first October meeting at Newmarket when he finished second to Persian Beauty, a filly of Mr. H. J. Joel's, in the Buckenham Stakes. In his only other race he was second to Anthelion in the Houghton Stakes.

In the spring of 1959 he was unplaced in the White Rose Stakes, fourth in the Royal Stakes at Sandown, won the Chester Vase, was second to Parthia in The Derby and then annexed the Irish Derby. It was a wonderful feat on Harry's part to carry off the Irish Derby-Oaks double twice in three years. At Epsom Fidalgo had every chance but was beaten by a better horse, whilst at The Curragh he showed his total supremacy over a moderate field. Subsequently he was unplaced behind Saint Crespin III in the Eclipse and second to Cantelo, whose St Leger victory was exceedingly unpopular and was greeted with disapproval after her Park Hill defeat. It had been the intention to keep Fidalgo in training as a four-year-old, but he sustained a tendon injury in October and was retired to stud, first at Phanton House Stud, and then at the Moreton Stud, before he was exported to Japan in 1966.

Saturday 26 September 1959 was one of the saddest days in Harry's life, for his son-in-law, twenty-nine-year-old Manny Mercer, was killed in a million-to-one freak accident whilst riding at Ascot. Born in Cheshire he had been apprenticed to J. Russell at Mablethorpe and rode his first notable winner when he scored on the 100-1 outsider, Jockey Treble, in the 1947 Lincoln. Russell's licence was withdrawn later in the year and Manny's indentures were transferred to George Colling at Newmarket, where he received an abundance of advice from Charlie Elliott who was first jockey to Colling.

He had the indefinable gift of being able to make horses run their best, and although less articulate than some of his contemporaries and less thoughtful as to tactics during a race, he possessed genius to such an extent that he quickly rose to the top of his profession. He rode horses in the same carefree manner that he drove fast cars, taking calculated risks that men of lesser courage and skill would not have attempted. In a race it did not matter where he was drawn. He was always in the correct position after the runners had gone a furlong — on the fence, running smoothly, with his horse settled and balanced. He rode 37 winners in 1950, 97 in 1951, and 90 in 1952 to be third in the Jockeys' Championship. In November 1952 he rode Wilwyn to win the inaugural running of the Washington D.C. International at Laurel Park. He won the 1953 One Thousand Guineas on Happy Laughter, the 1954 Two Thousand Guineas on Darius and in 1955 won the Lincoln on Military Court, trained by Harry, for H. H. Begum Aga Khan.

On Thursday 24 September 1959 the three-day Ascot Heath meeting had commenced in brilliant sunshine, and Manny had enjoyed a successful afternoon. He won the Buckingham Palace Stakes on Compere for Mr Tom Blackwell, and the Clarence House Stakes on Lord Rosebery's Diffidence to complete a double for Jack Jarvis, only failing to make it a treble when Lester Piggott beat him less than a length in the Marlborough House Stakes. He had no success on the Friday, and on the Saturday watched his younger brother Joe win the first race on Title Deed, trained by Harry for Mr R. B. Moller. The brothers both rode in the second race, the Blue Seal Stakes, with Manny unplaced and Joe beaten three lengths on a filly of Sir Percy Loraine's. Joe and Manny both had mounts in the Golden Gates Nursery, with Manny failing to reach a place on Mr Marcus Wickham-Boynton's Lentolia whilst Joe was again second, riding Chinky. Joe was to win the next race, the Queen Elizabeth II Stakes, on Rosalba, but for Manny, Lentolia was his final ride in a race.

The fifth race of the afternoon was the one and a half mile Red Deer Stakes, a handicap for three-year-olds, and for which there were eighteen runners. Geoff Lewis was riding Suki Desu, Scobie Breasley Peterman, Harry Carr, Joe Mercer's father-in-law, was aboard Hieroglyph, whilst Doug Smith, Eph Smith, Edward Hide and Peter Robinson also had mounts. Manny Mercer was riding Sir Foster Robinson's Priddy Fair, a filly upon which he had won twice early in the season. As the horses were parading in front of the grandstands before cantering to the start Priddy Fair seemed to stumble as she turned and to kick the prostrate Manny, who had been thrown to the ground as she tried to regain her footing. Simultaneously he struck his head on a concrete support post of the rails. He was taken to the Ambulance room where doctors pronounced him dead, the cause being cerebral lacerations due to multiple fractures of the skull.

Harry was one of the first to be told the tragic news, as the

Duke of Norfolk, Her Majesty's representative, walked to the Weighing Room and personally ensured that the announcement was given over the public address system. 'The Stewards regret to announce that the last race has been abandoned as E. Mercer has been killed.' A strange silence came over the racecourse as men raised their hats in tribute, and sadness was in the countenance of all. Eph Smith, who was next to Manny when the fall occurred, told Doug Smith at the start that he thought that Manny was very seriously injured, but none of the jockeys imagined that he was dead.

When the race was over, won by Geoff Lewis, jockeys huddled in groups sharing shock and a sense of disbelief. Doug Smith told a friend, 'Manny was so full of fun, and he and I always dressed in the same corner of the dressing room. It will be a much duller place now, and so will all the racecourse.'

Manny's balance on a horse and his uncanny judgement of pace had brought him to the top of the jockey' list, and in 1960 he was to be first jockey to Jack Jarvis, with every probability that he would have become Champion Jockey. Scobie Breasley, still badly shocked by the news of Manny's death, said as he left the racecourse, 'Race-riding is a nerve-racking strain, and in the heat of the moment released tension frequently results in heated Weighing Room disputes. Manny would have his arguments like the rest of us after a race, but he would never bear malice. He would make his point, and in the very next race if he was on a beaten horse he'd give way to a rider who he thought had wronged him half an hour earlier.'

More than a thousand mourners went to Manny's funeral at St Mary's Church, Newmarket. Susan Mercer was on the arm of her brother-in-law Joe, Harry supported Madge as they shared each other's grief. The Duke of Norfolk, Lord Derby, Captain Cecil Boyd-Rochfort, Jack Jarvis, Charlie Smirke, Clive Graham and Sir Foster Robinson were amongst the congregation who listened to the Vicar tell them, 'Manny Mercer was known as a very fine horseman as well as a jockey, and I understand that is quite an unusual thing. He had a strange sympathy for that wonderful thing God has created, the

Horse. Manny was more than a jockey. He was a gentleman, a gentle man in the true sense of the word.' In his will he bequeathed his entire estate, £36,727 net, to his widow, twenty-six-year-old Susan, who lived at Fordham Road, Newmarket with her two children.

10

Classic triumphs in the Sixties

In 1960 Harry had fifty horses in training, of whom twenty-six were two-year-olds. Only two of his horses, Title Deed and Pal Fast, were four-year-olds, and his three-year-olds contained no outstanding horse. However the two-year-olds included Cynara, Sovrango, Ambergris, Violetta III and Psidium, all of whom were to bring him further fame. Cynara, who raced in Mr Gerry Oldham's colours, was considered by Harry to be the fastest juvenile that he had ever handled. Sent up to the Newmarket Second October Sales by the Lambourn Stud, she had been bought by Peter Wragg for 3,300 guineas. By 1950, the three founders of the Lambourn Stud, Sir Hugo Cunliffe-Owen, Captain Ossie Bell and Major George Drummond, were dead, and the Stud was owned by Ossie Bell's widow, with Rockefella one of the stallions standing there.

Cynara won the Sceptre Stakes at Chester on her debut, the Queen Mary Stakes at Royal Ascot by five lengths from Crisper and Sweet Solera, and the Molecomb Stakes at Goodwood, before surprisingly being defeated in the Lowther Sweepstake at York by the Paddy Prendergast-trained Kathy Too.

Sovrango, also astutely bought by Peter Wragg for a mere 1,700 guineas, only raced twice in 1960 but showed promise when second to Cracksman at the Newmarket Houghton meeting. Ambergris, in the colours of Sir Percy Loraine, won at Newmarket and York in the spring, was second to Sweet Solera at the Newmarket First July meeting, resumed her winning ways at York in August and ended a successful season by scoring a triumph in the Champagne Stakes at the Doncaster

173

St Leger meeting. Violetta III ran seven times, winning at Kempton, whilst Psidium also ran seven times, scoring a solitary success at Ascot in October when he won the Duke of Edinburgh Stakes. Subsequently he proved to Harry that he was a colt full of promise by running second in the Dewhurst Stakes, but nevertheless Harry indicated that Sovangro was his Derby hope for 1961.

Lester Piggott had the mount on Sovrango when he scored a comfortable victory at Newbury in the spring of 1961 over twenty-seven other maidens. He then endorsed Harry's high opinion of him by a decisive victory in the Chester Vase, a race won in past years by Fidalgo, Alcide, Swallow Tail — and in the 1930s by Hyperion and Windsor Lad. Everything seemed set fair for a Derby victory, for his vanquished Chester opponents included Latin Lover, Bounteous and Gallant Knight. All his credentials seemed correct, for he was a three-parts brother to the dual Classic winner Musidora, and had shown that he had speed, stamina and resolution. His chances appeared even more bright when Noel Murless reluctantly announced that Pinturischio had been scratched from The Derby. Mystery has always surrounded the reasons for the stomach disorder suffered by Pinturischio and many 'Nat Gould' stories concerning possible doping became racecourse gossip.

Meanwhile, Psidium had been given an unorthodox Derby preparation. Harry saddled him for the Two Thousand Guineas Trial at Kempton, where he finished third, but significantly was running on strongly inside the final furlong. Mrs Plesch, Psidium's owner, thought that he should run in France, and consequently he was sent to Longchamp for the ten-furlong Prix Daru. Lester Piggott rode him, finished third, and reported to Harry that he did not stay the trip. Harry was disconcerted by Piggott's comment for he was convinced that Psidium had an abundance of stamina. Yet Piggott's comments were confirmed by both Peter and Geoffrey Wragg who had flown to Paris for the race, although they added that Lester might not have ridden the colt correctly, for he had kept him up with the leaders from the start. Nevertheless, when Mrs Plesch requested that

Psidium should run in the Two Thousand Guineas since he did not appear to stay ten furlongs, Harry agreed to her request, although privately he was angry, and thought that giving Psidium three races in less than a month was foolhardy. However he accepted that 'pipers call the tune'. Willie Snaith rode Psidium in the Newmarket Classic, and at the end of six furlongs his mount was a spent force through attempting to keep up with the leaders.

Psidium avoided all the Classic Trials, was galloped on the training grounds with Sovrango who was considered vastly superior although he needed some give in the ground and did not race again until The Derby. In the gallops Psidium was ridden by an apprentice and invariably was settled down at the rear of the field where he was content to remain. Doug Smith usually rode Sovrango, but was unable to accept the mount in The Derby as he had to ride Latin Lover for Lord Derby. One morning on the gallops the very experienced Heath Man, Mr Potter, watched Sovrango working with Psidium. He told Harry that Psidium seemed to him to be the better of the two.

Derby Day was warm and sunny, and huge crowds flocked to Epsom Downs. Many of them thought that the French favourite Moutiers, was a 'good thing', whilst others expected Dicta Drake, Sovrango, Pardao and Just Great to figure prominently. Lester Piggott, without a mount, for he had been booked to ride the non-runner Pinturischio, watched the race on television from his Newmarket home. When Harry met Mr and Mrs Arpad Plesch at Epsom they sportingly wished him good luck with Sovrango, the mount of George Moore, and were somewhat surprised when he told them that Psidium had far more than an outside chance and was definitely not a forlorn hope, particularly as Roger Poincelet had accepted the ride. In the paddock Mrs Plesch acted as interpreter in a three-cornered conversation between owner, jockey and trainer, for Harry's French was virtually non-existent, and Poincelet's English equally moderate. Broadly speaking Harry's instructions to Poincelet were to come late on the scene — à la Felstead! Nothing untoward occurred in the preliminaries, and Mr Alec

Marsh despatched the runners with promptitude. At the two-furlong pole George Moore, following the lengthy instructions given to him by Harry, drove Sovrango into the lead, and he looked to be the hero of the hour. Then Pardao, Latin Lover and Dicta Drake joined issue and it could be seen from the grandstands that Sovrango might not be able to withstand their challenges, for he was failing to accelerate on ground too firm for him. Suddenly Psidium, given a copy-book ride by his French jockey, burst through on the outside, cut down his rivals as though they were standing still, and at the winning post was two lengths clear of Dicta Drake.

It would be an understatement to claim that the result was temporarily greeted with shocked silence, but Sporting England rapidly recovered and those connected with the 66-1 winner Psidium received resounding applause as the colt was led into the hallowed winner's enclosure. Wearing a new green suit made for her by Balenciaga, and her lucky amethyst brooch, Mrs Plesch rushed out onto the course to greet her hero, muttering congratulations in fluent staccato French to her jockey whilst Harry seemed somewhat bemused, and Bunny Esterhazy, Etti's daughter, laughed happily alongside her friend Henrietta Tiarks. Afterwards Poincelet's story translated into English was, 'I dropped Psidium out on purpose and was last after half a mile, and still in the last few at Tattenham Corner. We then worked our way out despite being behind a dozen horses which gave me a job to get clear. But I was never worried ...' His remarks seemed to sum up the situation succinctly concerning a race which produced the longest-priced winner since 1913.

As the Two Thousand Guineas had also been won by a 66-1 shot bookmakers rejoiced, with the possible exception of the Epsom Downs bookie who had to pay out a considerable amount of money to a punter who had backed Psidium. He then asked the lucky punter why he had backed the 66-1 winner, and when told it was because he had served on a cruiser named *Psidium* during the war he retorted instantly, 'Pity it was not the Titanic'.

Harry was submerged under a sea of well-wishers, but later when he had recovered from the excitement of the occasion made it clear that credit must be given to Mr and Mrs Plesch for the fact that Psidium had contested the race. On being told by Piggott after the Prix Daru that Psidium was not a stayer, initially he had been inclined to withdraw the colt even though in his heart he believed that Psidium would stay twelve furlongs. When he explained his thoughts to Mr Arpad Plesch he was told, 'Train the horse for The Derby'.

Mrs Plesch became only the fourth woman in Turf history to own a Derby winner, the others being Mrs G. B. Miller, Mrs M. Glenister and Mme Volterra. On the night of The Derby the Plesches gave a huge party at the Savoy. They had not dared book even a table in advance, but once the race was over and the result known, the Savoy came up trumps. At Claridges before the party the winning owners were showered with congratulations, telephone messages, flowers and gifts which included a picture of Kisber!

The subsequent events concerning Psidium are tinged with sadness. It was decided to train him for the Gordon Stakes at Goodwood and the Great Voltigeur Stakes, and Harry began to make him settle. He was working brilliantly and Piggott — who had been unimpressed when he rode him in France — requested that he try him in a trial gallop. Harry said to Piggott:

'If you ride this feller the way I tell you, you'll find he is a different horse. I've put him with the same horses that he worked with before The Derby, so just drop him in behind and get him off the bridle, let him settle.' Psidium did this beautifully, and we worked on the same ground as before The Derby, on racecourse side. I said: 'Bring him out and challenge about a furlong from home and see what you think.' He really sprinted by the other horses at the finish. When Lester got off he said, 'This horse will never get beaten, he's a different horse to what I rode before The Derby, I'll tell you that.'

The next day Psidium had broken down, injuring a tendon, and was retired to stud, occupying the box once honoured by Prince Chevalier at the Cheveley Park Stud.

Sovrango went on to be unplaced behind Just Great in the Great Voltigeur Stakes and the St Leger, before failing in the Arc, where the ground was very firm. On soft ground he was a horse almost two stone better.

Two days before his Derby success Harry came near to achieving another major triumph when Ambergris ran second to Sweet Solera in The Oaks, beaten one and a half lengths. She had also been runner up to Sweet Solera in the One Thousand Guineas, and sandwiched between these races had won the Musidora Stakes at York. Sadly her owner, eighty-year-old Sir Percy Loraine, had died six days before her York victory, and so did not live to know of her future deeds, which not only included being second in The Oaks and third to Aiming High in the Coronation Stakes at Royal Ascot, but also a notable triumph in the Irish Oaks which she won comfortably. He also missed witnessing the head victory of the two-year-old Abermaid in his colours at Royal Ascot, where Harry saddled Mr Gerry Oldham's filly Futurama to win the Ribblesdale Stakes to add to his halcyon summer. In his will Sir Percy Loraine left his binoculars to Harry.

As Harry looked to the future it was another of Mr Gerry Oldham's colts who excited him the most. Miralgo, yet another perspicacious purchase by Peter Wragg, had been bought for 5,200 guineas at the Tattersalls Sales in early September, and had been submitted by the Kildangan Stud. He was a rather washy chesnut with a prominent blaze and four white stockings, and Harry gave him a gentle introduction to racing at the York Spring meeting. His home reputation had gone before him and he started a short-priced favourite but failed to gain a place. In his next race, the Granville Stakes at Ascot in July, he slammed his opponents to win by four lengths. He was somewhat unlucky to be beaten a neck and a short head by Sovereign Lord and Prince Poppa in the Gimcrack Stakes but ended the season in a blaze of glory when taking the inaugural Timeform Gold Cup from Escort and Prince Poppa. This added considerably to Harry's total of £91,645 for the 1961 season, a sum only £4,327 less than the prize money earned by Noel Murless. Another autumn winner who contributed to this total was Violetta III who dead-heated with Henry the Seventh for the Cambridgeshire.

Harry's owners now included his great friend Colonel Nat Frieze, Major G. Bradstock, Mrs J. A. Dewar, Lord Elveden, Mr R. B. Moller and R. Sigtia, in addition to his stalwarts, Mr Gerry Oldham, H. H. Begum Aga Khan, and Roderic More O'Ferrall, and he sent out innumerable winners for them.

In 1962 Miralgo was the star of the Abington Place yard, but to everyone's amazement he went through the season without a victory, although he was third to Silver Cloud and Young Lochinvar in the Chester Vase, second in the Lingfield Derby Trial, unplaced in The Derby, third in the Gordon Stakes at Goodwood, second to Hethersett in the Great Voltigeur and third in the St Leger. However the season brought Harry another Classic success when Abermaid won the One Thousand Guineas. She had won all her races as a two-year-old, and was fancied for the 1962 Free Handicap at the start of which she was badly bumped. Ridden in the One Thousand Guineas by W. Williamson, she won gallantly from Display and West Side Story. Although she started an even-money favourite for the Irish One Thousand Guineas she could only manage to finish third to Shandon Belle. At Royal Ascot she was second in the Jersey Stakes and finished her racing career by being third to Tournella, to whom she was conceding 14lbs in the Falmouth Stakes at Newmarket. Nevertheless she contributed much towards Harry finishing second in the list of Winning Trainers with £69,284 — only £922 below Dick Hern.

In 1963 Miralgo won the Hardwicke Stakes at Royal Ascot, and was runner up in both the Eclipse and the King George VI and the Queen Elizabeth Stakes before being bought by the Irish National Stud. Curiously, Miralgo did not race outside England even though Harry was being acknowledged as a pioneer of those prepared to attempt to plunder Continental races. One of the first raiders that he employed in these ventures was Mr Gerry Oldham's Espresso, a small but handsome colt who had been bought for a mere 1,000 guineas at the 1959

Ascot January Sales from Major Patrick Dennis's Greenmount Stud in Co. Limerick. As a three-year-old Expresso won the Craven Stakes, the opening race of the Goodwood July meeting, but did not 'hit the headlines' until 1962 when he scored victories in the Great Cheshire Handicap, the Newbury Summer Cup and the Alexandra Handicap at Doncaster's St Leger meeting. As a five-year-old he won the Vaux Gold Tankard, the Manchester Cup, in which he defeated Sovrango, and was a distant fourth to Mongo in the Washington D.C. International, after winning the Grosser Preis von Baden, which he also won in 1964. When Harry sent horses to Baden-Baden he flew them into a Canadian NATO airfield at Sollengen, only a few minutes from the racecourse, whilst other trainers were compelled to use Stuttgart or Frankfurt aerodromes, which were several hours away.

It had struck Harry forcibly that it was useless sending out a near champion to be second or third time after time in top-class English races when he could be sent to race on the Continent with far greater chance of success. Harry also thought that it was not degrading to run Classic horses in handicaps. Inevitably there were critics who attempted to compare the training career of Harry with that of Sir Gordon Richards at this period, but such comparison was purely academic. Harry had won far more prize money than Gordon who had won a greater number of races, and in addition Harry had twice narrowly missed being at the top of the Winning Trainers' List. On both these occasions he had saddled a fancied runner in the Manchester November Handicap — Flower Drum in 1961 and Expresso in 1962 — and if either of them had won he would have headed the List.

Atilla was another useful horse that Harry trained in 1965 and he sent him out to win the Vaux Gold Tankard at Redcar and the Gran Premio del Jockey Club in Milan. Atilla had been bred by Mr A. B. Askew and was out of Festoon who had won the 1954 One Thousand Guineas for Mr J. A. Dewar. Harry did not hurry him, and he did not run until he was a four-year-old, but he amply repaid Harry's patience by winning the Old

Harry discussing the purchase of yearlings with one of his patrons, Mr G.A. Oldham (*seated*) and his son Peter Wragg

OPPOSITE PAGE ABOVE The finish of the 1961 Derby with Psidium (R. Poincelet) beating Dicta Drake (M. Garcia) by two lengths with Pardao (W.H. Carr) a neck away third and Sovrango fourth

BELOW Mr R.B. Moller's Full Dress (R. Hutchinson) winning the One Thousand Guineas by 1½ lengths from Hecuba (L. Piggott) and Motionless (G. Lewis) to give Harry his fourth Classic success in England, Newmarket May 1st 1969

THIS PAGE Lester Piggott returns to the unsaddling enclosure on Mr R.B. Moller's Favoletta, trained by Harry, after winning the 1971 Irish One Thousand Guineas at The Curragh

ABOVE Susan Piggott presenting a silver salver to Harry's grand-daughter
Carolyn Jane Mercer, after she had won the 1973 Newmarket Town Plate on
Wood Ditton
BELOW Harry critically watching some of his horses at exercise on
Newmarket Heath

Newton Cup at Haydock before his Redcar victory. As Harry had already taken the race with Monterrico in 1962 and Espresso in 1963, Atilla's success implied that Harry had a penchant for it, an implication given more weight by the fact that he also saddled the runner up to Atilla — Twelfth Man. This colt of Mr R. B. Moller's was yet another horse that Harry had refused to hurry as a juvenile, and once again such patience paid handsome dividends. A big rangy colt sired by Fidalgo, Twelfth Man went on to win the Ebor Handicap at York and was well-backed for the Cesarewitch, but failed to gain a place behind Mintmaster. The next season, as a five-year-old, he won the Bessborough Stakes at Royal Ascot.

Atilla did not rest upon his laurels after winning the Vaux Gold Tankard. Harry sent him to Baden-Baden for the Grosser Preis von Baden in which he finished fifth, and then to Milan to contest the Gran Premio del Jockey Club. It was expensive to run horses abroad, particularly in Italy, and in consequence Harry always attempted to reduce costs by sharing an aeroplane. On this occasion he learned that a plane was flying to Milan without a cargo in order to bring back some army horses that had been appearing in a British Fair week in the city. The plane was due to leave Gatwick early on a Saturday morning, which was cutting things a bit fine as the race was to be contested on the Sunday, but it seemed sensible to use it. Atilla was sent to his owner's stud near East Grinstead on the Friday, and all appeared to be under control.

Unfortunately everything went wrong on the Saturday. The plane developed engine trouble whilst on the runway awaiting take off, and left almost five hours late. In flight the pilot was informed that Milan was fog-bound and that the plane would be diverted to Nice. From Nice the pilot was persuaded to fly to Genoa but on arrival the customs officer refused to allow Atilla off the plane because it was not scheduled to land there and all the documents were therefore out of order. Luckily, the travelling head lad, Arthur Taylor, could speak a little Italian having served in the army in Italy in 1944. Tremendous arguments ensued, phone calls were made and eventually Atilla was allowed off the plane. It was almost nightfall and no accommodation had been booked. However, the resourceful Arthur Taylor found a cow shed. The cow was evicted and Atilla installed. A box duly arrived from Milan into which an exhausted Atilla was put. He reached the racecourse only three hours before he was due to run. Meanwhile, Geoffrey Wragg who had flown to Milan on a Trident which reached the city just before it became fogbound the previous day, had been frantically trying to ascertain Atilla's whereabouts, but without any success.

In the paddock Atilla looked worn out, and Geoffrey told Frankie Durr that the only hope seemed to be to ride a 'non-trier' type of race, hope that the Italian jockeys made a nonsense of the pace, and ask Atilla to quicken inside the final furlong. There were three false starts but in the event Atilla was far superior to his rivals and won easily despite the chaos of his trip. After this race there was some confusion over his papers and documents and Harry decided that if he was to remain in Italy for a few weeks then he should contest the Premio Roma in which he finished second to the crack French colt Demi-Devil.

Harry had the presence of mind to realise that the Continent offered rich prizes for his horses who were just below championship class, and in addition he was perfectly prepared to send his potential Classic colts to race abroad. Deservedly he earned a great deal of money for his patrons by his initiative when some English trainers with horses of suitable merit were content to remain 'in their own back-yard'.

At home he put forward a suggestion to the Trainers' Federation designed to give apprentices encouragement and more opportunities to ride in public. His idea was that the winning of apprentice races should not involve penalties for other races, with the result that owners would be more willing to run their horses in races exclusively for apprentices. He was convinced that if owners knew that victory in an apprentice race would not penalise the winner then they would give such races greater support.

*   *   *

By 1966 Harry was recognised as the trainer to be most feared where the rich Northern handicaps were concerned, and his record in the Vaux Gold Tankard was outstanding, for he added to his tally of success in 1966 when he saddled Salvo at Redcar to win the £8,000 prize for the fourth time in five years. Salvo was one of Mr Gerry Oldham's first American acquisitions and had been purchased at Saratoga for $9,500. Bred by John W. Galbreath and Winston Guest, Salvo only had one race as a two-year-old, the Houghton Stakes at Newmarket in October 1965, in which he was beaten a head by Hermes in a field of twenty-four.

At the outset of the 1966 season Harry was training fifty-three horses, including some for Sir Philip Oppenheimer, David d'Ambrumenil and Basil Samuel. Several of his eighteen two-year-olds were by Fidalgo, whilst others were out of mares whom he had trained during their racing careers. He had the added advantage, therefore, of having first-hand knowledge of the traits and characteristics of many of the juveniles in his care. Salvo won the Craven Stakes in the spring of 1966, finished third to his Houghton Stakes conqueror, Hermes, in the Dante Sweepstake at York, and was then put away until the Vaux Gold Tankard which he won easily. Harry fancied him for the Ebor Handicap, but he was never a factor, and was a long way behind Lomond as the winning post was reached. He made amends by a convincing victory in the Newbury Autumn Cup, but caused Harry to come up before the Stewards of the Jockey Club. The local Stewards, not satisfied with the reversal of the Ebor Handicap form of Salvo with Lomond and Mehari, referred the matter to the Stewards of the Jockey Club who exonerated Harry after an hour-long hearing. Salvo ended his three-year-old career by being beaten a short head by the Russian champion Anilin in the Preis von Europa at Cologne in October. Anilin was repeating his 1965 victory in the race, but it was only by the narrowest of margins that Salvo failed to catch him. The judge called for a photo, but the print was very indistinct due to the gloom and when he gave his verdict to Anilin, many spectators thought his decision to be incorrect. Joe

Mercer, Salvo's jockey, was convinced that he had won by a neck.

As a four-year-old Salvo enjoyed a wonderful season. Beaten a head by Charlottown in the John Porter Stakes, he then proceeded to win the Yorkshire Cup, and the Hardwicke Stakes at Royal Ascot before finishing second to Busted in the King George VI and Queen Elizabeth Stakes. The eight four-year-olds who contested the race had between them won the 1966 Irish Derby and the St Leger, the Italian Derby, the Prix du Jockey Club and the Prix d l'Arc de Triomphe, not to mention the 1967 Eclipse, so that the field was of the highest quality. On a surface that did not suit him Salvo ran a marvellous race, and although well beaten by Busted ran on gallantly to finish a neck ahead of the Irish Sweeps Derby hero Ribocco. Harry then sent him to Germany for the Grosser Preis von Baden in which he beat Luciano by three-quarters of a length. A month later he ran one of the greatest races of his career when he finished second to Topyo in the Prix de l'Arc de Triomphe. The thirty runners included Anilin, Roi Dagobert, Ribocco, Frontal and Dedini, running in the colours of film star Omar Sharif. Salvo, ridden by Ron Hutchinson, may have been unlucky for at the entrance to the straight he had a wall of horses ahead of him and could see no daylight. Suddenly a gap appeared on the rails and Hutchinson squeezed through it. Salvo produced devastating acceleration but it was too late and he failed to catch Topyo by a neck. He was retired to stud, being sent to the Sandwich Stud before moving to Banstead Manor where he remained until departing for West Germany in 1975.

The next outstanding horse that Harry trained for Mr Gerry Oldham was Chicago, sired by Fidalgo out of Grischuna, subsequently to become the granddam of Sagaro. In 1960, Harry had persuaded Mr Oldham to buy a yearling filly, whom he named Grischuna, for 7,000 guineas from the Theakston Stud, for Harry believed that she came from a winner-producing family. Harry saddled Grischuna to make a winning debut at Newbury, but she never won again, although as a three-year-old she was second in both the Princess Elizabeth Stakes and the

Ebbisham Stakes at Epsom. Her first foal was Chicago, who in 1968 won the Henry II Stakes and the Cumberland Lodge Stakes in which he defeated Park Top. On the Continent he took the Gran Premio del Jockey Club in Milan and the Premio Roma in Rome. The following season he finished second to Park Top in the Hardwicke Stakes and was unplaced to her in the King George VI. He was sold at the 1969 December Sales for 17,000 guineas and exported to South Africa.

The last of the 'Oldham Champions' that Harry trained before Mr Gerry Oldham decided to concentrate his racing interests in France was Intermezzo, who won the 1969 St Leger. Sired by the great stayer Hornbeam, Intermezzo did not see a racecourse until August when he started at 10-1 and easily accounted for his twelve rivals in the Norfolk Stakes on the July course at Newmarket. In the valuable Wills Goblet Stakes at Newcastle a month later he trounced the opposition, and on the strength of these victories was made favourite for the Observer Gold Cup. He could not match the final burst of The Elk and was beaten into second place.

Intermezzo commenced his three-year-career by being a remote fourth in the Dante Stakes at York before being eighth to Blakeney in The Derby. In the Great Voltigeur Stakes he finished first but was relegated to fourth place for causing interference. Then came the St Leger. It seemed that Ribofilio had an easy task, but Harry had other ideas for he knew that the headstrong Ribofilio was not invincible.

He laid his plans with the maximum of skill, basing them on the fact that Ribofilio could be defeated if the race was run at a slow pace in the early stages. To this end he started Totalgo, ridden by G. Sexton, as a pace-maker. He told Sexton to set a very slow early pace, but to increase it at the end of six furlongs. He hoped that this increase in pace would confuse all Totalgo's rivals with the exception of Intermezzo. Ron Hutchinson had been told of the plan and was fully aware of its implications. With half the race completed and without the participation of High Line, who had refused to enter the starting stalls, he raced up to Totalgo whilst the jockeys on several of his rivals, including Precipice Wood, Blakeney and Reindeer, were uncertain of the tactics that they should employ.

By the time they had collected their wits Intermezzo was beyond recall and as they struggled amongst themselves, Ron Hutchinson had stolen an unassailable lead. Some of them appeared boxed in, others bumped and bored, with the result that whilst confusion reigned, Intermezzo was totally in command. Lester Piggott eventually extracted Ribofilio and attempted to get on terms with Intermezzo but failed honourably to do so by one and a half lengths.

Intermezzo's St Leger victory was the first Classic success enjoyed by Intermezzo's sire, Hornbeam, who had finished second to Cambremer in the 1956 St Leger, and prior to Intermezzo's success had been the sire of Merchant Venturer, Windmill Girl and Iskereen, all of whom had been runners up in the Classics. As a four-year-old Intermezzo was third in the Geoffrey Freer Stakes, runner up to Karabas in the Hardwicke Stakes and unplaced in the Grosser Preis von Baden. In 1970 he was sold and exported to Japan where he joined Miralgo.

Forty-two-year-old Ron Hutchinson, who rode Intermezzo, had ridden his first winner in Australia in 1943. Initially he had come to Great Britain to ride for Paddy Prendergast, for whom he won the 1960 Two Thousand Guineas on Martial — which was his first mount in England. From the moment that Ron first arrived from Australia, Harry was attracted to the unflustered style and waiting tactics that he adopted, and felt that in the fullness of time he should ride for the Abington Place stables. For many years Ron Hutchinson rode for the Duke of Norfolk's Arundel stable, once his association with Paddy Prendergast ended, but by the mid-1960s he was accepting mounts from Harry and scored his first notable success in 1967 when he won the Irish One Thousand Guineas and the Cambridgeshire on Lacquer owned by Mr R. B. Moller.

The association of the Moller brothers, Budgie and Eric, with Harry stemmed from the end of World War II. In the autumn of 1944 Eric Moller, acting on the advice of Nicky Morriss who owned the Banstead Manor Stud, bought a Panorama yearling filly to whom he gave the name Horama. Trained by Teddy Lambton she ran twice in the autumn of 1945 and on both occasions was ridden by Harry. As a three-year-old she ran eleven times, winning three times, but on none of these occasions was Harry her jockey. Retired to stud she became one of the outstanding broodmares in post-World War II Turf history, breeding ten winners of nineteen races between 1949-1965. These winners included Minstrel's Gallery, Urshalim, Close Up and Perspective. The year after the purchase of Horama the Moller brothers bought a three-year-old filly out of training named Sweet Cygnet. A daughter of Hyperion, she had won the Cheveley Park Stakes beating Sun Stream who was ridden by Harry. She was to prove a fine broodmare even if not as successful as Horama, with her progeny including Sea Swan, Feather Ball, Cadenza and Feather Bed — who as a three-year-old ran second to Homeward Bound in the Princess Elizabeth Stakes at Epsom, was also runner up to Royal Danseuse in the Irish One Thousand Guineas, was second to Derring-Do, sired by Darius, in the Hungerford Stakes, and won at Lingfield before finishing third to Linacre and Derring-Do in the Queen Elizabeth II Stakes at Ascot.

By the time that Mr Budgie Moller, who had been interned by the Japanese during the war, came back to England, his brother had created the foundations of their stud at his home, White Lodge near Cheveley. In the spring of 1948 an addition to the stud was made with the purchase of a filly named Test Match who had been bred by Lord Astor. Test Match had won only two minor races as a two-year-old, but she was impeccably bred, being by Big Game out of Traffic Light, heroine of the Park Hill Stakes at Doncaster. Test Match was to become the dam of Twelfth Man and Full Toss. Eight years later the Moller brothers purchased another filly who had raced in the Astor colours, Mitraille. The price at the Newmarket December Sales was 2,500 guineas. In 1961 she foaled a filly by Fidalgo to whom the name Fusil was given. Harry trained Fusil to win two races of little significance and she finished second in the Ribblesdale

Stakes to Windmill Girl before she went to stud, where she produced Full Dress II.

During these years Harry realised to the full the quality of all the horses that the Mollers sent him to train, but understandably was most in favour of those who traced back to Horama and Urshalim, who had been trained by Marcus Marsh, and who had won the Molecomb Stakes at Goodwood. Urshalim became the dam of Title Deed, Landlord, Violetta III, Lacquer, Sovereign, Relkalim and Funny Fellow. Lacquer, after finishing third to Fleet in the One Thousand Guineas, went on to win the Irish One Thousand Guineas by four lengths ridden by Ron Hutchinson. Later in the season she was fourth to Fleet in the Coronation Cup, and ended a great season by winning the Cambridgeshire. Meanwhile Sovereign was upholding Urshalim's reputation by easily winning the Queen Mary Stakes at Royal Ascot, scoring a record-breaking victory in the National Stakes at Sandown and triumphing in the Lowther Stakes at York to endorse her merit as the best filly of her generation. In 1968 Harry delayed her debut until the One Thousand Guineas in which she ran third to Caergurle, she disappointed in the Irish One Thousand, won the Coronation Stakes at Royal Ascot, and failed to cope with Petingo in the Sussex Stakes.

The Moller colours of 'chocolate, gold braid and sleeves, quartered cap' were now famous throughout Europe, and in 1969 were carried to victory by Full Dress II in the One Thousand Guineas. It was a dramatic race in the final yards of which Full Dress veered left from Ron Hutchinson's whip hand. Without doubt she crossed sharply in front of Lester Piggott's mount, Hecuba, although she was more than a length clear at the time. Piggott objected on the grounds of bumping and boring, but his objection was over-ruled after the Stewards had examined the camera-patrol film. Nevertheless the camera showed that the two fillies had come very close even if the result was in no way affected, and if the race had taken place in France, Full Dress would have been disqualified.

Full Dress II only raced twice after her Classic victory, failing behind Sleeping Partner in The Oaks, before finishing fifth to

Lucyrowe in the Coronation Stakes at Royal Ascot. Harry regretted that she had failed to train-on in mid-summer, but accepted the fact philosophically.

In many respects Harry was now a lonely man, for his wife Madge had died in 1968 after a brief illness. She had returned from holiday, complained that she felt unwell, and died within weeks. Abington Place seemed empty without her, and for a time he was inconsolable. There was a possibility that Geoffrey and his wife, Patricia, the daughter of Phil Lancaster, would move from their house in Hamilton Road, Newmarket, to join Harry, but the possibility never materialised. Years earlier the idea had been that Peter Wragg, who had spent a year at the Royal Dick veterinary college in Edinburgh, would ultimately succeed him, and for a time Peter acted as his assistant trainer, but he chose to make his career as a bloodstock agent, and his acumen brought him success through the acquisition as foals and yearlings of many top-class horses including Cynara, Plaza, the dam of Intermezzo, Grischuna, Miralgo, Czar Alexander, a winner in both England and the U.S.A., and Senador, winner of twelve races in Venezuela. In consequence Geoffrey Wragg joined his father as assistant trainer. Harry, who had contemplated buying a house in Barbados where he had enjoyed several winter holidays before the war, was now finding more time to relax on the golf course. During the year he did a hole in one for the second time at Newmarket, but was one of many who were incensed when thirty-one-year-old jockey Brian Taylor was blackballed from membership of Royal Worlington. Brian, a twelve-handicap player whose golf was improving rapidly until he was playing off five, had been proposed by Humphrey Cottrill and seconded by Atty Corbett. Cottrill stated, 'I can only suppose that he has been blackballed because of the old snobbishness about admitting jockeys. I thought all that died out when Harry Wragg and Bobby Jones became members.'

11

The final years

The 1970s opened with less success for Harry, and although Whitefoot, a daughter of Mitraille, won the 1970 Musidora Stakes, she failed to gain a place behind Lupe in The Oaks when her saddle slipped forward during the race. Stintino, a son of Cynara, was making a name for himself in France and won the Prix Lupin before finishing third to Nijinsky in The Derby, but he was trained for Mr Gerry Oldham by Francois Boutin at Chantilly rather than Harry. Gerry Oldham, who never had a bet and who drank a quart of milk a day, had lived in Bermuda for six years in the 1960s, but had moved to Geneva in 1968, because, 'even with the best telephone in the world, it is difficult to transact business seven hundred miles out in the Atlantic'. A compulsive jet-setter, he once remarked: 'I often fly to Ireland to talk horses. You can feel the horses better when you lean across a rail, or talk over a steak. It is not the same feeling when you talk about horses over the telephone. The Irish regard it as a new fangled instrument, so it is not much use anyway.' In 1970 Gerry Oldham, thought by many to be a confirmed bachelor, married Carolyn Hunter, who had formerly been married to old Etonian Christopher Glyn, and he decided he would prefer to have his horses trained at Chantilly in the future.

Harry sent Mr R. B. Moller's Popkins to Longchamp to contest the 1970 Poule d'Essai des Pouliches in which she finished third to Pampered Miss. Popkins had no Classic engagements in England, and in the course of the season made five trips to France. She won the Prix des Lilas at Longchamp, was second in the Prix de Royaumont at Chantilly, won the Prix de

190

Psyche at Deauville, and was the heroine of the Prix de la Nonette at Longchamp in September. Harry now set his sights upon the Sun Chariot Stakes at Newmarket which she won decisively, to prove herself the best racehorse sired by Romulus. Her dam, Peat Fire, was a daughter of Test Match.

Brian Taylor, who had been apprenticed to Harvey Leader, and who had achieved notable success on Palatch, Bringley, No Mercy, Command, Shoemaker and Ovaltine, began riding for Harry in the 1970s, and rode Cheveley Princess, a daughter of Busted and Feather Bed in the 1973 One Thousand Guineas. Later in the year she was to win the Nassau Stakes ridden by Lester Piggott. However Lester did not ride Moulton, the 'star' of Harry's stable in England in 1972 and 1973. Moulton was a big handsome colt bred by the Mollers. His dam was Close Up, a three-parts sister to Urshalim, already a prized broodmare through the exploits of Sovereign, Lacquer and Violetta III. Close Up's first foal, Promontory, won three races including the Premio Besnate in Milan. Her second foal, Closeness, won the Britannia Stakes at Royal Ascot and the Prix Sica Boy at Saint Cloud.

Her third foal was Moulton, who was backward as a two-year-old and only ran once. He made rapid improvement throughout the winter and in the spring of 1972 won at Newcastle and Ascot before being second to Rheingold in the Dante Stakes. He finished ninth in The Derby, ridden by Edward Hide, and subsequently won the Prix Ridgway at Deauville and the Prix Henri Delamarre at Longchamp where he was also second in the Prix du Prince d'Orange. Harry saddled him to win the Premio Presidente della Republica in Rome in May 1973 before he finished third in the Prix d'Ispahan and second in the Eclipse to Scottish Rifle.

Then came a memorable Benson and Hedges Gold Cup at York. The day had opened with the dramatic news that Roberto would not contest the race due to his dislike of anything but perfect or fast ground. Because of overnight rain Vincent O'Brien took the view that the ground was too soft for his champion and withdrew him. The Stewards considered this withdrawal to be unjustified, and fined him £50 — a ridiculously paltry sum in the circumstances, particularly as Roberto was to have been the 'star attraction' on the programme.

Lester Piggott had been engaged to ride Roberto, but had agreed with Harry that in the event of Roberto not being in the line up he would be prepared to ride Moulton. It was natural, therefore, that he should contact Harry and explain the position to him, reminding him that Geoff Lewis, who had been engaged to ride Moulton assuming that Roberto was in the field, would now be without a mount even though he had been promised the usual percentage of any winnings. However after Lester had contacted Harry to say that he would ride, the connections of Rheingold, hearing of Roberto's defection, decided that they would ask Piggott to ride their horse. This decision seemed incomprehensible to many people, for the ride on Rheingold had been promised to Yves Saint-Martin, who had already arrived at York racecourse, having flown from Paris. Saint-Martin, as one of the greatest jockeys in the world, was not accustomed to any attempt to 'jock him off' a horse at the eleventh hour.

Piggott had other ideas, and accepted the ride on Rheingold in preference to Moulton. His belief that Rheingold held a better chance than Moulton was understandable, for during the season Rheingold had won the Prix Ganay, the Hardwicke Stakes at Royal Ascot and the Grand Prix de Saint-Cloud (ridden by Yves Saint-Martin) for the second time, in addition to the John Porter Stakes. His only failure had been in the twelve-furlong King George VI and Queen Elizabeth Stakes at Ascot in July. Yves Saint-Martin was furious at Piggott's lack of courtesy, and complained bitterly to the Stewards who were powerless to insist that the original plans were adhered to, with Piggott on Moulton and Saint-Martin on Rheingold. They issued a statement deploring the belated change in the riding arrangements, but could do nothing else.

In the event poetic justice prevailed, for the one factor that Piggott had not taken into account was that Rheingold was a better horse at twelve furlongs than the ten furlongs of the

Benson and Hedges Gold Cup. Ron Hutchinson attempted to make all the running on his Eclipse Stakes hero, Scottish Rifle, but Geoff Lewis was biding his time on Moulton. When he realised there was a chance that he might be boxed in between Scottish Rifle and Sun Prince he sent Moulton to the front and was never headed. He defeated Scottish Rifle by two and a half lengths with Rheingold, who could never reach the leaders, in third place.

In the autumn Moulton was fourth in the Champion Stakes to Hurry Harriet. Moulton's dam, Close Up, also had success during the year with Freefoot who finished third in The Derby to Morston. However Harry's Oaks contender, Reload, a filly out of Fusil, failed behind Mysterious, so although both Classic runners had been given more than outside chances, they did not live up to expectations.

One result which gladdened Harry's heart at the end of the season was the victory of his grand-daughter, Caroline Mercer, in the historic Newmarket Town Plate. In 1972 she had won the race on Greenacre, and completed a double when scoring on Woodditton by a mere twenty lengths. She was presented with her prize by Susan Piggott who, as Susan Armstrong, had ridden the Town Plate winner in both 1961 and 1963. Caroline Mercer, who was to score another victory in 1975 when she rode Destino to win at a Doncaster evening meeting, had been taught to ride almost as soon as she could walk, being put up on a family pony called Flash.

In 1974 Harry almost gained another Classic success through Furioso, a daughter of his Cambridgeshire heroine, Violetta III, in The Oaks. Tony Murray, who had been engaged to ride Furioso, took up the running on the Moller filly a mile from home, and at the foot of Tattenham Corner was three lengths clear and going 'great guns'. All the way up the straight she battled on courageously, and only in the final fifty yards did Polygamy wear her down. Meanwhile Wille Carson was having a nightmare ride on Dibidale, who lost first her number cloth and then her weight cloth as her saddle slipped beneath her belly. Carson rode the final furlong bareback, and showed great horsemanship and courage to pass the post third. Inevitably he was disqualified and placed last as he was unable to draw the correct weight of nine stone with which he had weighed out. But for this disaster it is probably that Dibidale, a daughter of Priddy Maid, would have won The Oaks. Priddy Maid's dam was Priddy Fair, whom Manny Mercer was riding when he was killed at Ascot.

A month earlier Freefoot, a half-brother to Moulton, lost his maiden certificate when winning the John Porter Stakes ridden by Lester Piggott. Harry had forgiven and forgotten the 'Moulton incident', and was delighted that Piggott rode so brilliant a race at Newbury. Having held Freefoot up for a late run, Piggott rode a superbly-timed finish without making use of his whip and forced his mount up almost on the line to beat the 1973 St Leger winner Peleid by a head.

When the 1974 two-year-old Free Handicap was published Grundy headed the list with 9st 7lbs. Harry had three horses in the list, Silky, the superbly-bred filly by Nijinsky out of Close Up, being given 8st 3lbs, and two colts, Green Belt and Ra, bred by Sir Philip Oppenheimer at his Hascombe and Valiant Studs, both being allotted 8st.

Sir Philip Oppenheimer had originally joined the ranks of owners at the suggestion of Nicky Morriss who had also been responsible for introducing the Moller brothers to the English Turf. Philip Oppenheimer and Nicky Morriss had become friends whilst Cambridge undergraduates and their racing interests had stemmed from those carefree days. Philip Oppenheimer first registered his colours in 1959, and sent a few horses to Charlie Elliott to be trained. One of them was a Persian Gulf filly named Golden Sands who defeated Gerry Oldham's Plaza in the 1961 Red Oak Stakes at Ascot, and two months later beat Mr R. B. Moller's Violetta III in the Marlborough House Stakes at Ascot. Sir Philip Oppenheimer did not remain as a patron of Charlie Elliott for long, for the celebrated ex-jockey relinquished his trainer's licence in 1963 and the Oppenheimer horses went to Humphrey Cottrill and Harry. When Sir Philip

Oppenheimer first established a small stud he named it Valiant, a name derived from the Christian names of his two children Valerie and Anthony. In November 1965 Sir Philip's blood-stock interests gathered momentum when he bought the Hascombe stud 'lock, stock and barrel' from the executors of Sir John Jarvis. The stud, close to Banstead Manor and between the villages of Cheveley and Ashley, had been founded by Sir John Jarvis in 1936, and named after his Godalming estate. One of the best horses that he had owned was Old Reliance, conqueror of Mickey the Greek at Royal Ascot.

Early in the 1975 season Harry saddled Green Belt to win the Free Handicap for Sir Philip Oppenheimer. A fortnight later Green Belt finished a respectable fifth to Bolkonski in the Two Thousand Guineas, whilst Silky was nearer to last than first behind Nocturnal Spree in the One Thousand Guineas at the end of the week.

The entire week was an unhappy one in racing history and culminated with angry scenes on the day of the One Thousand Guineas when the stable lads went on strike. Luckily for racing the strike did not spread outside Newmarket, although the re-percussions were felt in the town for more than a year. Matters came to a head when the Newmarket Trainers' Federation refused to grant stable lads an extra £1.47 a week. The principal reason for this refusal was the conviction of the Federation that many owners would not stand for the increase, and would depart from ownership with the result that more stable lads would be made redundant. The area organiser of the Transport and General Workers Union refused to accept this reason, and implied that his union would support a strike.

In consequence as racegoers motored to the Rowley course on One Thousand Guineas Day they found the approach roads to the course picketed. At first they were amused by the antics of the stable lads but their amusement turned to fury when pickets became aggressive. One racegoer in a large Volvo attempted to by-pass the pickets who chased his car over the grass, sur-rounded it and were in the process of turning it upside down with the driver and his passenger inside when the police arrived. On the racetrack groups of pickets stood in line-abreast refusing to move despite requests to do so from the police. Militancy became the order of the day, as tempers flared, and 'rent-a-mob' hooligans who had never been to Newmarket before attempted to fan the flames of discontent. Trainers felt that it would be an intolerable situation to employ strike-ringleaders in their yards and a considerable number of sackings were made. Eventually after arbitration the dispute was settled, but the 'Battle of Newmarket' was not forgotten for a long time.

Hobnob, winner of the Chester Vase, was Harry's Derby contender that year, but the colt sired by Gyr was unplaced to Grundy, whilst Harry had no filly of sufficient merit to run in The Oaks. All trainers have a poor season from time to time, and 1975 was not a vintage year for Harry, although he sent out Shantallah to win the Cesarewitch in October. However, 1976 appeared to be more satisfactory, for Laughing Girl won the Lupe Stakes at Goodwood for the Moller brothers, and Sir Philip Oppenheimer's Fluellen ran consistently well, whilst his filly African Dancer took both the Cheshire Oaks and the Park Hill Stakes at Doncaster, in addition to being third to Pawneese in The Oaks, second in the Yorkshire Oaks and third in the Lancashire Oaks. Although she won the Park Hill Stakes her stubborness and near-refusal to enter the starting stalls resulted in her being reported to the Stewards. It had been intended to run her in the St Leger, and she was declared at the Four-Day declaration stage, but the Stewards insisted that she pass a stalls test before she was allowed to race again. After the Park Hill Harry remarked:

> The handlers tried to run her into the stall. She hit it and bounced back. Of course she reacted. You have to be kind with fillies, not rough, and she would have been better with a little bit of kidding.

A month earlier an Employment Appeal Tribunal held that eleven of Harry's stable lads, whom he had dismissed after the 'Battle of Newmarket', were not entitled to compensation for unfair dismissal. The Tribunal stated that Harry Wragg had not dismissed them because they were union members, and added that of the twenty-nine men he employed only fourteen had elected to go on strike. During the continuation of the strike after the Guineas meeting at Newmarket many of the horses in training at Abington Place had been sent away. However all of them had returned by 21 July to be prepared for races in September. Harry Wragg informed all the striking stable lads that he would dismiss them if they did not return to work. When they refused he employed others to fill their places. In consequence when the strike was over and they decided that they wished to come back into his employment he had no need of their services. They took him to arbitration and lost.

No matter how great or small the ability of the horses in his care, Harry took meticulous care of each and every one of them. His training methods included the use of two-way radios, stop-watches and weight-watching before and after each race. Geoffrey Wragg had a radio-telephone installed in his car which was linked with a mobile set carried by him when he went out onto the gallops. He was able to talk with his father in the car, who could phone the office at Abington Place whenever he wished. Both Harry and Geoffrey believed implicitly in the use of stop-watches, and regularly tried the horses against the clock in trial gallops. They believed that by timing horses' gallops on stop-watches much of the guesswork involved in training was eliminated, and it proved the most reliable guide to the merit and capability of each horse. Harry also believed in electronic warning and security systems in the stables and installed an elaborate one at Abington Place. He was also one of the first trainers to instal a Telex and to acquire a Magnetopulse machine to deal with horses' muscular complaints. Many of these innovations were suggested to him by Geoffrey, who had spent six months in California working on the Old English Ranch owned by Ellwood B. Johnston after completing his National Service.

At one time Geoffrey had thought of emigrating to the United

States, and had flown a group of horses to the Old England
Ranch, with a three-month visa. This was subsequently extended for a further three months, but gradually he became
homesick and returned to Newmarket. But if his elder brother
Peter had not decided to relinquish the job of being his father's
assistant it is possible that Geoffrey would have remained at Pye
Ltd, making a very successful career in the world of electronics.

In 1977 Harry trained three exceptional horses, Lucky
Sovereign, Cherry Hinton and Amaranda. Lucky Sovereign, a
three-year-old colt sired by Nijinsky out of Sovereign, was very
forward in condition and ran at Doncaster in March, finishing
second in the March Stakes. A week later he was fourth in a
Maiden Plate at Ascot, and next was third in the Craven Stakes
at Newmarket. His improvement was now remarkable for in his
fourth race of the season he won the Mecca-Dante Stakes at
York by five lengths to become a live candidate for The Derby.
He bitterly disappointed Harry at Epsom behind The Minstrel,
but at The Curragh ran Mr Robert Sangster's colt to a length
and a half in the Irish Sweeps Derby. Frank Durr, who rode
Lucky Sovereign, lodged an objection for 'bumping and taking
my ground inside the final furlong' but the objection was
over-ruled.

As a result of the form he showed in the Irish Derby Lucky
Sovereign was installed an odds-on favourite for the Gordon
Stakes at Goodwood but finished last of four to Pollerton. He
was third to Alleged and Classic Example in the Great Volti-
geur and fifth in the St Leger, to bring further prestige to the
Moller bloodstock empire.

Cherry Hinton, by Nijinsky out of Popkins, brought even
more renown. She was third on her debut at Haydock in
August, was second to John de Coombe, a very good horse sired
by Moulton, in the Convivial Stakes at York's Ebor meeting,
won a race at York in September, and ended her juvenile career
by a clean-cut victory in the Argos Star Mile at Ascot. Meanwhile Amaranda, a filly by Bold Lad out of Favoletta, was also
hitting the headlines. Lester Piggott rode her to a five-length
victory at York on her debut in May, and proved that she was a

brilliantly fast filly by scoring a three-lengths victory in the Queen Mary Stakes at Royal Ascot. She started 7-2 on at Goodwood but was beaten in the Molecomb Stakes by Hatta before returning to her winning ways by taking the St Hughes Stakes at Newbury in August. She was again made an odds-on favourite for the Flying Childers Stakes at Doncaster but was beaten three-quarters of a length by Music Maestro and sadly had to be withdrawn from the Cheveley Park Stakes due to injury.

Amaranda proved a disappointment to Harry in 1978 as did Old Bill, Fluellen and Court Barns. He gave Amaranda one race at Newmarket as a 'pipe-opener' for the One Thousand Guineas, but she was beaten into second place by Seraphima. Harry decided to withdraw her from the fillies Classic and run Cherry Hinton instead. As a result Amaranda contested the Palace House Stakes in which she received a bump which put paid to any chance that she might have had in the race. Rested until September she again disappointed when beaten by Saltation in the Marlborough Stakes, but happily won her final race at Haydock.

Meanwhile Cherry Hinton, after finishing second to Shapina in the Fred Darling Stakes at Newbury, had started a short-priced favourite for the One Thousand Guineas only to be beaten into fourth place behind Enstone Spark. There may have been some excuse as she returned to Abington Place running a high temperature and was speedily announced as a non-runner in The Oaks. At Royal Ascot she was third in the Ribblesdale Stakes to Relfo, before failing abysmally in the Yorkshire Oaks.

For Harry it was another poor season, but when it was rumoured that he was contemplating retirement he announced, 'Not on your life! I am still kicking and looking forward to the challenge yet again.' He added that as The Oaks still eluded him he intended to attempt to win it in 1979 with either Pine Grove, a filly by Brigadier Gerard out of Reload, or Topsy, by Habitat out of Furioso. The firm ground throughout much of the 1978 season had prevented some of his most fashionably-bred two-year-olds from running so that he faced 1979 with confidence and pleasure. He also gained much pleasure at the end of the season when his grand-daughter, Caroline Mercer, married Pat Eddery, whom he recognised as one of the best jockeys of the post-war years.

In 1979 Pine Grove did not live up to expectations, merely winning an insignificant maiden race at Salisbury in the spring, but Topsy improved steadily throughout the season and by the autumn was one of the best three-year-old fillies in training. On her debut she won the Fred Darling Stakes by five lengths. On her next outing she ran on strongly to be fourth in the One Thousand Guineas behind One in a Million. She ran badly in the Musidora Stakes but, after missing The Oaks, ran second to One in a Million after the disqualification of Harry's Buz Kashi. At Newmarket in July she finished second to Rose Above before winning the Prix d'Astante at Deauville. She returned to Deauville at the end of August where she was beaten by Bellypha. In her penultimate race she was defeated at York before winning the Sun Chariot Stakes at Newmarket.

The Coronation Stakes at Royal Ascot had proved to be a thoroughly unsatisfactory race. Harry saddled the 33-1 outsider Buz Kashi owned by Anthony Oppenheimer in addition to Topsy. Buz Kashi's maternal grand-dam was Golden Sands. Paul Cook rode Buz Kashi, made rapid headway once the straight was reached, squeezed through on the inside and was first past the post. Following a Stewards' Enquiry the luckless filly was disqualified. Harry and Paul Cook appealed against the disqualification but the appeal was turned down. Nevertheless, both Geoffrey Wragg, who was appearing for his father, and Paul Cook, who was legally represented, considered that they had received a fair and exhaustive hearing during which the Racecourse Technical Services head-on camera patrol film and the B.B.C. recording of the race were constantly referred to. Significantly the £75 deposits of both Harry and Paul Cook were returned.

The remainder of the year brought little notable success for Harry's yard, although races were won by Stetchworth, Romara, Good Lassie and Cragador, and in the 1979 two-year-old Free Handicap weights headed by Monteverdi and Super Asset his only representative was Sir Philip Oppenheimer's Cragador on 8st 9lbs. It was not surprising, therefore, that Harry did not saddle a runner in either the Two Thousand Guineas or the One Thousand Guineas that year.

During the 1980 season a juvenile for whom Harry had high hopes was Kirtling, a Grundy colt out of Silky, bred by Eric and Budgie Moller. Sadly, Budgie died on 13 March 1980.

> I got a terrific shock when I was told that Budgie Moller had died because nearly every week we used to play golf together. He had never been ill and was as strong as a bull. We only used to play for a golf ball, but he loved to beat me. He was so strong that he could hit a golf ball out of sight, and so powerful that his arms were as thick as my thighs. He claimed that his handicap, if he had one, ought to be twenty-four, but I thought it ought to have been about five and that he ought to have given me shots. He was my opponent one day when I did a hole in one. He 'confiscated' the ball and when I next saw it he had generously had it mounted on a little pedestal and gave it back to me.
>
> During my golfing career I have done a hole in one on three occasions, once at Doncaster and twice at Newmarket. I always seemed to play my best golf in competitions, and won the Turfite Trophy at Fulford, near York, twice. Sometimes I partnered Atty Corbett in matches against bookmakers. He was not such a good golfer as Bobby Jones, but off his handicap of eight he was invincible and we never lost a match.

In May, two months after Budgie Moller's death, Harry introduced Kirtling to the racecourse at York. He started favourite, and ran second to Parkdale after showing signs of inexperience. He made no mistake at Royal Ascot where he won the Chesham Stakes, but it was only by a short head that he beat Robellino. Harry rested him until September when he ran fourth to Gielgud in the Laurent Perrier Champagne Stakes. In his final race of the year he was fourth to Storm Bid in the Dewhurst Stakes. He wintered well and Harry took him to Stockton where he won the Rosebery Stakes at the Easter meeting. Harry thought that he had Classic potential, and ran him in the Guardian Newspaper Classic Trial. He ran a fine race but was no match for the ten-length winner Shergar. At Chester he won the Dee Stakes easily, before Harry sent him to Milan where Lester Piggott drove him home to win the Gran Premio d'Italia by a short neck. Undoubtedly one of the best of his generation it seemed that Shergar would beat him at Epsom, so that Harry persuaded his owners to withdraw him from the race. However, he laid down the gauntlet to Shergar in the Irish Sweeps Derby, but failed to reach the first three. At Saint Cloud a month later he finished fourth to Bellman, Al Nass and Church Parade in the Prix Eugen Adam, and showed that he was retaining his form by running second to Beldale Flutter in the Benson and Hedges Gold Cup at York. Harry kept him in training for the remainder of the season, with his objective the Champion Stakes, but although he led for seven furlongs he was a spent force at the Bushes and was virtually last behind Vayrann and Cairn Rouge.

Another colt who brought further credit to Harry during 1981 was Sir Philip Oppenheimer's four-year-old Pelerin, the second foal of Padrona who had been bought for 40,000 guineas at the dispersal sale of Lord Rosebery's bloodstock. After Pelerin had won at the 1980 York May meeting, Harry began to fancy him for The Derby. Pelerin, fitted with blinkers, repaid his confidence by finishing fourth at Epsom, less than three lengths behind Henbit. This performance made it seem certain that the colt running in Sir Philip's 'black and white halved, sleeves reversed, red cap', would win top prizes before the end of the season. Inexplicably he failed to do so, and in both the Irish Sweeps Derby and the King George VI he ran disappointingly. Subsequently it was thought that he might have picked up a virus, for he also ran badly in the Great Voltigeur at York. Sensibly it was decided to keep him in training as a four-year-old, with far happier results, for he seemed to be a reformed character and won the Hardwicke Stakes at Royal Ascot, in which he defeated Light Cavalry, Lancastrian, Nicholas Bill and Mrs Penny, the John Porter Stakes, the Ormonde Stakes and the Grosser Preis von Baden before being sold as a stallion to California.

Pelerin, however, was not the only horse to triumph for Sir Philip Oppenheimer during 1981, for the two-year-olds Dancing Rocks and On The House also brought success. Dancing Rocks won both her races, the Deinhard Green Label Stakes at Goodwood and the Blue Seal Stakes at Ascot, whilst On The House won at Newbury and York before finishing second to Woodstream in the William Hill sponsored Cheveley Park Stakes.

Both fillies were to bring notable success to Harry in his final season at Abington Place. Dancing Rocks ran third in the Coronation Stakes at Royal Ascot, won the Nassau Stakes at Goodwood, was fourth in the Yorkshire Oaks and second in the Virginia Stakes at Newcastle, before failing in her final race, the Sun Chariot Stakes won by Time Charter. On The House proved a better filly, for after running a moderate race in the Ladbrokes Nell Gwynne Stakes she slammed her rivals to win the One Thousand Guineas by two and a half lengths.

Greville Starkey and Pat Eddery had both turned down the offer to ride On The House and in consequence the mount was given to John Reid. Harry was not feeling at his best and decided to watch the race on television at Abington Place. He admitted:

> It took me five minutes to get my breath back after 'riding' this one today. I picked up my stick going into the Dip, and rode her out to the line.

Harry sent On The House to the Curragh for the Irish One Thousand Guineas in which she was beaten by Princess Polly and Woodstream before she contested the Coronation Stakes at Royal Ascot, in which she finished behind her stable-companion Dancing Rocks. She returned to her brilliant best in the Sussex Stakes in which she showed a clean pair of heels to Sandhurst Prince and Achieved, but sadly was not in the first four to Sandhurst Prince in the Waterford Crystal Mile a month later.

Although Sir Philip Oppenheimer was relishing the victories of Dancing Rocks and On The House, Harry was providing him with further success with Zinzara, an American-bred filly who had been purchased as a foal. Zinzara won the Sir Charles Clore Memorial Stakes at Newbury in May, finished fifth to Time Charter in The Oaks, was fourth in the Prix de Malleret at Longchamp, won the Prix de Psyche, a race that Popkins had won, and ended her career by being second to Dion at Kempton in September.

By the autumn it was common knowledge that Harry intended to retire at the end of the season, leaving Geoffrey Wragg, who had assisted him since 1954, to hold the trainer's licence at Abington Place. However it would not have been in Harry's nature to give up all interest in horses overnight, and in consequence he viewed the future prospects of his 1982 two-year-olds with as much interest as he had always shown. One in particular whom he believed had immense potential was Teenoso, bred by the White Lodge Stud, from their mare Furioso, already the dam of Topsy. Teenoso, sired by Youth, derived his name from the somewhat complicated fact that Youth implied a teenager, so that by taking the first four letters, Teen, and adding the final three of Furioso, the resulting word was Teenoso. The colt raced three times as a two-year-old. Unplaced behind Coquitos Friend on the July course in August and also unplaced in the Ribero Stakes at the Doncaster St Leger meeting behind Cock Robin he gave a hint of his ability when fourth behind Oula Owl at Newmarket in October.

Harry retired officially at the end of the 1982 season and spent the next month at Abington Place. He was eighty years of age, and as a jockey and trainer had graced the Turf for more than sixty years. Understandably lonely since the death of his wife, he was constantly reminded of his personal triumphs as he wandered around the house. On a grand piano in the drawing room were ash-trays on which were horseshoes from many of the

Gerry Oldham champions, including Salvo, Intermezzo and Chicago, and a cup commemorating Psidium's Derby victory. Cups and trophies took pride of place on his dining room sideboard, whilst oil-paintings of Rockfel and Felstead adorned the walls. In his office was a prized mug given to him by Sir Percy Loraine after Darius won the Two Thousand Guineas, and the framed letter from King Georve VI congratulating him upon his Royal victories in 1941. There were also photographs to remind him of some of the apprentices, including Peter Robinson, Paul Kellaway, Graham Sexton and Peter Boothman, whom he had put on the road to success.

Before Christmas Harry left the cold and damp of Newmarket for his annual holiday in California, where in January 1983 he was taken seriously ill. It was thought that he might not recover, and Geoffrey and Patricia flew out to be with him. Happily his health improved and by the commencement of the Flat season he was back at Abington Place. His vigour had returned, and his new lease of life made him take especial interest in the manner in which Geoffrey was training the horses. Teenoso was his favourite three-year-old, and he watched over him with fatherly care.

Geoffrey elected to give Teenoso his first run of the year at Haydock on 2 April in a ten and a half furlong Maiden Stakes. He ran on strongly from the distance but was beaten by a neck by Welsh Idol. Geoffrey was somewhat despondent, but Harry with typical understanding based on experience preached patience. At Newmarket a fortnight later Teenoso romped home by eight lengths to give the staff and stable lads at Abington Place far greater expectations. The May meeting at Chester was abandoned, so Teenoso was re-routed to the Highland Spring Derby Trial at Lingfield which he won decisively. Hopes for The Derby ran even higher, and knew no bounds when it was learned that Lester Piggott had accepted the mount. Harry was delighted for he had total faith in the brand of confidence that Lester displayed on the important occasion. He acknowledged that Lester was not only cool and confident but had the flair to be completely aware of everything that was going on around him throughout even the most emotional and exciting moments.

Teenoso's triumph at Epsom in The Derby reads like a fairy tale for Geoffrey Wragg in his first season as a trainer, but he was the first to admit the inestimable debt that he owed to his father. Harry did not feel fit enough to attend Epsom, but no sooner had he recovered from the excitement of watching The Derby on television than the telephone began to ring. It was Geoffrey calling him from Epsom, telling him of the Queen's congratulations, and her insistent suggestion 'let's watch the video recording of the race again.' Other memories of the great occasion include seeing Mrs Eric Moller clutching a favourite red rose picked from her garden that morning in one hand and the Derby trophy in the other, and jubilant Tricia Wragg and Susan Piggott awaiting Teenoso outside the hallowed unsaddling Enclosure. Twenty-two years earlier similar jubilation might have been shared by Tricia and Susan if Lester had ridden Psidium.

Geoffrey Wragg had been the victim of a nightmare drive to Epsom racecourse in the morning, for the congestion on the roads was chaotic. At one time he had told his chauffeur to double back on their tracks towards Reigate, and when he thought he was going to be very late, explained his predicament to a policeman who was totally unimpressed that it was the trainer of a Derby candidate requesting help. No help was forthcoming. However the return journey was far more exhilarating, and included dinner with Lester and Susan Piggott in London. Geoffrey went out to the chosen restaurant wearing his formal striped trousers and a jersey belonging to Lester!

The following morning Harry collapsed in the office at Abington Place and was rushed to hospital where he remained for a month. On his return he did not leave his home for any length of time, and became an armchair racing critic by watching television. One decision which incensed him was the disqualification of Vacarme at Goodwood, for he considered that Piggott had ridden a brilliant race. He began to spend time listening to the radio and his record player and found especial pleasure in the signature tune of the New York group Kids of Fame. The words 'You are going to live for ever, you are going to learn to fly' appealed to him. However, as the season continued Harry regained his strength and was obviously proud and delighted by Geoffrey's success.

In December his brother Sam died after a long illness. He had ridden the winners of the Cesarewitch, the Manchester November Handicap, the Stewards Cup and the Queen's Prize in addition to riding Rockfel to win the One Thousand Guineas and Pont l'Evêque to triumph in the New Derby, but perhaps the most significant colt with whom he had been associated was Star King, who subsequently founded a dynasty in Australia. He had retired from the saddle in 1953 and moved to Newbury where he lived quietly for the remainder of his life. He had always thought that following Harry's advice in the 1932 Derby had cost him the race on Royal Dancer who finished fourth but Harry did not accept this belief.

Saddened by the death of his brother Harry again wintered in California, returning in February 1984 refreshed after two months spent in the sun. Alert in his outlook his memory was as clear as ever, and as he remembered the champions whom he had ridden more than forty years ago he still insisted that Rockfel was the greatest horse with whom he had been associated, even though she was not the last champion whose saddle he graced. So often it is this last champion who is considered the greatest, but for Harry Rockfel was the ride of a lifetime. He liked to add that if he had never ridden her he would be hard pressed to name the best horse he ever rode, but whereas with all the others he needed his ability with head and hands, with Rockfel he was only required to sit still. After winning The Oaks he had said:

> I felt as though she was a part of me. I did not need to ride her. She just carried me along.

A few days later a friend who had known Harry for many years wrote, 'There is a side of Harry which always seems to be striving for the unobtainable'. In those now far-distant days he may not have obtained everything that he desired but today, as he looks back over his distinguished career as a jockey and trainer, even he as a perfectionist, must acknowledge that he has obtained the most treasured prize — a place in Turf history.

APPENDICES

Harry Wragg's Record as a Jockey

YEAR	WINNING RIDES
1919	1
1920	20
1921	14
1922	38
1923	58
1924	76
1925	78
1926	68
1927	73
1928	89
1929	103
1930	87
1931	110
1932	102
1933	64
1934	76
1935	102
1936	62
1937	102
1938	82
1939	62
1940	38
1941	**71 Champion Jockey**
1942	28
1943	19
1944	18
1945	50
1946	83
TOTAL	1,774

Harry Wragg was also second on 1,568 occasions and third on 1,500 occasions.

He rode in 11,658 Flat Races in Great Britain and Ireland.

Harry Wragg's Record as a Trainer

YEAR	SUCCESSFUL HORSES	RACES WON	VALUE £
1947	16	25	11,711
1948	18	29	16,919
1949	18	32	18,107
1950	17	36	25,016
1951	23	37	19,547
1952	16	24	11,736
1953	21	40	26,736
1954	24	43	38,080
1955	26	46	39,442
1956	19	33	23,030
1957	21	29	11,687
1958	20	34	15,254
1959	30	42	35,220
1960	19	28	30,226
1961	24	38	91,645
1962	19	38	64,284
1963	23	29	44,077
1964	16	25	21,454
1965	17	28	50,415
1966	22	37	44,164
1967	24	34	47,299
1968	21	33	37,870
1969	20	22	77,712
1970	17	27	39,815
1971	17	21	18,109
1972	16	27	31,008
1973	11	37	98,605
1974	23	36	45,008
1975	16	26	41,171
1976	20	30	64,994
1977	22	39	89,247
1978	23	34	65,951
1979	21	30	115,724
1980	18	33	71,284
1981	21	37	182,806
1982	20	30	259,572

INDEX

Index

Horses' names are given in italics

Abbot's Fell, 160
Abbots Worthy, 68
Abergavenny, Lord, 64
Abermaid, 178, 179
Abingdon Place, 21, 148-9, 197, 204
Achieved, 203
Adam's Apple, 79
Adare, 163
Admiral Drake, 144
Admiral's Walk, 107
Adriatic, 88
African Dancer, 196
Aga Khan, 30, 33, 42, 56, 58-9, 66, 70, 84, 92, 94, 96, 112, 123, 146, 155, 165
Aga Khan, Begum, 152, 153, 156, 165, 167, 170, 179
Aiming High, 178
Airborne, 140, 142
Al Nass, 202
Alcide, 167
Alleged, 198
Allison, Captain, 40
Almond Hill, 95
Aly Khan, Prince, 96, 102, 168
Alycidon, 151, 167
Amaranda, 198-9
Ambergris, 173, 178
Anilin, 183
Annie Oakley, 162
Anthelion, 168
Apperley, 68
Applause, 28, 29
Apple Sammy, 103
April the Fifth, 66
Aprolon, 145
Archer, Fred, 27, 83

Aristophanes, 156
Armagnac, 62
Armstrong, R.W., 12
Askew, A.B., 180
Asmena, 167
Astor, Lord, 22, 29, 30, 31, 66, 92, 187
Athford, 49, 51
Atilla, 180-2
Auction Pool, 59-60
Aureole, 161
Azam Pasha, 96

Baber Shah, 95
Bachelor's Buttons, 29
Bahram, 94, 95, 113, 119
Bailey, Sir Abe, 16, 64
Baird, Abington, 73, 148
Bakshishi, 152, 154
Bald Eagle, 167
Baldock, Teddy, 91
Baltazzi, Mr, 122
Banstead Manor stud, 187
Bay Meadows, 152, 153-4
Beadle, Ellen, 141
Beary, Michael, 44, 49, 52-4, 57-9, 66, 68, 89-91, 146
Beasley, P., 111
Beasley, Rufus, 74
Beausite, 117
Beaverbrook, Lord, 64-5, 73, 80
Beckhampton, 118
Bedford Lodge, 73-5, 76, 80, 108, 115, 147, 148
Bell, Sir J.P., 23, 42
Bell, Captain Ossie, 28, 42, 44, 47, 48, 85, 96-101, 118, 123, 149, 160, 173

215

Iskereen, 186

Jacopo, 61
Jai Mahal, 153
James, Mrs Arthur, 117
Janieri, 163, 164
Jardine, Douglas, 128
Jarvis, J.L., 23
Jarvis, Jack, 47, 61, 63, 65, 66, 68,
    74-5, 84, 85, 92-4, 104, 113, 123,
    131, 136, 142, 170, 171
Jarvis, Sir John, 96, 107, 195
Jarvis, Vivien, 84
Jarvis, W.R., 52
Jellis, Henri, 32
Jennifer, 167
Joel, H.J., 109, 168
Joel, Jack, 28, 48
Joel, Solly, 28, 29, 30-1, 43, 122
John de Coombe, 198
Johnston, Ellwood, 154-5, 197
Jonstone, Rae, 145, 152
Jones, Bobby, 21, 31, 55, 66, 76,
    77, 78, 90, 107, 140, 146, 189,
    201
Jones, Herbert, 26
Jones, Peter, 21
Joss House, 26
Just Great, 175, 178

Karabas, 186
Kathy Too, 173
Kellaway, Paul, 205
Khaled, 139, 140, 155-6
Khosro, 158
Ki Ming, 157
Kildangan, 157-9, 178
King of the Tudors, 161
King Salmon, 82-3, 85-6
King Sol, 43
Kirtling, 201
Kisber, 166
Knee Cap, 22
Knight of the Garter, 27
Knight of the Vale, 64
Kohn, Mrs Geoffrey, 152
Kyle, Alex, 77
Kyloe, 158

Lacquer, 186, 188
Lady Abbess, 48, 52
Lady Feo, 26
Lady Godiva, 157
Lady Sybil, 130-1
Lambert Simnel, 117
Lambton, Cicely, 63
Lambton, George, 32, 33, 45, 63,
    73-5, 102, 108, 113, 122, 127,
    131-4, 159
Lambton, Teddy, 187
Lambourn Stud, 47, 173
Lancaster, Phil, 77, 189
Lane, Fred, 66
Lang, Chick, 48, 49
Larwood, Harold, 82
Las Vegas, 145
Lascelles, Lord, 52
Latin Lover, 174, 175, 176
Laughing Girl, 196
Lavandier, 167
Leach family, 115
Leach, Bill, 116
Leach, Chubb, 13, 78-9, 103, 104,
    105, 115, 143, 145
Leach, Felicity, 116
Leach, Felix, 13, 48, 78
Leach, Jack, 13, 79, 143
Leach, Lily, 78-9
Leader, Colledge, 123
Leader, Fred, 77, 141
Leader, Harvey, 191
Leader, Jack, 48
Lentolia, 170
Lemonade, 22
Lewis, Geoff, 170, 171, 192
Lex, 53
Light Brocade, 84-5
Light Tackle, 88
Lilley, J.A., 162
Lillywhite, 159
Linacre, 187
Llanstephan, 153
Loder, Colonel Giles, 96
Lomond, 183
Londonderry, Lord, 70, 96, 98-9,
    151
Long, Sam, 76